Remaking France

Explorations in Culture and International History
General Editors: Jessica C.E. Gienow-Hecht and Frank Schumacher

REMAKING FRANCE
Americanization, Public Diplomacy, and the Marshall Plan

He objects to semiotic approach to Americanization or cultural transfer; what US did after WWII was material + economic change, not just new meanings Europeans gave to American culture (Pells, Kroes, etc).

Brian Angus McKenzie

Marshall Plan was overt propaganda and efforts toward free market capitalism + consumption in Europe. It created a benevolent myth of altruistic Marshall Plan.

Chapters address Marshall Plan effects on GIs, French counter move w/ Cannes Film Festival, tourism, labor, print culture

problem of assessing effectiveness of cultural + informational exhibits — ch. 2

Argues that American political + economic policies allowed success of cultural Americanization (Rapports, Sélection, comics.)

Marshall Plan "failed" because it succeeded in getting too much American material into France, allowing Fr ambivalence + not anti-Americanism

Berghahn Books
New York • Oxford

First published in 2005 by
Berghahn Books
www.berghahnbooks.com

Library of Congress Cataloging-in-Publication Data

McKenzie, Brian Angus, 1970–
    Remaking France: Americanization, public diplomacy, and the Marshall
Plan / Brian Angus McKenzie.
        p. cm.—(Explorations in culture and international history series ; 2)
    Includes bibliographical references and index.
    ISBN 1-84545-154-6
    1. United States—Foreign relations—France. 2. France—Foreign
relations—United States. 3. United States—Foreign relations—1945–1953.
4. Americanization—History—20th century. 5. Marshall Plan. 6. United
States—Foreign public opinion, French. 7. Public opinion—France—
History—20th century. I. Title. II. Series.

E183.8.F8M38 2005
327.7304'09'044—dc22   2005049340

British Library Cataloguing in Publication Data

A catalogue record for this book is available from the British Library

Printed in the United States on acid-free paper

ISBN 1-84545-154-6 hardback

*For Rae Ellen McKenzie and
in memory of Richard Angus McKenzie*

CONTENTS

LIST OF TABLES AND FIGURES

LIST OF ABBREVIATIONS

AFAA   Association française d'action artistique
AFL   American Federation of Labor
CAB   Civil Aeronautics Board
CFTC   Confédération française des travailleurs chrétiens
CGA   Confédération générale de l'agriculture
CGT   Confédération générale du travail
CIO   Congress of Industrial Organizations
CNC   Centre national du cinéma
CNPF   Conseil national du patronat français
CRS   Compagnies républicaines de sécurité
ECA   Economic Cooperation Administration
EDC   European Defense Community
ERP   European Recovery Program
FO   Force ouvrière
IATA   International Air Transport Association
NATO   North Atlantic Treaty Organization
OEEC   Organization for European Economic Cooperation
OSR   Office of the Special Representative
PAO   Public affairs officer
PCF   Parti communiste français
TA   Technical Assistance
USIA   United States Information Agency
USIS   United States Information Service
VOA   Voice of America

ACKNOWLEDGEMENTS

I am grateful for the support I received while completing this book. At Colby-Sawyer College I benefited from the encouragement of Judy Muyskens as well as from faculty research funds, which allowed me to spend valuable time in France during the final stages of the project. A grant from the American Foreign Policy Center at Louisiana Tech University enabled me to deepen my treatment of the U.S. side of the project. I relied on the assistance of many archivists but David Pfieffer was especially helpful at the National Archives and Records Administration.

I am humbled by and grateful for the advice, criticism, and encouragement I received from colleagues. I hope they will recognize their influences in the pages that follow as much as I do. Judy Stone's course on the French Revolution at Western Michigan University is the reason I became interested in French history in the first place. Richard F. Kuisel taught me the historian's craft patiently and thoroughly. His mentoring has served as a model and inspiration for my own teaching and his work continues to inspire me. Herman Lebovics, Ellen Furlough, and Michael Barnhart provided important suggestions and I am fortunate to have had the help of these outstanding historians. Brian Etheridge's comments on the theoretical aspects of my work were invaluable. Jessica Gienow-Hecht and Frank Schumacher also deserve praise. Their leadership has encouraged and enabled young historians to pursue an exciting agenda for the study of culture and international history. I am grateful for Marion Berghahn's support of this agenda. I also wish to thank Michael Dempsey at Berghahn Books for guiding me through the publishing process and Catherine Kirby for her copyediting.

Friends and family made life possible while I was working on this book. My brothers Dennis and Bruce provided joyful respites. Roy Roberts, Peter White, Joel Vessels, Hilary Aquino, Chad Wager, and Greg Barnes provided encouragement when I needed it and essential discouragement on occasion. My parents supported me under the most difficult of circumstances and I hope this book honors their sacrifices. I must also acknowledge the support I received from my family in Old Europe: Marie and Tony Cullen, and Maisy Kelly. My biggest debt is to Pauline Cullen. Her love, patience, and care made this work possible.

INTRODUCTION

The American empire is intangible, invulnerable, an influence over the minds and customs of mankind which is confirmed every time the world installs an adding-machine, dances to jazz, buys a bale of cotton, sells a pound of rubber, or borrows an American dollar.

John Carter, *Conquest: America's Painless Imperialism,* 1928

In 1951 Paris's only baseball diamond was located in the Bois de Boulogne, the expansive park outside the city. According to William Koren, a United States Information Service (USIS) official, the field was in poor condition: there was no dugout and the backstop was a sieve.[1] Baseball facilities beyond Paris were scarce. Worse still, in the eyes of this official, only a handful of Frenchmen were familiar with the game and there was virtually no place for students to practice. At a joint staff meeting between the USIS and the information division of Mission France (the lead body of the Marshall Plan in France) Koren proposed that Marshall Plan funds be used to encourage and promote baseball in France. He argued that baseball provided an excellent means of improving Franco-American relations. "Those Frenchmen," he argued, "who are already baseball players or interested in baseball have an interest in something particularly American that has spread to include an interest in other things American and a friendliness toward us that goes beyond that of the average Frenchman."[2] In short, baseball promoted "American" values. There were other benefits to promoting baseball in Europe. According to Koren, it could also promote European unity. As an American sport baseball transcended local European culture. "America's national sport" offered a potentially unifying pursuit for Western Europe.

The argument for promoting baseball in France was an example of the public diplomacy of the United States in France during the

USIA public diplomacy = propaganda

Marshall Plan. This book analyzes these efforts. "Public diplomacy," according to the United States Information Agency (USIA), "seeks to promote the national interest of the United States through understanding, informing and influencing foreign audiences."[3] Practitioners and scholars differentiate between cultural diplomacy, support for the arts and exchange programs, and public diplomacy, programs which can serve short-term needs in ways cultural exchanges cannot.[4] The distinction is arbitrary, except perhaps for bureaucratic reasons. The goal of both is to positively influence relations between the U.S. and other nations and to promote U.S. interests, broadly construed. During the Marshall Plan U.S. officials did not use the term public diplomacy. Rather, they identified their work as propaganda, information, psychological warfare, and publicity. A posteriori, I impose the term public diplomacy on U.S. programs during the Marshall Plan period as a matter of convenience, in effect treating cultural diplomacy as a subset of public diplomacy.[5]

In the 1950 state of the union address President Harry S. Truman gave a clear indication of public diplomacy's importance as a major axis of U.S. foreign policy. "Our aim for a peaceful, democratic world of free peoples," explained Truman, "will be achieved in the long run, not by force of arms, but by an appeal to the minds and hearts of men."[6] In the 1990s the United States neglected public diplomacy. The USIA was, in fact, subsumed by the State Department in 1999. What need was there for overseas information programs in a post–Cold War world?

The occupation of Iraq and the 9/11 attacks refocused attention on public diplomacy. Simply put, the United States is one of the most hated nations on the planet, and apathy often prevails where hatred is absent. Such have been the consistent findings of the ongoing Pew Global Attitudes Project.[7] Summarizing the results of a forty-four nation poll, the researchers concluded: "Images of the U.S. have been tarnished in all types of nations: among longtime NATO allies, in developing countries, in Eastern Europe and, most dramatically, in Muslim societies."[8] Testifying before the Senate Committee on Foreign Relations, Andrew Kohut, the director of the Pew Research Center, explained that the "spread of U.S. ideas and customs is disliked by majorities in almost every country included in this worldwide survey."[9] Such antipathy bewilders most Americans. "Why do they hate us?" is a common topic for U.S. newspaper editorial pages. The inability of the United States to convince its allies, let alone the rest of the world, of the soundness of its foreign policy, politics, and social order prompted President George W. Bush to create the Office of Global Communications. Its mission is to advise the President "of the most effective means for the United States Government to ensure consistency in messages that will promote the interests of the United States abroad, prevent misunderstanding, build support for and among coalition partners of the United States, and inform international audiences."[10] The period under consideration in this book reminds us that such efforts are not new. Truman's Campaign of Truth, launched in 1950, made "cultural infiltration" a central, if underfunded, component of U.S. foreign policy.[11]

Focusing on France, this book examines the programs of the U.S. State Department and the Marshall Plan, which was formally called the European Recovery Program (ERP) and was administered from Washington by the Economic Cooperation Administration (ECA). The largest component of American public diplomacy belonged to the Marshall Plan. As David Ellwood argues, the Marshall Plan was "the greatest international propaganda operation ever seen in peacetime."[12] The Marshall Plan provided the United States with an unprecedented opportunity to intervene in the affairs of Western Europe. It was not only an effort to reconstruct European economies; the plan was also an attempt by the United States to reorder European society. From chicken farming to class relations, the United States deployed the Marshall Plan in an attempt to provide economic and technical assistance that would end class conflict, cement peaceful European relations, check the rise of communism, and promote American interests.

American public diplomacy was developed both as a means of accomplishing specific political, social, and economic policy goals and as an end in itself for furthering transatlantic understanding. U.S. programs included films, exhibits, publications, travel promotion, and educational/technical exchange programs. The budget of the Marshall Plan program (funded by the local currencies of participating countries and known as counterpart funds) far exceeded that of any other American agency devoted to similar work. A clause in the bilateral agreement between the United States and participating countries allowed for American publicity programs in the participating countries. It also established a 5 percent pool from the total counterpart funds that was available for information and administrative work in participating countries. The budget of the ERP's French Mission (Mission France) in 1951, for example, included the counterpart equivalent of $10 million for information and special projects.[13] Italian information programs ranked second at $7.6 million, followed by the West German mission.

A primary topic of this book is the development and scope of U.S. public diplomacy in France, and its connection to U.S. foreign policy. One group of questions deals with policy issues. How did France and the United States negotiate the implementation of this policy, an operation that stretched from Paris to the smallest village in provincial France? What goals did the program hope to achieve? Who, both French and American, formulated public diplomacy? How did politicians of the Fourth Republic, engaged in their own efforts to reproduce French national identity, respond to the American program? What was the relationship between the operations of various U.S. agencies in Europe and the administration in Washington, D.C.? A second group of questions deals with the impact of U.S. public diplomacy and its French reception. How did French and American officials assess the program: did it gain support for Washington's larger political, economic, and social goals? How did long-standing transatlantic stereotypes affect not only the production and content of American policy, but also its French reception?[14] Finally, to what extent did the U.S. programs contribute to the Americanization of France?

Although the literature on the Marshall Plan and France is extensive, few authors treat its cultural components.[15] A recent volume edited by Dominique Barjot and Christophe Réveillard examines the Marshall Plan and Americanization by focusing on the Technical Assistance Programs.[16] Yves-Henri Nouailhat provides a study of the emergence of U.S. cultural policy in France from 1945 to 1950 without examining the specific programs of the Marshall Plan.[17] Several authors treat France in the context of Franco-American relations. Richard F. Kuisel examines Franco-American relations since the Second World War, combining a study of policy with an analysis of how Americanization raised questions of national identity.[18] However, Kuisel's chronology is broad, and public diplomacy during the Marshall Plan is not his focus. Irwin M. Wall and William I. Hitchcock provide detailed studies of the economic and political interventions of the U.S. in France from 1944 to 1954, but they devote little attention to the question of public diplomacy.[19] Reinhold Wagnleitner's *Coca-Colonization and the Cold War* addresses public diplomacy as well as the question of Americanization in Austria.[20] However, the conditions in Austria—an occupied country—that Wagnleitner studies were radically different from those in France. Other studies similarly highlight the importance of national studies.[21]

While the formation and strategy of public diplomacy has recently gained attention from diplomatic historians, policy makers, and the public, questions still remain about its impact, reception, and broader cultural implications. Even contemporary proponents of public diplomacy are at pains to demonstrate the effectiveness of their programs. "Unfortunately," notes the director of the Foreign Policy Centre in *how to assess public diplomacy*

London, a strong advocate of public diplomacy, "it is very difficult to evaluate public diplomacy activity. While it is possible to measure changes in public opinion over time, there is no way of being certain what factor or combination of factors may have influenced this."[22] The State Department now uses a contact-management system that tracks the participation of various "target groups" at previously identified events (movies, lectures, and so on).[23] During the Marshall Plan an indirect means employed by U.S. planners for demonstrating the success of the program was to assess the level of Communist reaction it provoked. Another barometer of success employed was the quantitative distribution of U.S. material, both in an autonomous form such as pamphlets and as items carried in the French press.

I use local and national press, opinion polls, letters, radio programs, diplomatic records, and oral histories in an attempt to assess the efficacy of U.S. public diplomacy vis-à-vis foreign policy objectives, which included the goal of shaping French perceptions of American society. The majority of official records consulted were from the files for the Information Divisions of Mission France and the Office of the Special Representative (OSR), supplemented with the records of the USIS, U.S. State Department, the French Foreign Ministry, and the French Interministerial Committee for Economic Cooperation (SGCI). This study does not eschew quantitative measures. However, numbers fail to indicate anything about reception or changes in attitudes. Einstein's aphorism "Not all that counts can be counted, and not all that can be counted counts" is particularly relevant to the study of public diplomacy. American and French officials, as we will see, were at pains to demonstrate the effects of U.S. programs. And yet the seriousness with which such officials fought or embraced these programs is not difficult to assess. U.S. and French officials clearly believed in and "witnessed" the impact, negative and positive vis-à-vis policy objectives, of such programs.

The Marshall Plan and Americanization

Efforts to Americanize Europe were not without their American and European critics. Koren's baseball proposal was eventually rejected. The head of Mission France's information division, Helen Kirkpatrick, informed Koren that funds were not available. However, private discussions between Kirkpatrick and other officials revealed that deeper issues had been raised by the proposal to send baseball to France. In a probing interpretation of the dangers of Americanization one U.S. official suggested that transmitting baseball to France would corrupt the sport: "Some things are ineradicably local. Some things are sacred."[24] Logically then there were also French institutions, traditions, and attitudes that were local. In examining the public diplomacy of the United States in France, this study reveals how the programs of the United States interacted with the sacred and the local in France.

This book challenges a number of conceptions of Americanization. I use the term to refer to social, political, economic, and cultural changes that arose from the spread of a specific version of modernity promoted by the United States through public and private policies and practices. Americanization, of course, is a contested concept, and the use of the term by postwar critics of the United States further complicates its use by scholars today.[25] Following Victoria De Grazia, Eli Moen, and Harm G. Schröter, this study treats Americanization as a historically delineated concept.[26] For De Grazia, the term Americanization is applicable from 1920 to 1970 when "the U.S. was not only a paradigm of development, but also exerted powerful pressures for change, its consumer durables and cultural industries vastly accelerating the globalization of markets and the pressures exercised thereby on local economies and cultures."[27] For Moen and Schröter, Americanization does not refer to "unchanged imports" from the U.S., but a convergence of how comparable issues are treated in the U.S. and other countries.[28]

As an aspect of modernity Americanization is closely related to globalization.[29] If globalization, following Philip Gordon and Sophie Meunier, refers to "the increasing speed, ease, and extent with which capital, goods, services, technologies, people, cultures, information, and ideas now cross borders," then Americanization refers to the centrality of the U.S. in this process, which has been prominent at specific historical moments.[30] As Henry Kissinger has put it, "What is called globalization is really another name for the dominant role of the United States."[31] Polls indicate that it is the threat of Americanization that makes the French most apprehensive about globalization.[32]

For some scholars, however, modernity remains the primary category of analysis. As Rob Kroes explains, critical theory since Marx has argued that capitalism and imperialism possess an expansionist logic. Therefore the changes attributed to Americanization were not dependent on the United States all.[33] Americanization is merely an "imprint" that makes the U.S. and American culture the scapegoat for changes caused by modernization.[34] However, this argument minimizes the exceptionalism of American capitalism and society identified by key figures in critical theory.[35] More fundamentally, this argument errs between counterfactual and denial. Clearly many social

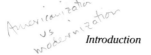

phenomena are too complex to blame only on American culture. However, in other cases American influence is demonstrable. Would the Belgian and French fast-food chain Quick have arisen without a McDonald's to copy? And if so, would its name be "Rapide"? Would its menu still have Le SuperGiant, KingFish, Long Bacon, and Long Chicken? Some modern cultural trends are not intrinsically American, as Reinhold Wagnleitner points out, but many are because the United States occupies the dominant location in the capitalist culture of consumption.[36]

In the 1950s and 1960s American mass culture became one of the most visible signs of the social transformations affecting France. Many French intellectuals and political leaders confronted American mass culture with apprehension.[37] Leaders of France's Fourth Republic had reason to be insecure. A weak executive office, disastrous colonial policies, and divided political parties condemned it to a troubled, brief existence from 1946 to 1958. As France began to modernize during the Marshall Plan years and became dependent on the U.S. for security during the 1950s, critics worried that the Americanization of French society was the inevitable outcome. American mass culture may not have been the driving force behind the transformation of French society during the "thirty glorious" years of economic growth, but it was certainly a material component of this transformation. The Marshall Plan provided support for French modernization while U.S. public diplomacy simultaneously presented the American way of life as the most desirable outcome.

Historians and other commentators disagree on the extent to which American culture transforms other cultures. An important distinction must be made at the outset. When discussing cultural transformation, scholars often conflate two phenomena. One relates to the transformation of cultural meaning, the other to the material transformation of culture. This book presents a number of examples of the latter, and it infers some of the former. As such it disputes the work of Rob Kroes, Richard Pells, and others who minimize the transformative effect of American culture while emphasizing the transformation of meaning.[38] They argue that American culture has become global but poses little danger for other cultures. Europeans transform American culture; "they re-contextualize it," Kroes contends, "and re-semanticize American culture to make it function within expressive settings entirely of their own making."[39] For these scholars Americanization is primarily a semiotic process. American culture, which Kroes sees as a configuration of symbols and myths that reinforce collective identity in the United States, has became a global collection of "free-floating signifiers."

Kroes does criticize the commodification of the political ideal of freedom. Yet even here there is a silver lining. The connotations of American mass culture—"freedom of choice" and "choice of freedom"—make this culture inherently subversive and offer the potential for cultural rebellion.[40] American mass culture provides the tools for younger generations to challenge the status quo:

> Boys or girls with the name *Coca-Cola* on their T-shirts are not the unpaid peddlers of American merchandise. Quite the contrary; they have transcended such trite connotations and restored American icons to their pure semiotic state of messages of pleasure and freedom. Within this global youth culture the icons that youngsters carry are like the symbol of the fish that early Christians drew in the sand as a code of recognition. They are the members of a new International, geared to a postmodern world of consumerism rather than an early modern one centered on values of production.[41]

Reinhold Wagnleitner offers a similar understanding of the subversive character of American mass culture, but with a significant difference. Unlike Kroes's "free-floating signifiers," Wagnleitner materially and historically grounds the subversive aspect of American mass culture in the postwar years.[42] Perhaps more importantly, Wagnleitner shows the limits of subversion by showing how traditional gender roles remained intact.

Kroes and Pells save their sharpest criticisms for the efforts of politicians and intellectuals to limit the spread of American mass culture. They are certainly correct to point out the elitism in many criticisms of mass culture. As an example of this Kroes cites François Mitterrand's argument, articulated during trade negotiations on audiovisual goods, that a nation must represent itself in images or cease being a nation.[43] Kroes objects to the paternalist implications of this stance. Such a conception of national identity, he contends, requires a centrally imposed definition. Intolerance of foreign cultures and influence is also inherent in this view. Kroes is not only critical of European politicians who advocate protectionism. He also criticizes Europeans who protest the policies of transnational financial institutions.[44]

Linking cultural essentialism with cultural protectionism is a common argument employed against the critics of Americanization. I suggest that this line of thinking commits two errors. First, it sets up a straw man. Not all those who resist the spread of American mass culture are essentialists. Some of its opponents certainly do belong to the antimodern forces Benjamin Barber identifies as "Jihad"—dogmatic and violent particularisms.[45] Yet not all those who defend cultural uniqueness do so in the name of the Al Qaeda. Even in France politicians who advocate protecting the "cultural exception" recognize the diversity of French culture.[46]

The defenders of American mass culture posit a strong link between the success of American mass culture and the agency of consumers. Although post-structuralist theorists have argued for an understanding of subjectivity that takes into account power, hegemony, and symbolic orders, scholars such as Kroes and Pells posit agents that possess a Cartesian power to create meaning.[47] No one forces Europeans to watch American movies or to eat at McDonald's. They do this because they want to; to state otherwise is to fall back into the errors of cultural imperialism and elitism. Because this perspective stresses the transformation of American culture by Europeans, it follows that even if only American products were available they would be understood in a distinctly French (or Irish, Italian, Polish, or perhaps even "European") way. The defenders of American mass culture emphasize the "heroic" side of the "antimony of political correctness" identified by Frederic Jameson.[48] Representations that emphasize victims or suffering are the other side of this antimony. According to the heroic perspective, the latter emphasizes the defensive weakness of non-American cultures. This risks making subaltern populations appear even more powerless.[49] Jameson argues, however, that both strategies of representations are necessary, but present at different points in the struggle against colonization, with different political consequences. Walter Benjamin illustrates this concern when he writes, "The contemporary who learns from books of history to recognize how long his present misery has been in preparation (and this is what the historian must inwardly show him) acquires thereby a high opinion of his own powers. A history that provides this kind of instruction does not cause him sorrow, but arms him."[50]

A consequence of perspectives that emphasize consumption is to exclude a whole sphere of action in the social and political realm indicative of group and individual agency. My study argues for an understanding of agency that does not limit the heroic to the act of consumption. Many examples of reception/transformation provided by the consumption school are either superficial or surprisingly passive. Drinking Coke or eating at McDonald's may indeed provide French youth with an opportunity to rebel against conservative parents. Nevertheless, the positive correlation between the spread of fast-food chains and increases in adolescent obesity indicates the price of such rebellion.[51] While a semiotician sees a seven-year-old girl's admiration of an American pop star as "an experiment in creative identification with their admired examples," others would see a girl in a media environment saturated with dangerously thin and/or surgically enhanced women.[52] Furthermore, the evidence provided for the subversiveness of American mass culture and for the transformation of "free floating signifiers" is vague, like the signifiers themselves. The message sent—notions of freedom associated with the American west in the case of Marlboro cigarettes—is the message consumed. In many instances "active reception" does not seem to alter meaning significantly. After interviewing visitors to Tokyo Disneyland and Disneyland Paris, Alan Bryman concluded that "the dominant frame within which the parks are read is very much in tune with what Disney seeks to promote."[53] Furthermore, Bryman shows that the popularity of the theme parks increased after Disney ceased attempting to incorporate local culture. Illustrations of the transformation of meaning and the subversive nature of American consumer goods are applicable to Eastern Europe during the Cold War, for example, but this was linked to the nature of Communist regimes, the political economy of consumer goods, and the often tangible risks associated with possessing such goods.

As an approach for studying Americanization, political economy does have its limitations. It is easy to demonstrate the ubiquity of Hollywood movies, *Reader's Digest,* and American tourists. The transfer of the values deemed to be implicit in these vessels is less easy to demonstrate. For Pierre Guerlain Americanization is "jeans-deep."[54] It was, after all, the inability of the cultural imperialism approach to take into account the "self-understanding" of indigenous people that led to its widespread rejection.[55] However, an emphasis on agency does not necessarily reveal the transformation of cultural meaning. The native of Paris, Texas, receives culture and transforms its meaning in a process similar (mechanically, that is) to that of the native of Paris, France. That individuals construe the world and culture in different ways is the starting point (and a rather banal one) not the finish line. Historically, resistance or, more basically, agency has never been limited to the realm of culture.[56] Thus Frantz Fanon criticizes those who think it possible to give "new values" to "native culture" within a "framework of colonial domination."[57]

It is difficult to talk about agency or self-understanding without reference to a cultural, social, or historical context broader than that of an individual.[58] It is not surprising, therefore, that examples that purport to show the transformation of meaning often rely on the researcher to tell us the content of the new meaning, just as the cultural imperialists told us about the imposition of values. Furthermore, skepticism about our ability to discern intent, meaning, and causality is just as applicable to the analysis of our contemporaries as it is to historical subjects. Generalization, interpretation, mediation, inference, and reference to ideology are impossible to avoid unless we accept that emphasizing agency and self-understanding makes a person capable of commenting only on the content of their own head. The latter position is similar to the "theoretical egoism" identified by Arthur Schopenhauer in the nineteenth century. The need for epistemology arises precisely because knowledge is bound to an individual. This is why the skeptic will always be able to refute causality, and the skeptic's position itself is irrefutable. This is an argument in need of a cure, not a refutation.[59] Schopenhauer recommends that the skeptical argument be regarded as a polemical refuge: "Admittedly the fortress is impregnable, but the garrison can never sally forth from it, and therefore we can pass it by and leave it in our rear without danger."[60]

This study understands Americanization in relation to the material and historical circumstances, the power, behind American hegemony and the very real transformations in culture that resulted from it.[61] The Marshall Plan in France provides a number of such examples. This was a period of unprecedented American influence and Americanization remains an important and useful concept for understanding it. Americanization is not a bulldozer, but more akin to a scattergun. It is not, in my use, a narrative that explains all social change, nor does it necessarily dictate meaning. Incorporating political economy at least has the benefit of showing which voices were privileged and which were silenced. It helps us explain the material transformation of culture. The effects of this on individual values may remain implicit or inferred, but they are no less certain because of this, much like unseen solar bodies whose existences are known only by their gravitational effects on other objects.

Chapter 1 provides the context for understanding U.S. public diplomacy in France. It begins by looking at efforts to cope with the presence of American GIs in France, a key area of cooperation between France and the United States. I also illustrate the emergence of U.S. public diplomacy during the early years of the Cold War as a high priority for American policy makers. The bilateral clause in the Marshall Plan allowed the United States to conduct a program that reached from small villages in the Massif Central to the floor of the Renault factory outside Paris. The battle against communism, both in France and throughout Europe, had to be fought by showing the superiority and desirability of the American way of life.

The first chapter also details French reactions to U.S. programs, and it looks at an example of the Fourth Republic's cultural policy, the creation of the International Film Festival at Cannes. The center-right governments of the Fourth Republic were sympathetic to American anticommunism, and they embraced policies and programs that they hoped would limit the strength of the French Communist Party (PCF). However, some French officials saw American programs as a challenge to the sovereignty of France. They accepted American hegemony, but attempted to develop strategies that would safeguard and extend French interests while limiting the American presence. This chapter also considers covert American sponsorship of a French organization to examine how American aid could be manipulated and co-opted.

The next chapter, "The True Face of the United States," takes its name from a traveling exhibit the United States used in France. This chapter examines American efforts to promote the American way of life in France through exhibitions. The first traveling exhibit began in 1949 and traveled across France stopping at small villages. Other exhibits, targeted at both the urban and rural populace, followed. I argue that because American planners were unfamiliar with the political culture of rural France these exhibits often failed to gain support to the desired extent for U.S. policy goals. Rather, I show how these exhibits acted as metanyms for modernity which in turn strengthened French discourses about the threat of Americanization. In addition, the exhibits provoked violent reactions: violent protesters destroyed three, including "The True Face." However, by the end of the Marshall Plan in 1952 the American exhibits had undergone an important transformation which increased their efficacy. Where previously American officials had provided explanations of Marshall Plan funding mechanisms and refutations of Communist charges, they now displayed consumer goods. This chapter also looks at the development of "high culture" exhibits in France such as an exhibit of the life and work of Frank Lloyd Wright, which the architect himself attended, and an exhibit sponsored by the Congress for Cultural Freedom entitled *L'oeuvre du XXe siecle.*

"Creating a Tourist's Paradise" examines the promotion of American tourism to France. American and French planners held that tourists served dual purposes. They benefited France and the U.S. economically, and they also contributed to international understanding. An important development for international tourism was the creation of so-called tourist-class airfares. American and French planners also emphasized the cultural benefits of tourism. I show how French tourism publicity in the United States presented French vacations as an opportunity for middle-class American consumers to increase their cultural capital.

Labor relations and productivity were a central concern of the Marshall Plan. The fourth chapter looks at efforts to gain support from

French labor. Labor officials from the American Federation of Labor (AFL) and the Congress of Industrial Organizations (CIO) worked directly with French labor to promote non-Communist labor organizations. At higher levels American officials concerned with the disparity of wealth in France worked to create economic policies that would increase the size of the middle class.

"The Makers of Stories" examines the print media, at the time still more influential than television or radio. The chapter discusses American publications such as *Sélection du Reader's Digest* and official U.S. publications. American publications, I show, received competitive advantages from the intervention of the U.S. State Department. In turn, their popularity (and the political economy of consumer choice is central to my analysis here) provoked French imitation. This chapter also examines how U.S. officials and private interests undermined the efforts of French legislators who sought to pass laws that limited the importation of foreign children's publications. In examining French reactions to the presence of American publications this chapter illustrates and assesses an early articulation of French cultural protectionism in the face of Americanization.

The public diplomacy of the United States created a Marshall Plan myth that endures to this day. Since 1948 world leaders have proposed "Marshall Plans" for the Middle East, Russia, the Balkans, South Africa, Cambodia, and others. There is even a campaign for a "Global Marshall Plan." Yet historians and economists question whether the Marshall Plan was essential for postwar reconstruction. Since the publication of Alan Milward's *The Reconstruction of Western Europe, 1945-1951,* a consensus has emerged that Europe was well on its way to recovery before the Marshall Plan began.[62] Scholars conclude that it retarded growth in Belgium, for example, and its effects in Italy were negligible.[63] Furthermore, as this study will show, U.S. public diplomacy itself often failed to achieve its goals, and was often counterproductive. Nevertheless, U.S. public diplomacy proved to be a powerful tool. It created the myth that the Marshall Plan was a panacea for Europe's economic woes and an extreme act of generosity and sacrifice by a rich nation rather than a politically motivated act of self-interest. U.S. public diplomacy did indeed make a deep impact. It created an image of the American way of life as a utopia of gratified individuals leading lives of mass consumption, and then promised it to European populations. In France and beyond, U.S. public diplomacy created a *mentalité,* or discourse, of what it means to be modern.[64] This discourse was and continues to be contested, but it has proven to be very durable indeed. When states fail, infrastructure crumbles, and populations starve, the myth of the Marshall Plan will always be on offer.

Notes

1. Counterpart funds for baseball, memo from William Koren to William R. Tyler, USIS, 24 January 1951, National Archives and Records Administration (NARA henceforth), record group (RG. henceforth) 84, entry 2462, box 27.
2. Ibid.
3. Planning group for integration of USIA into the Department of State, 20 June 1997, quoted in Mark Leonard, Catherine Stead, and Conrad Smewing, *Public Diplomacy* (London: the Foreign Policy Centre, 2002), 1.
4. Juliet Antunes Sablosky, "Recent Trends in Department of State Support for Cultural Diplomacy: 1993-2002," *Cultural Diplomacy Research Series,* Center for Arts and Culture, www.culturalpolicy.org, 1–2.
5. As Hans N. Tuch explains, "American public diplomacy combines cultural exchange and information programs in an integrated process of mutually reinforcing long- and short-range activities," "American Cultural Policy Toward Germany," in *The United States and Germany in the Era of the Cold War, 1945-1990,* ed. Detlef Junker (Cambridge: Cambridge U.P., 2004) 2: 276.
6. Harry S. Truman, Annual Message to the Congress on the State of the Union, 4 January 1950. The Truman Library, http://www.trumanlibrary.org/whistlestop/tap/1450.htm.
7. "What the World Thinks in 2002," "A Year After Iraq War," "Views of a Changing World 2003." These reports are available from The Pew Research Center for the People and the Press, www.people-press.org
8. "What the World Thinks in 2002," 11.
9. "American Public Diplomacy and Islam," Hearing before the Committee on Foreign Relations, U.S. Senate, 108th Congress, 27 February 2003.
10. "Executive Order: Establishing the Office of Global Communications Office" Office of the Press Secretary, 21 January 2003, http://www.whitehouse.gov/news/releases/2003/01/20030121-3.html.
11. Walter L. Hixson, *Parting the Curtain: Propaganda, Culture, and the Cold War, 1945-1961* (New York: St. Martin's Griffin, 1997), xi–xii, 232.
12. David Ellwood, "The Impact of the Marshall Plan on Italy; the Impact of Italy on the Marshall Plan," in *Cultural Transmissions and Receptions: American Mass Culture in Europe,* eds. Rob Kroes, Robert Rydell, and Doeko F.J. Bosscher (Amsterdam: VU University Press, 1993), 100.
13. Revised 1951 fiscal year obligations by activities, Budget and Fiscal Section ECA, NARA, RG. 469, entry 1193, box 44.
14. For a recent discussion of this issue see: Richard F. Kuisel, "What Do the French Think of Us? The Deteriorating Image of the United States, 2000-2004," *French Politics, Culture and Society,* 22, no. 3 (Fall 2004): 91–119.
15. The most thorough treatment of the economic policy of the Marshall Plan in France is now Gérard Bossuat, *La France, l'aide américaine et la construction européene 1944-1954* (Paris: Comité pour l'histoire Economique et financière de la France, 1992). Bossuat also provides a useful discussion of Franco-American relations during the Marshall Plan, but treats cultural policy only in passing. See also Gérard Bossuat, *Les aides américaines, économiques et militaires à la France, 1938-1960: Une nouvelle image des rapports de puissance* (Paris: Comité pour l'histoire Economique et financière de la France, 2001); Barry Eichengreen, ed., *Europe's Postwar Recovery* (Cambridge: Cambridge University Press, 1995); Martin Schain, ed., *The Marshall Plan Fifty Years After,* introduction Tony Judt (New York: Palgrave Macmillan, 2000).
16. Dominque Barjot, ed., *Catching up with America: Productivity Missions and the Diffusion of American Economic and Technological Influence after the Second*

World War (Paris: Presses de l'Université de Paris-Sorbonne, 2002); on the same topic see Henri Morsel, "La mission de productivité aux États-Unis de l'industrie française de l'aluminium," *Histoire Economie et Société* 18, no. 2 (1999): 413–417.

17. Yves-Henri Nouailhat, "Aspects de la politique culturelle des Etats-Unis à l'égard de la France de 1945 à 1950," *Relations internationales,* Spring 1981: 77–88.

18. Richard F. Kuisel, *Seducing the French: the Dilemma of Americanization* (Berkeley: University of California Press, 1993).

19. Irwin M. Wall, *The United States and the Making of Postwar France, 1944-1954* (New York: Cambridge University Press, 1991); William I. Hitchcock, *France Restored: Cold War Diplomacy and the Quest for Leadership in Europe, 1944-1954* (Chapel Hill: University of North Carolina Press, 1998).

20. Reinhold Wagnleitner, *Coca-Colonization and the Cold War: The Cultural Mission of the United States in Austria after the Second World War,* trans. Diana M. Wolf (Chapel Hill: University of North Carolina Press, 1994); and more recently Günter Bischof, Anton Pelinka, Dieter Stiefel, eds., *The Marshall Plan in Austria* (New Brunswick: Transaction Publishers, 2000).

21. Gerald K. Haines, *The Americanization of Brazil: A Study of U.S. Cold War Diplomacy in the Third World, 1945-1954* (Wilmington: Scholarly Resources, 1997); Bernadette Whelan, *Ireland and the Marshall Plan, 1947-1957* (Dublin: Four Courts Press, 2000).

22. Leonard, *Public Diplomacy,* 90; see also Mark Leonard, "Diplomacy by Other Means," *Foreign Policy* 132 (Sept./Oct. 2002): 48–56.

23. Leonard, *Public Diplomacy,* 92.

24. Undated memo from Harold Kaplan, Mission France Information Division, to Helen Kirkpatrick, NARA, RG. 84, entry 2462, box 27.

25. For a review of this literature see Jessica C.E. Gienow-Hecht, "Shame on *US?* Academics, Cultural Transfer, and the Cold War—A Critical Review," *Diplomatic History* 24, no. 3 (2000): 465–494.

26. Victoria De Grazia, "Americanization and Changing Paradigms of Consumer Modernity: France, 1930-1990," *Sites* 1, no. 1 (1997): 191–213; Eli Moen and Harm G. Schröter, "Americanization as a Concept for a Deeper Understanding of Economic Changes," *Entreprises et Histoire* 19 (1998): 5–13.

27. De Grazia, "Americanization," 198.

28. Moen and Schröter, 6.

29. Robert J. Antonio and Alessandro Bonanno, "A New Global Capitalism? From 'Americanism and Fordism' to 'Americanization-Globalization'," *American Studies* 41, no. 2/3 (2000): 33–77; Kuisel, "Americanization for Historians," 514–515; Robert W. Rydell, "'The Americanization of the World' and the Spectacle of the American Exhibits at the 1900 Paris Universal Exposition," in *Ceremonies and Spectacles: Performing American Culture,* eds. Teresa Alves, Teresa Cid, Heinz Ickstadt (Amsterdam: VU University Press, 2000): 93–100; Walter L. Hixson, "Whose World Is It, Anyway?" Feature Review, *Diplomatic History,* 26, 4 (2002): 645–647.

30. Philip H. Gordon and Sophie Meunier, *The French Challenge: Adapting to Globalization* (Washington: Brookings Institution Press, 2001), 5.

31. Quoted in William K. Tabb, *Unequal Partners* (New York: New Press, 2002), 14.

32. Gordon and Meunier, 42.

33. Rob Kroes, "American Empire and Cultural Imperialism: A View From the Receiving End," in *Rethinking American History in a Global Age,* ed. Thomas Bender (Berkeley: University of California Press, 2002), 298.

34. Ibid.

35. Max Horkheimer and Theodor W. Adorno, *Dialectic of Enlightenment,* ed. Gunzelin Schmid Noerr, trans. Edmund Jephcott (Stanford: Stanford University Press, 2002), 105; Cf. Antonio Gramsci, "Americanism: [Babbitt]," "Americanism: Bab-

bitt Again," in *Selections from Cultural Writings,* eds. David Forgacs and Geoffrey Nowell-Smith, trans. William Boelhower (Cambridge: Harvard University Press, 1985): 278–280.

36. Reinhold Wagnleitner, "The Empire of Fun, or Talkin' Soviet Union Blues: the Sound of Freedom and U.S. Cultural Hegemony in Europe," *Diplomatic History,* 23, no. 3 (1999): 499–524.

37. Jean-Philippe Mathy, *Extrême Occident: French Intellectuals and America* (Chicago: University of Chicago Press, 1993), *French Resistance: the French-American Culture Wars* (St. Paul: University of Minnesota Press, 2000).

38. See also Tyler Cowen, *Creative Destruction: How Globalization is Changing the World's Culture* (Princeton: Princeton University Press, 2002).

39. Kroes, "American Empire and Cultural Imperialism: A View From the Receiving End," 466.

40. Kroes, *If You've Seen One You've Seen the Mall,* 125.

41. Ibid., 126.

42. Reinhold Wagnleitner, "The Empire of Fun, or Talkin' Soviet Union Blues: the Sound of Freedom and U.S. Cultural Hegemony in Europe," 515–516.

43. Kroes, "American Empire and Cultural Imperialism: A View From the Receiving End," 467.

44. Kroes, "Advertising and American Icons of Freedom," in *"Here, There and Everywhere" The Foreign Politics of American Popular Culture,* eds. Reinhold Wagnleitner and Elaine Tyler May (Hanover: University Press of New England, 2000), 286.

45. Benjamin Barber, *McWorld vs. Jihad: How Globalism and Tribalism are Reshaping the World* (New York: Ballantine Books, 1995), 9.

46. The "cultural exception" in French political discourse refers to exempting culture from the harsh forces of international competition. It also indicates active support by the government for French culture, such as subsidies to French filmmakers.

47. For a discussion of the question of agency and resistance in terms of "complicit postcolonialism" see Aletta J. Norval, "Hybridization: the Im/Purity of the Political," in *Sovereignty and Subjectivity,* eds. Jenny Edkins, Nalini Persram, Véronique Pin-Fat (Boulder: Lynne Rienner, 1999): 99–114.

48. Frederic Jameson, "Globalization and Political Strategy," *New Left Review,* 4 (July/August 2000), 52.

49. Ibid.

50. Walter Benjamin, *The Arcades Project,* trans. Howard Eiland and Kevin McLaughlin (Cambridge: Harvard University Press, 1999), 481.

51. Eric Schlosser, *Fast Food Nation* (New York: Harper Collins, 2002), 242; "U.S. Eating Habits, and Europeans, Are Spreading Visibly," *New York Times* 31 October 2003.

52. Kroes, "American Empire and Cultural Imperialism: A View From the Receiving End," 266; "Globalization of Beauty Makes Slimness Trendy," Norimitsu Onishi, *New York Times,* 3 October 2002.

53. Alan Bryman, "Global Disney," in *The American Century,* eds. D. Slater and P.J. Taylor (Oxford: Blackwell, 1999), 270.

54. Pierre Guerlain, "The Ironies and Dilemmas of America's Cultural Dominance: a Transcultural Approach," *American Studies International* 35 (1997), html full-text retrieved from Wilson Select Plus.

55. Ryan Dunch, "Beyond Cultural Imperialism: Cultural Theory, Christian Missions, and Global Modernity," *History and Theory* 41 (2002), 323.

56. Amory Starr, *Naming the Enemy: Anti-Corporate Movements Confront Globalization* (New York: Zed Books, 2000), 36.

57. Frantz Fanon, *The Wretched of the Earth,* trans. Constance Farrington (New York: Grove Press, 1963), 244.

58. Volker Depkat, "Cultural Approaches to International Relations," in *Culture and International History,* eds. Jessica C.E. Gienow-Hecht and Frank Schumacher (New York: Berghahn Books, 2003), 182–186.

59. Arthur Schopenhauer, *The World as Will and Representation,* trans. E.F.J. Payne (New York: Dover, 1958), I: 104.

60. Ibid.

61. As do the essays in Ronald H. Chilcote, ed., *The Political Economy of Imperialism: Critical Appraisals* (London: Rowan and Littlefield, 2000); Susan L. Caruthers, "Not Like the U.S.? Europeans and the Spread of American Culture," *International Affairs* 74, no. 4 (October) 1999: 883–892; Richard F. Kuisel, "Not Like Us or More Like Us: America and Europe," *Diplomatic History* 22 (Fall 1998): 617–621.

62. Alan Milward, *The Reconstruction of Western Europe, 1945-51* (London: Methuen & Co., 1984).

63. See the essays in Barry Eichengreen, ed., *Europe's Post-War Recovery* (Cambridge: Cambridge U.P., 1995); David W. Ellwood, "The Limits of Americanisation and the Emergence of an Alternative Model: the Marshall Plan in Emilia-Romagna," in *The Americanisation of European Business: the Marshall Plan and the Transfer of U.S. Management Models,* eds. Matthias Kipping and Ove Bjarnar (New York: Routeledge, 1998), 149.

64. John Gray, *Al Qaeda and What It Means to Be Modern* (New York: The New Press, 2003).

Chapter 1

FRANCE, THE UNITED STATES, AND THE DEVELOPMENT OF U.S. PUBLIC DIPLOMACY

Secretary of State George C. Marshall launched what would become the Marshall Plan at Harvard University on 5 June 1947. In a moving speech he called for a program to aid European reconstruction. A year later Congress passed the Economic Cooperation Act, which created the European Recovery Program (ERP), and an administrative organization, the Economic Cooperation Administration (ECA). The immediate goals outlined by Marshall were to provide relief—food and fuel—to Europeans and to aid in the reconstruction of their economies.

Yet the Secretary of State's call for reconstruction included an important cultural component. Years of war and hardship, Marshall argued, had caused Europe to lose confidence in its future. The crisis in Europe was a threat to "modern civilization" because it invariably led, in Marshall's words, to "disturbances arising as a result of the desperation of the people concerned."[1] The program to aid European reconstruction, therefore, needed to address not only economic matters, but also the social and political threats to European stability. Marshall asserted:

> The truth of the matter is that Europe's requirements for the next three or four years of foreign food and other essential products—principally from America—are so much greater than her present ability to pay that she must have substantial additional help or face economic, social, and political deterioration of a very grave character. The remedy lies in breaking the vicious circle and restoring the confidence of the European people in the economic future of their own countries and of Europe as a whole.

Notes for this section begin on page 56.

[handwritten: Marshall Plan was anti-communist]

Convinced of the link between the deterioration of socioeconomic conditions and the increase in support for national Communist parties (the French Communist Party was already the largest party in France), U.S. officials sought to create conditions conducive to the growth of a free market economy and democracy. "At the most basic level," explains Charles S. Maier, "the Marshall Plan embodied a belief that economic assistance could help prevent Communist political advance in Europe."[2]

Eighteen states, every European country outside of the Soviet bloc except Spain, participated in the Marshall Plan, including neutral nations such as Sweden and Ireland. After the initial "offer" by the United States, leaders from the Soviet Union, Britain, and France met in Paris during June 1947 to consider the proposal. The Soviets, however, did not stay long. Foreign Minister Vyacheslav Molotov concluded that the Marshall Plan was an attempt to relieve a crisis in the capitalist mode of production and an attempt by the United States to alter the postwar status quo. It was not clear, in any case, that western European leaders were eager to have Soviet participation.[3] The offer demanded a high level of cooperation among participating nations and a willingness to involve the U.S. in national economic planning. These were conditions that were difficult for some U.S. allies to accept, and there was never any question that the Soviet Union would participate in the Marshall Plan, or that the U.S. Congress would fund it with Soviet participation. The countries that decided to participate formed the Organization for European Economic Cooperation (OEEC) to coordinate and distribute Marshall Plan aid among participating countries. From 1948 to 1951 U.S. funding for the Marshall Plan amounted to $12.5 billion, roughly 3 percent of its gross domestic product for this period. American officials hoped the Marshall Plan would strengthen ties with its European allies and insure their strategic political and economic value.

In this sense, the Marshall Plan was a continuation of immediate postwar programs for U.S. allies.[4] France, because of its importance, illustrates this development of U.S. aid from the immediate postwar to the Marshall Plan. As early as 1945 American leaders began providing economic assistance to the French government. This aid preserved the solvency of the French government and provided emergency funds for food and fuel purchases. Of the $920 million in foreign aid that the United States earmarked for Europe in September, 1945, France received $550 million.[5] This increased to $650 million for 1946 and early 1947.[6] The U.S. doubted that France could even purchase staples. For the fourth quarter of 1947 and the first quarter of 1948 the United States estimated that France would need to import the equivalent of $190 million worth of coal, $172 million in grain, and $32 million in fats and oils, but France would collect only $380 million in receipts.[7] Bread rations declined from 300g to 200g over the course of 1946 to 1947, and Americans put the average daily caloric consumption of the French at about twenty-one hundred.[8] Given these circumstances, France could not be expected to contribute financially to the occupation of Germany, or to meet other commitments, including foreign debt payments. French officials shared a similar assessment of their country's plight. A 1948 report described U.S. aid as "indispensable."[9] It had prevented widespread food shortages and "grave political and social consequences."[10]

Was France's situation that much worse than that of other European countries? Not necessarily. Visiting Washington, D.C., in August 1945, Charles de Gaulle told Truman that French coal production had reached two-thirds of its prewar level.[11] American officials estimated that food was more available in France than Italy in 1947.[12] The U.S. recognized that other countries had pressing economic needs, but officials targeted aid to Western European countries where they feared a Communist takeover. In the eyes of American officials, a strong Communist party and material deprivation created an unstable political environment. The State Department policy statement on France explained: "Today, though at peace, France is the scene of an internal political battle, the outcome of which is of the greatest importance to the United States. The world drama of Russian expansion is being played in miniature on the stage of France."[13] To make matters worse, in the eyes of American officials, the extreme right was also a threat. Summarizing the situation in 1947 a State Department memorandum explained, "In France there is a possibility that the forces of the extreme right, grouped around General de Gaulle, might temporarily seize power. But is difficult to imagine this taking place without civil war."[14] American aid was seen as essential to preserve the political stability of France.

Indeed, the French Communist Party (PCF) was strong. It received 28.8 percent of the vote in the November 1946 elections for the new National Assembly.[15] The Communist François Billoux was the Minister of Defense, and the PCF held three additional portfolios. For American politicians the strength of Communism was a symptom of European weakness, not necessarily the cause. Western Europe had been in decline since the First World War, according to American officials, and it was now in need of spiritual and cultural renewal. In the eyes of Republican Senator A.H. Vandenberg a "corroding gloom" that threatened "Western Civilization" pervaded Europe.[16] The Marshall Plan offered Europe the United States as a social, cultural, and economic model to be emulated. From labor relations to chicken farming, the Marshall Plan exported American ideas and "know-how" as the cure to Europe's ills. Above all, American support could provide the hope needed by depressed Europeans. The more Americanized Europe could become, the better off it would be. It was this premise that enabled an American official to argue that counterpart funds spent on backstops and dugouts as well as steel mills were wise investments.

Political developments increased France's importance to the U.S. In May 1947, the prime minister Paul Ramadier dismissed Communist ministers from his cabinet. Then, in October, the PCF began a policy of government opposition. In the United States there was widespread agreement in official circles that if France was "lost" to Communism the rest of continental Europe would follow. According to Robert Lovett, the acting secretary of state in 1948, France was the "keystone of continental Western Europe."[17] Thus, when the final appropriations were made France received the largest portion of continental aid from the Marshall Plan, just over $2.9 billion.[18]

As was the case with American economic assistance, U.S. public diplomacy in France preceded the Marshall Plan. Initial postwar public diplomacy was, in fact, a continuance of wartime public diplomacy. A key issue from 1944 to 1967 (with a brief interlude) was the relationship between French civilians and the U.S. military. American soldiers are just now being recognized by scholars as important vectors for Americanization.[19] Olivier Pottier's *Les bases américaines en France (1950-1967)* offers the first complete study of American troops in France during the Cold War.[20] Pottier demonstrates that efforts to limit contact between GIs and the local populace were successful, but that ironically this did not constrain the Americanization of the locales where the troops were stationed.

A July 1945 military study of the attitudes of GIs revealed the need for a dedicated public diplomacy program. Just over a year after D-Day U.S. military officials concluded that American soldiers had an overwhelmingly negative opinion of France: "If strong measures are not put in effect during the next eight or ten months," the report explained, "the vast majority of U.S. soldiers will come home with stories of a corrupt, shiftless, unfriendly France."[21] According to the U.S. military, American GIs viewed the French less favorably than the Russians, English, and even the Germans.[22] U.S. authorities called for "an all-out campaign" in cooperation with the French to alter the opinion of the GIs before they returned home. "France's part, in this campaign, can be as important as she wants it to be."[23]

French officials responded to the American proposal with alacrity. Plans were quickly worked out with the U.S. military to show two short films to American GIs. French officials expected to reach thirteen million soldiers this way.[24] For French officials, this was an unprecedented opportunity to influence American opinion in favor of France.[25] In June 1945 the French provisional government had created the *Comité français de bienvenue aux allies* (COFBA).[26] In cooperation with American authorities COFBA pursued a number of programs. It organized visits to ski resorts in the Alps for GIs on leave. It also offered courses in cooperation with American universities to over five thousand Americans in France. Armed Forces Network featured French music programs. American film students worked with COFBA to produce the short documentary *A Nation Rises Again,* which was shown to GIs stationed in Germany.

The Allied Liaison Section showed exhibits at Reims, Marseille, and Le Havre that summarized the French effort during the war and emphasized the deep history shared by the two nations. Officials claimed that fifteen hundred GIs per week visited the exhibits. Twelve resistance leaders gave twenty lectures to thirty-six thousand soldiers. The Information and Education section of the U.S. printed one hundred thousand copies of a pamphlet entitled *112 Gripes About the French* which explained to GIs "that most of the gripes they utter against France have no basis, are the result of distorted information, or the unavoidable consequences of four years of occupation."[27]

U.S. soldiers returned to France at the end of 1950 to give meaning to the North Atlantic Treaty, but in truth GIs had stayed in France for years after the liberation. A shocking incident occurred in February 1947 when French police tried to arrest four "visibly intoxicated" GIs speeding around the town of Maison-Carrée.[28] The GIs were taken into custody after a long fight with the gendarmes. A few hours later another group of GIs tried to "rescue" their jailed comrades. One reportedly threatened French authorities with his Colt pistol. Further violence was avoided only with the arrival of more French gendarmes and some U.S. officers. As late as 1949 the Foreign Ministry received complaints about the presence of U.S. military police and their jeeps in the French capital.[29]

Marshall Plan public diplomacy inherited this issue. U.S. officials identified a number of concerns that the presence of American troops would raise in France. Local inflation, housing shortages, and criminal acts were some of the issues they hoped to assuage. U.S. officials recommended a targeted propaganda campaign in locations where U.S. troops were in close proximity to the French population: Donges, Melun, Bordeaux, La Pallice, Orléans, Châteroux, Metz, and Verdun.[30] Helen Kirkpatrick, the head of the Information Division at Mission France, provided an "Information Operational Plan" to guide U.S. policy in Iceland, the U.K., France, Italy, Germany, Austria, Trieste, and Morocco.[31] The presence of U.S. troops made tensions with the local population inevitable. The crucial task, therefore, was to educate European populations about the contributions of U.S. soldiers to their own security. The plan recommended the following general "treatments":

A. The American soldier, sailor, airman is a positive force for peace through strength.
B. The American soldier, sailor, and airman with other military forces of NATO assures security against aggression.
C. The American soldier, sailor, and airman respects the national status and prestige of the country in which he is stationed.
D. The American soldier, sailor, and airman always pays his own way.
E. American military forces in Europe are the best trained, equipped, and led forces ever sent abroad by the U.S.

In late 1952 France and the U.S. established a Franco-American Troop Relations Committee. Its first recommendation was to use the Institut Français d'Opinion Publique (IFOP) to conduct a poll to determine the "points of friction" between the French populace and U.S. soldiers.[32]

The involvement of French government and military officials on publicity programs to address the presence of GIs contrasted greatly with other aspects of U.S. public diplomacy. It was not just that the U.S. recognized the complexity and significance of this issue. This was an area that the Fourth Republic viewed as crucial. Its vigilance in other areas was not as pronounced, however. With the arrival of the Marshall Plan the United States unleashed a campaign without precedence during peace.

Each country mission possessed a staff which was responsible for conducting public diplomacy. In theory the ECA Information Division in Washington, D.C., set the strategic goals for the programs which were then coordinated with individual country missions by the Information Division of the Office of the Special Representative (OSR) in Paris. Alfred Friendly and then Roscoe Drummond served as the chief of the OSR Information Division. Uniformity was often a problem with American material. However, because country missions possessed their own budgets for information and administrative expenses they were also able to develop national projects. Marshall Plan film documentaries were often produced by local filmmakers rather than Americans. The OSR then dubbed those it deemed to be of superior quality for distribution to other Marshall Plan countries. Similarly, the OSR shared publicity ideas among country missions. The programs that emerged were innovative if not always successful in achieving their goals.

American officials concluded that pubic opinion in France merited special attention. A 1946 policy statement by the State Department concluded that public opinion in France was generally unfavorable to the United States.[33] "The American way of life," the report explained, "is generally regarded as essentially materialistic and hedonistic." According to the State Department, both left and right wing political parties were increasingly adopting an anti-American line as a result of "chauvinism" and a desire for "national recognition and prestige." The State Department recommended an information and cultural program not only to combat French misconceptions of the American way of life, but also to illustrate how U.S. goals for Europe were in line with French desires for recovery and prosperity.

The Smith-Mundt subcommittee (Senator Alexander Smith of the Senate Foreign Relations Committee and Representative Karl Mundt of the House Foreign Affairs Committee) confirmed these conclusions and recommendations. The group toured Western Europe in 1947 to study the effectiveness of American information services, determine the necessity for the Marshall Plan, and investigate the status of European education and the position of labor.[34] The Smith-Mundt group spent four days in Paris conducting interviews with French and American officials, newspaper publishers, and radio and broadcasting executives. Paul W. Thompson, the European representative for *Reader's Digest*, told the committee that Communist propaganda was effective and well organized.[35] During a meeting with French newspaper editors the head of a provincial daily bluntly informed the Americans, "Everywhere you hear—even from the smallest villages—people say 'America has done nothing for France.' ... You hear anti-American talk everywhere and nobody denies the lies the Communists tell about the Americans."

American businessmen provided specific suggestions at a luncheon. The European representative of Standard Oil told the group: "If we are going to fight against another way of life we should show our way of life as being the best in the world." He suggested that the U.S. make a film about a day in the life of a "typical" American worker. Such a film could show the worker arriving at a factory in a car and illustrate the high wages he earned as a result of high productivity. The executive suggested this could be illustrated by a graphic comparison of the number of work hours required for a laborer to purchase a dress for his wife, or provide a vacation for his family.[36] The businessmen urged Smith and Mundt to require the French government to accept a French language U.S. publication as a condition of aid. As we will see, the American magazine *Rapports: France–Etats-Unis* became one of the most widely circulated periodicals in France.

The congressional group received similar advice from American officials in other European countries: communism was pervasive and American motives were suspect. Its members returned to the United States as strong proponents for legislation that would fund American cultural and propaganda programs in Europe. The result was the 1948 Information and Educational Exchange Act, also known as the Smith-Mundt Act.[37]

To the frustration of American officials, the beginning of the Marshall Plan did not result in an increase in favorable French opinion of the United States. According to a Senate report, Communist criticisms of the Marshall Plan in France during 1948 to 1949 attained a high level of public acceptance.[38] The attacks centered on two themes. According to one, the Marshall Plan was merely a desperate attempt by the United States to dump industrial and agricultural surpluses on Europe. The second propaganda line was more general. It argued "the Marshall Plan is war." The Marshall Plan was an attempt to buy European military allies, provide funds for rearmament, and integrate Germany into an anti-Soviet alliance bent on war. The North Atlantic Treaty, signed in 1949, was, according to this argument, a preparatory step for the next world war. U.S. officials concluded that these attacks had met with success because the French population was quite simply ignorant of the provisions of the Marshall Plan: "On the other side of the ocean, much of an entire nation remains in ignorance of the objectives of the plan designed to assist the participating countries, and is either apathetic or hostile."[39] Marshall Plan officials were also pessimistic about the publicity value of the reconstruction program in the absence of a dedicated public diplomacy program. According to both Averell Harriman, the Special Representative in Europe (OSR), and Paul G. Hoffman, the head of the ECA in Washington, the Marshall Plan was "less successful, less understood, and less appreciated in France than in any other Western European nation."[40]

Because of this assessment the Marshall Plan possessed a number of services that contained cultural and public diplomacy components. First, each country mission contained an information officer, as well as posts devoted to radio, exhibits, and other visual media. A second element was the European representative of the Marshall Plan, the Office of the Special Representative, located in Paris. The OSR contained an information office and a division devoted exclusively to labor information. Finally, the administrative body of the Marshall Plan in Washington, the Economic Cooperation Administration

(ECA), included staff that addressed public diplomacy. The State Department supplemented the public diplomacy of the Marshall Plan with the Voice of America, while the United States Information Service, a separate agency, provided printed material and funded American libraries, among other activities. The Public Affairs Officer (PAO) of the American embassy in Paris was particularly active in cultural affairs. The ECA was independent of the State Department, and ECA control from Washington of its missions was often tenuous.[41] The perspectives of these agencies often reflected different priorities, and as a result American public diplomacy did not possess a unified voice.

The crisis in public opinion was exacerbated, in the eyes of American officials, by the refusal of the French government to assist in pro-American publicity. Jefferson Caffery, the American ambassador in France, reported that the French government could not be expected to conduct anti-Communist propaganda.[42] The French had established an interministerial committee (SGCI) to work with the ECA. It coordinated economic planning and managed counterpart funds. Georges Elgozy, of the SGCI, appears to have had cordial relations with Mission France officials, but Elgozy was not in charge of French publicity. He occasionally vetted American material informally.[43] In private conversations Elgozy explained that pro-American propaganda by the French government would only confirm the Communist charge that the Marshall Plan rendered the government subservient to U.S. interests.[44]

Article VIII of the bilateral agreement outlined France's publicity requirements to support of the Marshall Plan.[45] Both governments recognized that publicity "was in their common interest." The agreement also stipulated that the French government would publicize Marshall Plan projects and relief aid. Following the demands of the U.S., French and ECA officials established a *comité de travail* in December 1948. It was composed of representatives from the SGCI, Mission France, the French foreign ministry, and the state secretary for information (*secrétaire d'Etat à l'information*). The *comité* had three tasks: to coordinate the publicity of French governmental services relative to the Marshall Plan; to "follow" private publicity initiatives; and to create publicity in areas not already covered by governmental or private efforts.[46] The French allotted twenty million francs for Marshall Plan publicity in 1949. This amount would remain unchanged each year through 1952. In contrast, Mission France used over seven and a half billion francs in counterpart funds for publicity in 1950 alone.[47]

In 1948 Prime Minister Henri Queuille informed François Mitterrand, the state secretary for information, of the measures necessary to comply with Article VIII.[48] He stated that Mitterrand need only meet "periodically" with the SGCI, the Ministry of Foreign Affairs, and the Commissariat au Plan to determine which aspects of economic cooperation should receive publicity. Queuille also cautioned Mitterrand about sharing authority with the ECA: "You should not, in any way, directly or indirectly submit your planned initiatives for Marshall Plan publicity to the American authorities."[49]

The U.S. Congress raised concerns about Marshall Plan publicity. In February 1950, the head of the Economic Cooperation Administration, Paul G. Hoffman, testified before the House Committee on Foreign Relations. The Committee was particularly interested in the "informational activities" of the ECA in Europe. Congressmen pushed Hoffman to clarify how this program differed from existing programs run by the State Department through embassies and cultural attachés. Duplication was a potential problem, Hoffman admitted, but he argued that an independent information program was essential for the ECA: "It is quite impossible to tell the story of what the Marshall Plan is doing for Europe without getting across the story of the American democratic way of life."[50] The ECA retained an independent program not only because U.S. officials accepted it, but also because its operations were financed by counterpart funds.

The Evolution of U.S. Public Diplomacy

Promoting the American way of life, productivity, and explaining the operations and benefits of the Marshall Plan were the foci of U.S. public diplomacy from 1948 to 1952, but beginning in 1950 other themes were emphasized as well. The onset of the Korean War drastically increased tensions between the United States and the Soviet Union. As a consequence, the planning of informational activities by the U.S. began to emphasize psychological warfare. The U.S. also sought to create support for rearmament in Western Europe (particularly of Western Germany) and the North Atlantic Treaty. Yet the policy of Mission France was also shaped from below, that is from the reaction of the French public and officials and the assessments of embassy and Mission France officials. The tensions between these two forces—geopolitical policy planning in Washington and local, often anecdotal, assessments of French opinion and politics—were significant. Mission France officials, working closely with embassy personnel, resisted directives from Washington about the content of American material if they thought they could harm French opinion. Mission France rejected U.S. films or publications, for example, which dealt with French colonial possessions. Officials in Washington, particularly in the ECA information office, rarely ceased calling for high-visibility, high-volume campaigns in support of rearmament and other issues that were difficult to implement in France. The relative autonomy of the country missions created lacunae between the priorities established in Washington and the material developed by each country mission.

This was especially clear when it came to promoting European unification. The unification project was a priority for many French and American leaders at the highest levels of government. "European cooperation" was an explicit demand of the Marshall Plan, and some supporters of unification saw the Marshall Plan as a first step toward creating a federated Europe. For Paul G. Hoffman recovery was impossible without European cooperation. Addressing the OEEC in 1948, he declared, "New patterns of intro-European trade and exchange must be found and new directions in the use of Europe's resources."[51] European cooperation on trade was to be the precursor to European political unification. Indeed, the first great success (the creation of the European Coal and Steel Community) and failure (the European Defense Community) of the European project occurred during the Marshall Plan under French leadership. My concern here is not, however, one of causality. I am not interested in debating the extent to which the Marshall Plan was responsible for the move toward unification.[52] Rather, I am concerned with the role played by U.S. public diplomacy in promoting unification.

Both the ECA office in Washington, D.C., and the OSR in Paris decreed that unification was a key "theme" of U.S. information work in 1950. Ironically, the Communist invasion of South Korea in June 1950 was more of an impetus for emphasizing unification than the announcement of French Foreign Minister Robert Schuman's plan to merge French and German steel and coal production in May 1950.[53] As European recovery became synonymous with European rearmament, support for unification also shifted to military initiatives. A French plan to create a European Defense Community (EDC) became the favored initiative of the U.S.[54] It would resolve French concerns about West German rearmament and thus allow for the creation of a Western European military capable of facing the Soviet Union.

The emphasis on rearmament and European military unification— safety before prosperity—was difficult to implement in France. In contrast to other themes, Mission France practiced a subdued campaign in support of unification. There were several reasons for this. The most important one was the simple realization that European unification would have to be achieved by Europeans, not American statesmen or propagandists. The U.S. ambassador to France, David Bruce, warned

American officials in 1950 that the French must have the "appearance" of being in control of the EDC negotiations.[55] A year later another U.S. embassy official concluded that U.S. support of the EDC was counter-productive.[56] In 1953, amid difficult negotiations, denunciations of the EDC by French communists, and wavering public opinion, the U.S. embassy warned of "a growing feeling in France that the United States is attempting to pressure the French government into ratification of the EDC agreements, which generate little enthusiasm among average Frenchmen."[57]

In an attempt to minimize its profile in France and elsewhere, U.S. officials relied on national governments and the press office of the OEEC to promote unification.[58] The amount of material, unsurprisingly, generated by such efforts was practically insignificant relative to the propaganda conducted by the U.S. on other topics. OEEC countries displayed examples of their pro–Marshall Plan publicity at a Paris meeting and the OEEC sponsored a train exhibit which, we will see, disappointed U.S. officials. The topic of European unification was present in U.S. exhibits and publications, but it received much less attention than productivity and general Marshall Plan and pro-American information. According to the head of Mission France's information division, productivity, defense, and unification were three aspects of one policy, "a stronger Europe," and one necessarily implied the other.[59] In practice, Mission France treated unification in the context of something else, usually intra-European trade and productivity. Mission France did promote unification when it could be assured of a sympathetic audience. The Mission France magazine *Rapports France–Etats-Unis* editorialized in favor of unification and carried a number of articles on the topic. However, it was productivity, the American way of life, and explanations of the Marshall Plan—not European unification—that dominated U.S. public diplomacy in France.

Given the problematic nature of promoting European unification, it is not surprising that the majority of American support for it took the form of covert actions. "By the early 1950s," explains Richard Aldrich, "promoting European unity was the largest CIA operation in Western Europe."[60] By funding the European Movement and the European Youth Campaign the CIA used Europeans to further the goal of unification. Such indirect means became standard practice for the CIA, and Mission France also used this technique on a smaller scale. The U.S. ambassador in France was the "sole link" between the CIA and the French government.[61] By design the USIS and Marshall Plan missions were not involved. Indirect sources may have protected the U.S. from harming public opinion in sensitive countries, in the short term, but their efficacy was questionable. Covert operations attract the attention of historians for good reason, but it is easy to exaggerate their importance. Indeed, Aldrich concludes that the European Movement exerted little influence on public opinion or the negotiations surrounding the Schuman Plan.[62]

Even when the various U.S. agencies agreed on content they disagreed on how the effectiveness of American propaganda could be assessed. In Washington, ECA and State Department officials relied on quantitative measurements to judge the success of propaganda. In addition to using attendance and distribution figures, and counting press items, ECA officials used the level of Communist reaction to American propaganda as an indicator of successful propaganda work. The chief PAO of the American embassy in Paris, William R. Tyler, rejected such methods. As we will see, he argued that in many cases it was impossible to assess the effectiveness of American propaganda; only the failures of American propaganda revealed themselves. Nevertheless, the disagreements between Mission France and the ECA and State Department were not apparent until the events of 1950 generated the change in U.S. policy.

Both the head of the ECA, Paul G. Hoffman, and Averell Harriman, the special Ambassador to Europe, emphasized the quantitative success of the information program. Testifying before the House Committee on Foreign Relations, Hoffman stated that the purpose of information activity was to increase awareness of the Marshall Plan in Europe. "We are under way today with an extensive program of information activity," he explained, "to blanket Europe with information about the Marshall Plan."[63] Harriman, in front of the same committee, stressed attendance figures for exhibits, the number of ERP documentaries shown, and the amount of press coverage it received.[64] The head of Mission France, Barry Bingham, testified that a clear indicator of the success of the information work was a Gallup poll that showed 88 percent of the French were "aware" of the Marshall Plan.[65]

Despite the efforts of some officials, the militarization of U.S. foreign policy did affect the development of U.S. public diplomacy. Even before the outbreak of the Korean War the United States had begun to emphasize rearmament as an element of foreign aid. In late 1949 Hoffman complained to the secretary of state, Dean Acheson, that ECA appropriations were becoming laden with military appropriations.[66] Following the outbreak of war it became difficult for the Truman administration to justify anything but military aid to Congress. In 1951 the Mutual Security Act extended Marshall Plan aid, but also focused the aid on military procurements. Congressional oversight also shaped the tone and language of American public diplomacy. Edward Barrett, the assistant secretary of state for public affairs, cited the difficulties in obtaining congressional approval for "pure" cultural policy (for example, sending American performers abroad or the establishment of libraries). He explained that "if you dressed it up as warfare, money was very easy to come by."[67] Anticommunism thus provided a political consensus for the support of the Smith-Mundt Act and other U.S. public diplomacy measures, but it also ensured that cultural relations and public diplomacy were subsumed under "psychological warfare."[68]

Following the outbreak of the Korean War and as a result of the increased tension with the Soviet Union, the United States increased its information programs in September 1950. In 1949 George F. Kennan, in a pessimistic appraisal of U.S. foreign policy, had urged Acheson to view propaganda as a necessary tactical and strategic "weapon of policy."[69] President Truman responded to the new developments by launching the Campaign of Truth, which expanded funding and outlined broad psychological objectives.[70] As Walter Hixson suggests, during this period psychological warfare as an instrument of American foreign policy was reborn.[71] A 1950 directive, "Psychological Offensive," instructed the country missions of the ECA to increase the output, audience, and effectiveness of their information programs.[72] The increased militarization of American information material and the fusion of public diplomacy with this material had important consequences for the practice of cultural relations. The most immediate effect was a decrease in the flexibility of field officers to respond to a country's unique cultural and political context.

William R. Tyler of the American embassy in Paris objected to "the assimilation of both categories of endeavor within a single framework."[73] "Terms and conceptions," he explained, "which are essentially applicable only to informational activities are applied in practice to 'cultural' activities even when there may be no valid relationship." The comments of William C. Johnstone, the head of State Department exchange programs, at a meeting of the Committee on Books Abroad provided a good example of the outlook Tyler opposed:

> We are not interested in getting books into the hands of people abroad because we like books or we think they are nice to have; we are not interested in having films because we think it is nice for people to look at films; we are not interested in sending students abroad and bringing students here because we subsidize scholarships.... You can describe it as propaganda or psychological warfare or you can describe it as information and conveying information. It is a little bit of everything when you come right down to it. A book on American Government put into the hands of the right person at the right time is a potent psychological weapon so to speak because what that person reads in the book, if he reads it at the right time, may be instrumental in changing

his ideas which he in turn will convey to a lot of other people, so in that respect the book is a weapon. The ideas in a book are weapons which we have to use.[74]

Johnstone and other advocates of psychological warfare emphasized the transmission of ideas and externally induced cultural change.[75] The State Department's top policy study group prepared a document, "Areas of World Concern: Priority of Target Areas, Target Groups and Most Effective Media," that also reflected the shift to psychological warfare.[76] Speaking of a program that had previously entailed only libraries, student exchanges, and documentary showings, the policy planning staff stated, "The USIE program must be geared to psychological war, which it is not prepared for today. To be effective against the foe, it must be coordinated with a covert program."[77]

This language and outlook also inflected the programs and policy of the information offices of the ECA and the OSR (the Office of the Special Representative in Europe, the operational office of the ERP in Paris). An ECA policy paper circulated in mid-1950 explained three ways "psychological pressures" could help achieve policy objectives:

1. By fixing realistic psychological objectives in line with policy objectives.
2. By providing "incentives" which will make other people feel that they want to move in the direction of our objectives.
3. By exercising persuasion.[78]

The paper outlined three policy objectives and their corollary psychological objectives. For example, the policy objective "To establish a healthy international community" contained the psychological objectives: "To build up the impression that the United States stands for peace, for freedom, for human welfare," and "To encourage a spirit of self-help and self-reliance in free nations."[79]

In 1950 Mission France and the USIS began official coordination of information activities in France.[80] The USIS, critically underfunded, could now access the 5 percent pool of counterpart funds to finance projects. Mission France, on the other hand, could make use of embassy staff and resources to expand the scope of their program beyond the economic field of the ERP. As William R. Tyler explained: "The progressive consolidation of the USIS-ECA/F information organization and activities means that the policy planning and programming of U.S. information and cultural activities in this area are more sharply defined and cover a much wider range than if each agency were carrying out a program independently of the other."[81] This cooperation was a key development for American public diplomacy in France.

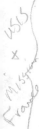

Kirkpatrick and Tyler were in fundamental agreement about the methods and means for conducting successful public diplomacy in France. Both stressed the need for indirect, French sources of material. In part, these were lessons learned from the experience of U.S. exhibits and participation in regional fairs. By late 1950 Kirkpatrick was advising that "blatant publicity" be avoided.[82] Americans now recognized that the French had been subjected to nearly five years of intense propaganda during the German occupation.[83] They were, in a sense, "allergic" to straight propaganda. Tyler responded to the "Psychological Offensive" directive by telling the State Department that "extreme flexibility" and local control were the key elements to successful information work.[84] He warned that the USIS should avoid explaining activities in terms of the relationship between "media" and "targets." He supported such efforts as the covert funding of the organization France—Etats-Unis and attempts to win over opinion makers to American policy through exchange programs. For Tyler, information programs were practical and successful to the extent that they simulated and facilitated French efforts to shape French opinion in ways favorable to U.S. foreign policy.[85] The positive impact of a propaganda campaign per se was both fleeting and difficult to assess:

> It is true that you get a large number of people going through exhibits just as you get large numbers of people watching lonely fishermen fishing in the Seine. But it does not necessarily mean that what they are looking at is understood or that if it is understood, it is making a deep impression on them, or that if it is making a deep impression on them, that they are the people we most want to reach. Statistics here as elsewhere can be the enemy of true assessment.[86]

During the closing months of 1950 Mission France and the American embassy fought a turf-guarding campaign against the ECA information office in Washington. At issue was who would determine the content and form of American public diplomacy in France. Robert Mullen, the head of the ECA Washington information division, and Roscoe Drummond, the head of the OSR information division, favored a direct, "fast media" campaign stressing productivity, rearmament, and European integration.[87] "Fast media" included radio, film, and press advertisements, as opposed to the "slow media" of high culture and educational programs.[88] Mullen also favored a voluntaristic approach by industry and the use of paid advertising.[89] In July he created an advisory committee for the ECA with the Advertising Council.[90] It included consultants from the J. Walter Thompson Company, *The Washington Post,* and General Mills. Later Life International participated in planning.[91]

The Advertising Council was a coalition of businesses formed during the Second World War to mobilize war bond sales and conduct public service campaigns.[92] Following the end of the war it continued its efforts to mobilize the American public, thus making the transition from building wartime unity to creating a Cold War consensus.[93] The Advertising Council possessed close links to the Eisenhower administration and the ECA. Among other projects it was an important fund-raiser for Radio Free Europe.[94] The pamphlet, *Advertising: a New Weapon in the World-Wide Fight for Freedom,* summarized the goals and premises of the Advertising Council:

> The world-wide fight for freedom *can* be lost—and defeat would bring an end to our political and economic system. The battle, therefore, amply justifies the active cooperation and help of American industry. But management has a further justification to its stockholders for the expenditure of corporate funds in helping counteract misconceptions and deliberate distortions with the truth about American life and motives. Industry's support of this campaign will help to hold present markets, develop new markets, and create good will in every country still free from Communist control.[95]

At the behest of Mullen, the Advertising Council sent a series of consultants to Europe to begin planning an advertising campaign in foreign publications. Many of these consultants were from the J. Walter Thompson Company. A study of French public opinion by the consultant Virgil Reed was one such mission, but others soon followed.[96]

Tyler and Kirkpatrick pressed the ambassador to restrict the ECA campaign. Tyler told the ambassador that the ideas of the ECA information office were "as foolish as they were dangerous."[97] Tyler presented his case in a lengthy memorandum where he restated his preference for an indirect, local approach to information work.[98] He criticized the ECA for lacking knowledge of European countries or languages. The material mass-produced by the ECA and OSR was "stereotyped" ("language captions to be fitted in according to the country") and ignored specific cultural contexts. Similarly, Kirkpatrick warned the chief of Mission France about the introduction of paid advertising in France.[99] This problem of mass-produced material was not just limited to the ECA, either. In 1952 the State Department distributed a questionnaire on "key words in American and Free World propaganda." It asked embassy officials to rank the importance of various terms for American propaganda, for example "peace" and "democracy." American officials in Paris pointed out that some of the terms were not equivalents when translated literally.[100] The term "Republic" to describe the United States, for example, did not have the same significance as "République" to describe France. Embassy officials in France refused to provide responses to the questionnaire, and they warned that the context for the reception of these key terms varied from one place to another.

These efforts were successful in maintaining the autonomy of the joint USIS/Mission France information program. Following the direct intervention of the ambassador, all material originating from ECA Washington for use in France was subject to Kirkpatrick's approval.[101] J. Walter Thompson received a limited contract with Mission France to consult with the Association française pour l'accroisement de la productivité (AFAP) to develop productivity publicity.[102] One of the first newspapers it consulted about running advertisements was the Communist paper *La Marseillaise*.[103] The Mission France contract with J. Walter Thompson was terminated less than a year later.[104]

The conflict between the ECA and Mission France was more than just turf-guarding and bureaucratic intrigues. The resistance of Tyler and Kirkpatrick was part of an important development in American public diplomacy. At issue was not only the control of material, but also its form. As Robert H. Haddow has demonstrated, during this period the United States began to move away from forms of information that had characterized the practices of the Office of War Information and the immediate postwar years.[105] Where previously the United States had sought to counter Soviet material and information programs on a point-by-point basis and explain the noble intentions behind the Marshall Plan, American material now began to present a more complex message about the nature of American society. In particular, information specialists began to emphasize elite culture and the cultural achievements of the United States alongside a presentation of American consumerism and material prosperity, while at the same time increasing anti-Communist programs in central and Eastern Europe.[106]

In practical terms, the shift in American information policy in France entailed focusing on two "target groups." The first was labor. The Labor Information Division of the OSR handled this area with limited success, as we will see. The other field, as described by Tyler, consisted of "the highly articulate, particularly chauvinistic and consciously superior minority grouped under the heading 'the intellectuals.'"[107] For Tyler and other American information specialists, the task was not to convert Communist intellectuals or workers, but rather to sway the sector of these groups that registered "undecided" in the IFOP and Gallup polls. Programs should be undertaken, he suggested, to reach each group in their respective cultural milieus through exchange programs and carefully planned events. Tyler argued that such methods offered the only possibility of making a deep impression on the target groups: "We cannot reach the psychological bloodstream of opinion so long as the patient is aware that he is receiving an injection."[108] Tyler accepted that these were programs whose "effectiveness" would be difficult if not impossible to assess.[109]

The meetings of the U.S. Advisory Commission on Educational Exchange, of which Helen Kirkpatrick was a member, illustrated the issues confronting American public diplomacy. Kirkpatrick told the Commission, which included the Assistant Secretary of State for Public Affairs, that the Soviet Union was capitalizing on "Europe's ingrained skepticism" of American values.[110] She described the prevalent mood as "the fear of most Europeans that Americans, brash and materialistic and uncultured, were attempting to swamp Europe with materialistic values." Soviet sponsorship of the Arts outstripped anything the Americans had been able to accomplish, and not just in France. From Iceland to East Berlin, the Soviets sponsored musicians, dancers, and other artists, including entries in the Cannes Film Festival. Kirkpatrick stated that the neglect of high culture risked destroying the gains previously won by American information programs. The Soviets, she explained, appeared to have dropped propaganda "in the political sense" from their activities in Western Europe. The Soviet line, "The Americans come in with troops, we bring you music and art," was proving quite effective.[111] She recommended that the State Department dramatically increase its support of the fine arts. Other field officers agreed with Kirkpatrick's assessment. The remarks of a former PAO in Rome demonstrated pessimism as well as a narrow understanding of culture: "We have already made the point all over the world about U.S. technical superiority and don't need to labor it any further. One thing we haven't been able to do is to convince other areas of the world that we have American culture." State Department officials acknowledged the strength of these arguments to a point. Yet the chair of the Commission, Harvey Branscomb, resented what he thought was an "apologetic state of mind" and told the group that they were "exaggerating." He nevertheless conceded that an effort needed to be made "to convince Europe that we are a cultured people."[112] The Assistant Secretary of State for Public Affairs was more receptive to their suggestions. However, he stated that high culture initiatives were "exactly the kind of thing" that Congress would refuse to fund. It would require "a good deal of education" before members of Congress understood the value of such programs.[113]

The Commission next discussed ways to fund these programs. Johnstone, also a member of the Commission, suggested that the Ford Foundation be contacted as a possible source of funding for a large-scale fine arts program. The Ford Foundation possessed close

[handwritten margin note: need to convey American high culture]

links with the State Department and the ECA. Paul G. Hoffman had resigned from the ECA in 1950 to become the Foundation's first director. The Foundation routinely consulted with the State Department before awarding grants.[114] According to Johnstone, Ford Foundation officials in New York were enthusiastic during initial discussions.[115]

During the postwar years, at least until the establishment of the President's Emergency Fund for International Affairs in 1954, the United States relied on private sponsorship to conduct exhibitions and demonstrations of America's cultural achievements.[116] The irony was that, contrary to European stereotypes, the United States did possess a vibrant and eclectic artistic life, in some ways more radical than contemporary European work.[117] The U.S. possessed such culture, but its politicians simply proved unwilling to support it. Eisenhower's 1954 creation of a "President's Fund for International Affairs" to promote cultural tours received only begrudging acceptance from the Congress. Analyzing 1955 Congressional hearings on the fund, one historian concludes that they "revealed not only profound ignorance about the arts but also active hostility toward them."[118] However, by the midway point of the Marshall Plan it was clear to many U.S. officials that the "American way of life" represented as material prosperity and productivity could not be successfully sold to Europe in a high-cultural vacuum.

A key problem with U.S. public diplomacy in France was its multiple sources. In addition to the projects of Mission France, the Office of the Special Representative Europe and the American embassy (before it began coordinating its efforts with Mission France) conducted information programs in France. Although Congress criticized the "redundancy" of ECA and State Department programs, this was not accurate.[119] Each agency's contribution to the din was unique. A more pressing concern, as evidenced by the struggles of Tyler and Kirkpatrick, was the lack of local, direct control and production of American programs by individuals sensitive to the culture of the country in question. Although the creation of the USIA in 1953 solved the bureaucratic question of redundancy, it was a beginning, not an end, in the search for effective public diplomacy.

This is not to say that the efforts of Mission France in this field were predestined to fail, or that political information programs conducted poorly were without consequences. Helen Kirkpatrick and William R. Tyler were some of the first American officials to recognize the danger of American material turning French public opinion against the U.S. They were instrumental in changing the American program from one of mass-produced material designed to support psychological objectives to a program that attempted to register and react to specific sectors of French opinion. Over time they moved away from overt propaganda as the major element of public diplomacy and sought to increase the cultural presence of the United States in other ways such as the promotion of American tourism in France and the introduction of American publications.

The cultural turn in American public diplomacy proceeded on other fronts too. Although elite culture remained an emphasis, particularly in the capitals of Western Europe, the U.S. began to incorporate mass culture into its propaganda arsenal. Jazz, previously shunned by U.S. officials, was by the late 1950s a staple of U.S. cultural tours.[120] The State Department also began to employ professional athletes, particularly black athletes, as "ambassadors of good will." American participation in fairs and international exhibits also demonstrated a growing sophistication by 1952. Overt propaganda was toned down and consumer goods, the trappings of the American way of life, were emphasized. Far from morally vapid, American exhibit planners attempted to present consumer culture in ways that conformed to traditional European sensibilities about gender roles and family values.[121] For example, the Marshall Plan film *Productivity, Key to Plenty* illustrated how a woman's productivity in the kitchen could be increased.

The Devolution of French Public Diplomacy

How did the development of French public diplomacy compare to the U.S. program? French officials, as we saw, were unenthusiastic about the requirements for publicity contained in Article VIII of the Franco-American bilateral agreement. In fact, with the exceptions of Italy and Britain, no participating country provided enough government-sponsored publicity to satisfy the United States.[122] According to Gérard Bossuat, this resistance arose from an understanding of French public opinion. Pro–Marshall Plan publicity would only contribute to Cold War divisions and endanger the larger project of modernization.[123] The governments of the Fourth Republic had reason to be cautious when it came to public opinion. The official paper of the French Communist Party, *L'Humanité*, was ubiquitous. Not only was the government vulnerable to Communist attacks, but neutralism, a recent development, had gained currency in France with the onset of the Cold War.

Although a number of other influential journals and newspapers also shared this outlook, neutralism was largely the product of the newspaper *Le Monde* and its editor, from 1944 to 1969, Hubert Beuve-Méry.[124] Beuve-Méry founded *Le Monde* in December 1944 with financial assistance from Charles de Gaulle's resistance government. Neutralism represented a desire to chart a course independent of the United States and the Soviet Union. Editorializing under the pseudonym Sirius, Beuve-Méry was one of the harshest critics of U.S. foreign policy during the period. He railed against the presence of U.S. bases, NATO, and Western European (especially West German) rearmament. These policies made war more likely, according to Beuve-Méry, and the cost of rearmament prevented West Europeans from fully recovering from the war. The "Anglo-Saxons" were preparing to win a war while the Western Europeans wanted to prevent war.[125] He was not silent on the Soviet Union, but he refused to condemn it. *Le Monde* was also critical of the governments of the Fourth Republic for their pro-American foreign policy.

U.S. officials tried to comprehend neutralism, but it did not fit into their Manichean world. A U.S. official described neutralism as "we-don't-want-to-be-occupiedism" and offered this bitter assessment: "My belief is that these people are acting almost precisely the way most individuals act when they begin to look like 'has beens,' or are afraid they are going to look like 'has beens.'"[126] Embassy personnel met with Beuve-Méry to attempt to bring him into the fold. "What I object to," Beuve-Méry reportedly explained during one conversation, "is not our alignment with the United States in interests of a common defense, but the abject subordination of our government within that alliance. I consider the present course of our government to be fatal to France.... We are just being treated like Liberia, as an appendage, as a satellite."[127]

From 1948 to 1952 U.S. officials became increasingly frustrated with neutralism. It went beyond *Le Monde*. Christian pacifists, existentialist philosophers, and others espoused the neutralist perspective. Many European politicians, particularly socialists, were sympathetic to the creation of a "third force" between the superpowers. According to one U.S. analysis, European unification itself was indicative of the "passive neutrality" of "Third-Force-ism."[128] It is safe to say that by 1951 Beuve-Méry had become a bogeyman for U.S. officials. Rumors and accusations of his involvement with the Communist Party became common. The French politician Paul Devinat "leaked" Beuve-Méry's communist affiliation to the State Department in February 1951. U.S. officials asked the Paris embassy to investigate the claim: "That B-M's policies serve the CP causes, no-one can deny. But what a beautiful jolt it would be to many avid *Le Monde* readers and disciples of neutralism if they suddenly found out they were buying, reading, and swallowing a well-starched version of *L'Humanité*."[129] In 1952 the Director of the CIA asked French officials to help in a campaign of "attack, ridicule, and exposure" against Beuve-Méry to have him removed as *Le Monde*'s editor.[130]

Sandwiched between neutralists and communists, it is easy to understand the French government's reluctance to conduct pro–Marshall Plan propaganda. Nevertheless, the French had developed a program for Marshall Plan publicity in 1948. In fact, the French effort at that point was better articulated than the American effort. French officials agreed that publicity would center on five basic messages:

1. American aid constitutes only a small portion of the French effort for reconstruction.
2. American aid is a gift, and as such there is no risk that France would be controlled by American capitalists.
3. France receives only the commodities it requests.
4. France imports only raw materials, not manufactured goods that it could produce itself, or purchase from other European countries.
5. The Marshall Plan complements France's own plans for reconstruction. It does not replace them.[131]

French officials also established a plan to collaborate their efforts with the non-Communist unions Force ouvrière and the CFTC.[132]

French publicity proceeded on other fronts too. The Marshall Plan was a frequent topic on French radio programs. Mission France's Information Division complained to French officials that the Marshall Plan was not being featured.[133] He evidently did not listen to many of the radio broadcasts. For if the Marshall Plan did not feature in the title of the broadcasts, the reconstruction of France and topics central to its success were common. The nature of the Soviet Union and the social transformation of France, for example, were topics on the program *Tribune de Paris*. One *Tribune de Paris* devoted to "The Truth About the Soviet Union" featured a contentious debate about political liberties between Maurice Clavel, Jean-Marie Domenach, and the Communist Jean Bruhat.[134] The *Tribune de Paris* focused on "Social Groups in France" for three broadcasts in August and September 1948. The programs featured Raymond Aron, who discussed the relationship between economic growth and the growth of the middle class.[135] "The Condition of Workers in the Year 2000" featured Jean Fourasitié, a key player in the French productivity program.[136] The French method demonstrated a characteristic of successful public diplomacy, to wit the use of indirect means and discretion. The ECA and Mission France, on the other hand, wanted headlines.

Granted, official, explicit French government publicity on the Marshall Plan was minimal. An official summary of French efforts claimed that "the largest publicity" had been given to the Marshall Plan. The publicity had been done with care to avoid creating the impression that it was propaganda, "which would have prevented it from reaching the French public."[137] Documentation Française, the official service of the French government, produced eighteen "documentary notes" containing texts of speeches by Marshall and Truman, as well as reports that summarized the economic aid France received. It distributed between seven and ten thousand of these to industry, educational, and other public and private establishments.[138]

The emphasis on indirect means was a French strategy, but it also reflected the limited budget available for Marshall Plan publicity. The twenty million franc budget was drawn from the prime minister's "special funds," which avoided budgetary oversight.[139] Discussing the French effort in 1948, François Mitterrand stated that the twenty million francs the French government devoted to Marshall Plan publicity was sufficient to meet its Article VIII obligations while meetings with the U.S. allowed France to retain control of the propaganda campaigns.[140] Nevertheless, throughout 1948 and 1949 American officials pressed the French to increase their efforts. Pierre-Paul Schweitzer of the SGCI told Mission France officials that French publicity efforts, for example the publication of information in *Documentation française* and radio broadcasts, and the meetings of the French and American working group "fully satisfied" the obligations of Article VIII.[141] Mission France threatened French officials that unless more publicity was issued "under the auspices of the French government" the U.S. Congress was likely to raise concerns during the next round of hearings on foreign aid.[142] French officials at the SGCI feared that the American Congress might set benchmark figures for publicity expenditures that the French had to meet in order to receive economic aid. They recognized that the twenty million franc budget was "totally inadequate" for a dedicated publicity campaign (a single brochure could easily cost that amount).[143]

In December 1949 Pierre-Henri Teitgen, in charge of information in the Bidault cabinet, requested eighty million francs for Marshall Plan publicity—a fourfold increase but still a paltry sum compared to the American use of counterpart funds for publicity.[144] This request, however, was rejected.[145] The foreign minister favored increased funding, but the SGCI noted that obtaining the funds necessary to finance a formal propaganda campaign would require official budget oversight and even the creation of a new bureaucracy.[146]

The question was not how much money was necessary to finance a campaign, but whether such a campaign was useful at all. A 1949 memorandum warned that a publicity campaign premised on quantitative distribution would sow confusion and create unrealistic expectations. "We must not lose sight," the memo noted, "of the fact the Marshall Plan is far from a panacea."[147] In 1948 François Mitterrand warned, "A campaign that escapes [France's] authority risks, if it does not take into account the legitimate susceptibilities of our population, damaging national pride and even undermining the proposed goals."[148]

French concerns over publicity reflected an astute tactical grasp of the political context. The French government may have been relatively quiet on the Marshall Plan, but the United States had little reason to doubt the commitment of French officials to its goals. In 1953 Mission France provided a "checklist of French government anti-Communist activities since 1950 aimed at reducing Communist strength and influence" to reassure U.S. officials of France's dedication to the Western camp. Under "Public Activities" the checklist described 145 actions from 11 March 1950, "Passage of law on state security, directed against Communist anti-militarist activity and agitation," to 1 October 1953, "The Seine Prefecture suspended for two weeks the Communist Deputy Mayor ... for utilizing the *Marie* for partisan purposes."[149] Items 90, 105, 107, 113, and 137 described the bombing or burning of PCF headquarters, "Perpetrators were not identified" and "cause unknown," respectively. Other actions included suspending teachers for participating in demonstrations, purging Communists from government bureaucracies, and general measures of intimidation:

> 91. February 26, 1953. Posters were affixed to the doors of ten Jewish Communist doctors in Paris who approved the sentences given the Soviet doctor-murders. The posters bore the legend: "Here lives Dr. X who, in approving the condemnation of the Soviet doctors, has renounced his religion and betrayed France."[150]

Many of the items on this checklist were probably the work of the anti-Communist organization Paix et Liberté. Created in September 1950 by Jean-Paul David, the secretary of the Rassemblement des gauches républicaines, the mission of this organization was to conduct a full-blown anti-Communist propaganda campaign across France. The group received most of its funds from the "secret funds" of Prime Minister René Pleven, but the CIA also contributed to its budget.[151] Paix et Liberté partially satisfied American concerns that the French were not interested in fighting communist publicity. Most importantly, the group provided a French outlet for propaganda in favor of such delicate issues as rearmament. David, the Prime Minister's office, and U.S. officials established an "unofficial" committee to coordinate anti-Communist propaganda.[152]

However, in dealing with publicity French officials had made a strategic error. As a tool for restraining American publicity the *comité de travail* proved useless. The French had underestimated the amount of publicity the United States was willing to generate when left to its own devices. They had also underestimated the creativity of Mission France and the extent of its demands—access to schools, colonies, homes—the public diplomacy of the United States permeated the public and private sphere in France. Mitterrand had warned that Marshall Plan publicity must not escape the control of the French government. Yet this is exactly what happened. If the original premise of the French approach was to ensure the success of the larger program—the modernization of France—then it must be acknowledged as a double failure. For the French effort did little or nothing to control or limit the American effort and, if their analysis was correct, the unrestrained American effort made the objectives of the French government and the Marshall Plan more difficult to achieve. Why then did subsequent governments—there were twelve between 1947 and 1952—not attempt to control or limit the American campaign? Initial French decisions had cast the government in the role of bystander rather than gatekeeper. It was easier to stay in this role than challenge the U.S. on access to the French public in fulfillment of Article VIII, but it was also politically dangerous to associate fragile governments with a program that, at the best of times, the French public regarded with ambivalence. A truce existed. American officials complained about the lack of French publicity but ultimately did not make it a major issue; French governments refused to conduct publicity but granted the U.S. unprecedented access to its citizens.

Nevertheless, it seems that the French realized their error and, perhaps, regretted not contesting Article VIII in 1948. There is more than a hint of bitterness in some of the French documents. A 1952 memorandum from the SGCI recommended the reduction of the twenty million franc budget for Marshall Plan publicity in France. A sum of ten million francs was sufficient for France, according to the SGCI. The remaining ten million franc balance should be spent in the U.S. "to make the American public aware of the effects of the ERP in France."[153]

At the beginning of 1952, a French official, J. Constant, filed a report with the French foreign ministry about American propaganda in France.[154] The official had spent five months working with Americans on various projects: with Labor Information (OSR), the USIS, and Mission France. According to Constant the program had two goals. The first was the fight against communism. The second goal was an effort to increase Franco-American understanding. His assessment of the program was pessimistic, and he judged that it had failed in both its missions.

According to Constant, American propaganda aimed at communism was "sterile." It emphasized "facts, 'undeniable facts'" rather than attacking communism on an ideological plane.[155] More critical, however, for a successful fight against communism was to "understand and love" the country in which the ideology had taken root. As Constant explained, "It is indispensable to know its history, traditions, and principles, but even more important and difficult is to sense the beat of its heart."[156] In Constant's opinion, the United States had not provided anyone with the requisite sensitivity to successfully combat communism in France.

Americans understood neither the necessary tactics for fighting communism nor the context in which this fight occurred: "During my five months of collaboration with American film propaganda in France," declared Constant, "I never met an American who knew our history or understood our civilization."[157] This may not have been an exaggeration. It was difficult for the ECA to get American film technicians who were willing to work in France, possessed a union card, and spoke French.[158] "American anti-Communist propaganda by film," concluded Constant, "is not efficacious. Infinitely more grave, it often damages public opinion and furnishes the adversary with the substance of its counterpropaganda."

For Constant, the American's misunderstanding of communism in France and their unintentional slights to French pride hampered their efforts to increase Franco-American understanding. The intelligence and abilities of the Americans were great, but they were nevertheless of an "essentially American formation." This limited the applicability of American propaganda: "If we are persuaded that this form of propaganda gives marvelous results when it is applied to the American masses, we can affirm that it is not only ineffective in France, but that it also damages public opinion."[159]

According to Constant, the reason U.S. programs elicited such poor reactions was because "the French refuse to admit that without America France would not exist."[160] Well-educated French shrugged their shoulders, while others reacted "violently." By Constant's tally, three-quarters of the films produced by the ECA were such an insult to French national pride that they could not be shown in France.

ECA films, he concluded, "provoke antipathy and risk creating a climate of enmity that is dangerous to the security of our alliance."[161]

The Association France–Etats-Unis

The Americans, for their part, adapted to the limited publicity offered by the French government. In addition to the expansive programs of Labor Information and Mission France, the U.S. courted private sources. *Reader's Digest* and *Réalités* were two publications that benefited from U.S. assistance, but Mission France also provided covert funding to the organization France–Etats-Unis. This organization illustrates that, like other programs, U.S. interventions went to the heart of French civil society. For the historian, France–Etats-Unis also provides a useful case to examine the issue of cooptation. Did the organization's leaders fulfill U.S. expectations or, in the name of anticommunism, did they milk a cash cow to increase their own power?

The Frenchman Robert Geffroy created the organization, originally entitled France–U.S.A., in late 1945.[162] For the next two years the organization hosted several American speakers and disseminated whatever pro-American literature it could find. The initial purpose of France–U.S.A. was to uphold the spirit of the Liberation by increasing the cultural ties between the two countries. However, by 1947 the original organization had collapsed because of the questionable loyalties of its regional directors, some of who allegedly possessed links to Vichy. Financial difficulties were also rumored to have been a factor.[163]

France–U.S.A. was reconstituted as France–Etats-Unis in 1947 under the presidency of Paul Claudel, the celebrated writer and former French Ambassador to the U.S. Jefferson Caffery, the American ambassador to France, was personally involved in the reorganization of the group.[164] Claudel, however, appeared to have little to do with the group. Instead, Cyrille Makinsky, a White-Russian émigré, provided the day-to-day leadership. Makinsky's political loyalties were never in doubt. While Cyrille sought to increase links between the United States and France through a cultural association, his brother sought the same result through commercial means as head of French operations for the Coca-Cola Corporation.[165] The United States funded the organization by subscribing to forty thousand copies of its periodical, *France–Etats-Unis*.[166] France–Etats-Unis used these funds to host guest speakers and distribute pamphlets, primarily in Paris. The activities of France–Etats-Unis remained limited to this area until Mission France increased its support in 1950.

   Helen Kirkpatrick, the chief information officer of Mission France, argued that the organization was essential to the American propaganda effort because it provided a French face for the ECA. Pro-American propaganda was more effective, she explained, if it was produced and disseminated under French rather than American auspices, particularly when it concerned matters such as rearmament or the North Atlantic Treaty.[167] In 1949 Helen Kirkpatrick wrote Elgozy to request assistance for the organization.[168] She prefaced her request with a review of the failures of the French government to produce newsreels and other publicity material in support of the Marshall Plan. The French government had recently prevented Makinsky's group from posting anti-Communist posters in train stations. France–Etats-Unis carried out "fine work," according to Kirkpatrick, and the French government should provide as much assistance as possible: "Such assistance would be consistent with the under-taking of the French government to disseminate information on the ECA, without at the same time engaging the French government in that type of direct propaganda which the government has hitherto felt impossible to conduct."[169] France–Etats-Unis thus offered a solution to the relative silence of the French government, the other potential source for pro-American propaganda. According to Makinsky, Elgozy told him that Article VIII of the bilateral agreement creating the Marshall Plan was unacceptable because it required the French government to conduct publicity for the U.S.[170] He reportedly told Makinsky, "No French government, because of diverse political interests, has ever really wanted to implement paragraph eight of the Bilateral Accord and thus be accused of subservience to the American government."[171]

   In 1950 Mission France supplied France–Etats-Unis with over twenty-eight million francs of counterpart funds to establish eight regional information centers in Toulouse, Rouen, Rennes, Nice, Clermont-Ferrand, Poitiers, Le Puy, and Montpellier.[172] Additional information centers were planned over the next years. These regional centers were intended to function like USIS libraries, providing a reading room of American material and a stock of pamphlets. The association received ten million francs to show Marshall Plan documentaries, print pamphlets, and translate American books. France–Etats-Unis received an additional six million francs to expand its program of hosting guest speakers and creating exhibits.[173] According to American officials, the organization possessed twenty thousand members in early 1950.[174] By 1951 Makinsky boasted that 108 sections of the organization existed through France.[175]

   The group actively contributed to the American effort. In 1951 France–Etats-Unis produced an illustrated booklet, *Amitié Franco-*

Américaine. The group distributed twenty-four thousand copies of the publication to locations in France where U.S. troops were stationed.[176] The wording was simple and direct. *Amitié* attempted to address Communist criticisms of American troop deployments in France. The troops, it explained, were not "new occupiers." "In fact," it stated, "American soldiers and their equipment protect France against a potential aggressor, the USSR, which has retained a large army."[177]

Despite the considerable resources given to this organization, American officials—particularly regional USIS officers—were disappointed with the results achieved by France–Etats-Unis. Far from representing a neutral source of pro-American propaganda, most French assumed it was a U.S. front in the same way that the organization France–USSR was a front for the USSR. Philip Dur, an American consular officer, stressed the fact that the links between France–Etats-Unis and Mission France were assumed. "I wonder who is covering whom?" he asked U.S. officials in Paris. [178]

At the regional level France–Etats-Unis was the source of a number of headaches for American officials. Makinsky was connected to the Parisian elite but his ability to coordinate regional offices was marked with more enthusiasm than ability. Opportunistic conservatives and other anti-Communists controlled the regional operations of France–Etats-Unis. One American official warned, "A superficial examination of the association France–Etats-Unis leads one to believe that it holds within itself many disturbing and potentially explosive characteristics."[179] After donating two million francs to the organization, Makinsky made one notable, a certain Monsieur Pico, the chief of the Toulouse information center and gave him the title "délégué général de France–Etats-Unis."[180] The American USIS officer in Bordeaux, Ted Arthur, characterized Pico as "an amiable enough man, but one who by virtue of a private income has never worked in his life, is very easy about the purpose and function of France–Etats-Unis, and has absolutely not one grain of political sense."[181] Arthur doubted that there was any liaison between Makinsky and the regional offices of France–Etats-Unis. "I do wonder," Arthur concluded, "as the show begins to unfold, if we are not due for some trouble." The assistant public affairs officer in Paris shared these concerns, sardonically commenting that he was "impressed by the possible over-enthusiastic way in which [Makinsky] spreads himself so thinly all over France and makes efforts to participate on an international scale as well."[182]

The participation of France–Etats-Unis in fairs and exhibits was indeed troubling for Mission France. At fairs in Rennes and Tours, the France–Etats-Unis delegate represented herself as an ECA representative in addition to speaking under the auspices of France–Etats-Unis, clearly not the same as appearing as a France–Etats-Unis official delivering a pro-American speech.[183] She delivered an anti-Gaullist speech and urged voters to support Georges Bidault. A Mission France staff member described her methods as unsound and haphazard.[184] She was reportedly "over-zealous" in her dealings with local newspapers, insisting that they cover the France–Etats-Unis presentations.

Philip Dur, the American cultural attaché in Lyon, worked closely with France–Etats-Unis and he too was unimpressed with the organization. At Le Puy, France–Etats-Unis hosted Jacques Dutheil, author of *La grande Parade américaine*. Dutheil, speaking as an authority on the United States, slandered blacks and Jews. "The bad impression made by Dutheil," reported Dur, "reflected on the U.S."[185] Dur called for an increased supervision of France–Etats-Unis, not by Makinsky but by the American authorities in France. The genie was out of the bottle, so to speak, and Mission France needed to take control of the situation. Dur explained:

> The very existence of a group which takes the title France–Etats-Unis engages the responsibility of American representatives on the spot. Whatever its profession of independence, a Franco-American association is inevitably considered to speak for the United States. American representatives have thus only two choices—either to encourage the group or to discourage it. In the case of France–Etats-Unis the choice has been made. Since American representatives ... cannot abdicate their mission of presenting a full and fair picture of American life, they must exercise some supervision.[186]

For Dur, the speech by Dutheil and other incidents demonstrated the risks involved. Thus while some public affairs officers were hesitant to cooperate with France–Etats-Unis, Dur increased his contact with the group.[187] France–Etats-Unis presented him as the featured speaker at a number of gatherings: Montbrison, Montbéliard, and Saint-Chamond.[188] The non-Communist press commented favorably on these speeches. Dur's fluency in French and lack of accent was especially noted.[189] *La République,* under the story "The brilliant exposé of M. Dur," stated that his knowledge of the "nuances and evocations" of the French language was remarkable.[190] Dur's speeches covered the standard American repertoire. He spoke at length about trade unions, the standard of living in the U.S., and its geography and political structure. He explained that industrial productivity was the basis of America's prosperity, and that if France emulated its methods it too could enjoy prosperity.

During the summer of 1950 Makinsky began plans to organize a "grande manifestation d'information" in Lyon.[191] Makinsky intended the rally as a chance for parliamentary deputies and veterans to show their support for the United Nations intervention in Korea. Documentaries about the war were to be shown and printed material distributed. Makinsky invited over thirty organizations and several dignitaries, including Édouard Herriot, the president of the National Assembly, to participate.[192] Dur obtained assurances from Makinsky that the manifestation would not proceed unless its success was guaranteed and no backing or participation from the USIS or Mission France was evident.[193] American officials in Paris were also worried about a public-relations backlash. One reported that he was "impressed by the charming reticence of groups to identify themselves with such an evidently propagandist and political gathering."[194] The participation of David's Paix et Liberté added a strident note. The Communist press "revealed" the ties between France–Etats-Unis and the USIS and printed Makinsky's invitation to Herriot.[195] Herriot was thus placed in the position of either participating or being seen to have rejected an invitation from the USIS. Although some U.S. officials worried that the opera hall rally was over the top, Kirkpatrick concluded that the rally was a success.[196]

Throughout 1951 and 1952 France–Etats-Unis continued its film showings and lectures. The regional information centers continued to attract a small but steady audience of like-minded individuals.[197] France–Etats-Unis focused most of its activity in the Paris region, evidently because Makinsky's ties with embassy personnel remained strong.[198] The group held twelve public meetings and twenty film showings. During this period Mission France placed twenty-seven million francs (close to ninety thousand dollars) at its disposal.[199] The United States financed eighty percent of the group's efforts, and U.S. officials urged Makinsky to seek private sources of funding.[200] Nevertheless, the budget and activities for 1953 were similar. Cities with France–Etats-Unis offices expanded to include Cannes, St. Etienne, and Marseille.[201] Then, suddenly, funding for France–Etats-Unis was terminated at the end of 1953 at the recommendation of the embassy. Charles K. Moffly, who had recently replaced William R. Tyler as Public Affairs Officer, bluntly explained: "Any subvention given to France–Etats-Unis is of very marginal value indeed."[202]

From Blum-Byrnes to Cannes

For all of the acquiescence of the Fourth Republic to U.S. hegemony during the Marshall Plan years, examples of France charting its own course do exist. As American culture and propaganda washed over

France, its leaders were still able to develop some initiatives that preserved, indeed strengthened, France's international status. The International Film Festival at Cannes is an example of this. However, the Cannes festival is also a good example of American power. The influence of the U.S. government and the Motion Picture Association of America (MPAA) was significant. Their participation was essential for the success of the festival, but they also affected its very structure. The festival thus illustrated the tensions created by conflicting domestic and international contexts. Concern for the dominance of Hollywood was tempered by a rudimentary anticommunism: a desire to purge the French film industry of Communists and limit the influence and appeal of communist films, originating either in France or abroad. Just as the first Cannes festival was conceived in 1939 to challenge fascist control of the Venice Film Festival, so the postwar Cannes festival came to serve a similar function but with a different target, communism. The festival was an important weapon in the cultural cold war, allowing Western nations to challenge communism in an important field of mass culture. [203]

France's postwar film industry, according to recent scholarship, was either yet another victim of Americanization or an area where the Fourth Republic, and indeed the French public, rejected American mass culture. In 1946 Léon Blum traveled to the United States to negotiate a trade and aid agreement with Secretary of State James Byrnes. Film policy was an element of this agreement, but Blum was more concerned with getting credit from the U.S. Export-Import Bank, the fate of Lend-Lease items, and reducing France's debt. Blum possessed a manifestly weak negotiating position, and he readily reduced France's initial demand for a minimum seven-week per quarter screen quota for French films. [204] As a result France became a dumping ground for Hollywood films.

French theater owners, faced with a shortage of films, welcomed the influx of Hollywood films.[205] Many French men and women welcomed the films too. In her autobiography Simone de Beauvoir described the desire felt by many to see Hollywood features: "Except for the Capra series *Why We Are Fighting* and some old Mack Sennet shorts, the cinema had very little to offer. Patience! There were fantastic stories of the wonders taking place in Hollywood. A twenty-seven-year-old genius named Orson Welles had revolutionized the cinema."[206] However, enthusiasm for Hollywood features waned rather quickly: "It was the first Spring of peace. They were showing Prévert's *Les Enfants du Paradis* in Paris, and at last some American films: *I Married a Witch*, *My Girl Friday,* and *The Old Maid,* with Bette Davis.

I was a little disappointed. Where was the revolution that was convulsing the cinema?"[207] Simone de Beauvoir's experience appears to have been shared by many in France.

By 1952, when France and the United States began another round of trade negotiations on film, France was willing to eliminate the screen time quota altogether. American experts were quick to alert the State Department that this was hardly a concession on France's part. John McCarthy, the vice president of the Motion Picture Association of America, reported that French audiences preferred French films to Hollywood features.[208] The U.S. embassy in Paris reported that under competitive conditions French films occupied between six and seven weeks of screen time per quarter.[209]

Nevertheless, despite this preference, by 1951 French and American experts, Communist and non-Communist alike, agreed that the French film industry faced a financial crisis which seriously limited production. The United States was limited to importing 121 dubbed films per year, yet the French film industry produced only 108 features in 1950.[210] In addition to the dubbed films, Hollywood was able to annually import hundreds of films *version originale* so long as they passed French censorship requirements. By 1952 Hollywood had a backlog of 2,600 films awaiting entry into France.[211] Thus in 1950 there were 330 Hollywood features in France compared to 108 French features. These figures remained roughly consistent through the early 1950s.[212] Limited production hurt French competition at home and abroad and the industry and the government looked for ways to regain prewar markets.

A parliamentary commission investigated the "crisis" in early 1952. Led by Guy Desson, a conservative deputy, the Commission contained eighteen subcommittees investigating every conceivable aspect of the film industry: distribution, production, exhibition, export/import, government subsidies, and more. Issued in May, during the conservative administration of Antoine Pinay, the Desson Report condemned the Centre national du cinéma (CNC) for being influenced by "syndicale, political," forces, i.e., the French Communist Party (PCF) and the Confederation générale du travail (CGT).[213] The film industry, because of its propaganda value, roused the interest of a "passionate minority" at a time when "insidious and brutal actions" threatened the very constitution of the Fourth Republic. Desson called for the reorganization of the CNC (created in October 1946) and its director, Michel Fourré-Cormeray, was sacked in July 1952 and replaced by Jacques Flaud of the moderate party the Mouvement républicain populaire. Desson argued,

> The cinema constitutes one of the principal and most attractive means
> of diffusing culture and information to the public. The existence of a
> strong national motion picture industry is, for a country, an important
> element for the defense of freedom of thought and one of the means of
> preventing screens from becoming a closed field for foreign propaganda.
> The present international situation and the eminent role which France
> is destined to play in the defense of peace and Western civilization mil-
> itates strongly in favor of a prosperous motion picture industry.[214]

More than foreign competition, however, Desson blamed the Loi
d'Aide of 1948 for the current crisis in the film industry because it
encouraged speculation. According to Desson, producers used very
little of their own capital to produce movies, relying instead on government subsidies and funds obtained through "usurious loans,
tainted money, backing on behalf of young persons with as little tal-
ent as virtue, money from shady speculations, gun smuggling, fiscal
frauds, racket enterprises, and bordellos." There was no qualitative
judge of a film's merits—any producer could receive the subsidy.[215]
Desson pointed out that French film producers had increased from
125 to 224 from 1950 to 1951 while production stagnated. Desson was
not silent on foreign competition; indeed he emphasized that "the projection of foreign films in their original versions is a serious handi-
cap because it immobilizes a number of first-run cinemas." Finally,
Desson concluded that the diminishing influence of French culture
and language reduced the market for French films. The minister of
industry and energy, Jean-Marie Louvel, used the Desson report as
a basis for a legislative push that reshaped state support for and administration of the film industry.[216] There was, nevertheless, little
hope that the situation would change. Reviewing the recent expansion
of Hollywood's markets, Desson remarked, "It is difficult to change
such a situation which is in reality a consolidation of what already
existed."

This brief review of the film crisis provides the context for understanding French goals for the Cannes festival. This context, I suggest,
consists of a desire to increase French prestige which was tempered
by an acknowledgement of U.S. hegemony, and an increasingly virulent anticommunism in French officials.

Planning for the festival began as early as 1944 but the organizers encountered a number of difficulties relating to transportation,
lodging, and the purges. Hotels in Cannes were in disrepair, and the
availability of screening rooms was questionable. The Cannes Festival was simply not possible in 1945. To make matters worse, Italy an-
nounced that it would resume the Venice Festival in 1946 at the same
time as the proposed gathering in Cannes. The Foreign ministry dis-
patched a team to negotiate a deal with the Italians. The two sides

agreed to consult on future dates to avoid overlap, but the Italians also agreed to remove any official sponsorship from the 1946 Venice festival.[217]

The foreign ministry took the lead in funding and organizing the festival in 1946. For French officials the festival was intended to symbolize France's postwar recovery.[218] The Association française d'action artistique (AFAA), a government funded agency created in 1922 to disseminate French culture abroad, organized the 1946 and 1947 festivals. In 1946 the AFAA had been placed under the control (and budget) of the cultural relations section of the foreign ministry.[219] It provided eight million of the seventeen million franc budget for the 1946 festival.[220] The education ministry provided an additional four million, and the information minister provided three million. The foreign ministry remained intimately involved in organizing the festival even after it ceded nominal control to the Centre national du cinéma in 1949. As late as 1955 it still exercised a veto over films chosen by the French selection committee.[221]

Tensions existed between organizers, those who stressed the festival's role as a key element in France's international cultural policy and syndicates that wanted to use the festival to increase protectionist measures in support of French domestic film production. The latter urged the organizing committee to adopt a motion acknowledging the Festival's international significance but declaring that the defense of the French film industry was also a key goal.[222]

Official invitations went out in May 1946, and the Festival opened in September. Works from twenty-one nations, including the United States and the Soviet Union, were presented at Cannes in 1946, but only twelve official delegations attended.[223] Despite a slew of technical difficulties French officials declared that the Festival was a success. It was clear that the construction of additional facilities was necessary and the foreign ministry balked at funding the 1947 Festival unless success was assured.[224] The 1947 Festival was a limited affair, but the foreign Ministry resumed substantial funding for the festival in 1948, which allowed Cannes to construct a new theater for 1949.

The Motion Picture Association of America influenced the jury structure of the festival. Competition was an essential aspect of the Cannes Festival. Initially the festival was structured such that the risk of a boycott based on awards was minimal.[225] An international jury awarded a "Grand Prix du Festival International du Film" for the best film from each country that had entered at least four features. This structure was not repeated, however. In 1947 the awards were distributed by category: comedies musicals, dessins animés (to Walt

Disney's *Dumbo*), film d'aventures et policiers, films psychologiques et d'amour, documentaries, and films sociaux. Edward Dmytryk won the award for films sociaux with *Crossfire*. After a break in 1948 (no official festival was held as part of the agreement reached with the Venice Festival) the prizes were changed yet again in 1949. The MPAA informed the French that it would boycott the festival if the jury remained international. Hollywood films would not be screened, nor would their stars grace the venues, unless the jury was composed of French members deemed to be "politically objective" by the French government.[226] French organizers worried that such a change would harm the prestige of the festival, but they readily admitted that an MPAA boycott could ruin the festival. They adopted the change in early 1948. *The Third Man* won the only Grand Prix du Festival in 1949, while awards were given to Edward G. Robinson (*House of Strangers*) and Isa Miranda (*Le Mura di Malapaga*) for best male and female roles. After another official break in 1950 the festival resumed in 1951 with virtually the same award structure.

Within two years of its creation the festival was a politically charged international affair. The delegations and receptions attracted as much attention as the films. The influential film critic André Bazin condemned the early festivals as spectacles for diplomats and tourists.[227] In addition to offering an indication of France's international aspirations, the festival also reflected domestic cleavages. Labor divisions in the French film industry mirrored the rest of French industry: a strong CGT presence challenged by weaker FO and CFTC groups, and the French foreign ministry used the selection process and excluded communist films.

Soviet participation in the 1951 Festival upped the ante at Cannes. Heretofore the Soviets had sent only films, not an official delegation. According to U.S. officials, Soviet participation at Cannes had become part of its cultural offensive.[228] The Soviet delegation consisted of Nicolas Semenov, the assistant minister for motion pictures, the director Vsevolod Poudovkine, and other officials. The delegation attracted a lot of attention from public and press alike. The U.S. public affairs officer, William R. Tyler, claimed that the Soviet film showings did not generate much enthusiasm. He conceded, however, that the official receptions offered by the Soviets were popular and well-attended events where international officials schmoozed with leading directors, actors, and critics.[229] "The Soviets scored heavily at the various social functions: press conferences and receptions," explained Tyler, "Its 'monster buffet' was so inexhaustible that it could not be wholly plundered."[230] In contrast, U.S. participation at Cannes was a "fiasco."[231] Neither Hollywood nor the State Department coordinated activities.

In fact, there was no official U.S. delegation. Last-minute attempts to fly in Bette Davis (*All About Eve* was a smash hit at Cannes) fell apart. In addition to the Soviets, virtually every other national delegation hosted gala receptions—except the United States. A last-minute donation from a private citizen allowed the U.S. to offer a reception.[232] Tyler concluded that U.S. prestige had suffered at Cannes, and that the lack of an official U.S. delegation had "left the door open to untrammeled Soviet propaganda."[233] Tyler's argument was convincing; the U.S. sent official delegations to subsequent festivals.

Anti-Communist cooperation between French and Americans increased after 1951. For the 1953 festival the U.S. petitioned to have the Golden Laurel Award and the Silver Laurel Award presented. Founded by David Selznick, the producer of *Gone With the Wind,* these awards were given to European producers who had "made the greatest contribution to mutual understanding and goodwill between the peoples of the free and democratic world."[234] The CNC agreed to the request as long as the awards did not appear on the official program. The U.S. also asked the foreign ministry to use import controls to prevent the entry of two Japanese films: *Children of the A-Bomb* and *Paintings of the A-Bomb.* Similar interventions in 1951 had prevented the showing of *Free China.* The Japanese films, the State Department argued, were merely an attempt to drive a wedge between allies "in common opposition to Communist advances."[235]

By the early 1950s the International Film Festival at Cannes had indeed become France's postwar recovery. The festival was also a key element of France's international cultural policy and a key instrument for French administration of the film industry. Officials from the CNC used the 1952 Festival, for example, as the initial venue for the renegotiation of its film trade agreement with the U.S.[236] At a time when the Fourth Republic, awash in U.S. and communist propaganda, possessed little control over the dissemination of information within its own borders it had, nevertheless, established an annual event that garnered it considerable international prestige. U.S. participation was essential for the success of the festival, whether it was the films of Orson Welles or the massively popular press conferences of Hollywood stars like Kirk Douglas and Gene Kelly. Of course many Fourth Republic leaders viewed Communists within France as an equal or greater threat to the regime than the Soviet Union. This anti-Communist imperative refracted the outlook of those who saw the festival as a way to challenge the U.S. on trade policy or the cultural leadership of the "free world." For the foreign ministry and the early organizers of the festival, good politics were just as important as good films.

Had the Fourth Republic more clearly divined the consequences of acquiescing to Article VIII its prestige could also have been more secure on the home front. What the French realized too late was that for many U.S. officials, public diplomacy was just as important as its economic aid. Having accepted Article VIII, however, and more fundamentally having chosen the path of anticommunism, the governments of the Fourth Republic could only hope to measure and perhaps mitigate the American influence. In January 1949 Schuman ordered French diplomatic officials in Marshall Plan countries to assess its impact. Schuman was particularly interested in discovering "the factors ... which favored or compromised" the economic and cultural expansion of the U.S.[237] A month later he concluded that the Marshall Plan was a central means by which the United States expanded its presence (cultural, economic, military) in Europe.[238] Given the magnitude of the U.S. operation in France it is not surprising that French politicians wanted to know the nature of successful or unsuccessful resistance in other countries. This was the crux. The Marshall Plan was not just about anticommunism, Schuman finally concluded, it was about extending American influence.

Notes

1. The Organization for Economic Co-operation and Development (OECD), http://www.oecd.org/about/marshall/speech.htm.
2. Charles S. Maier, "Premises of the European Recovery Program," in *Le Plan Marshall et le relèvement économique de l'Europe,* eds. René Girault and Maurice Lévy-Leboyer (Paris: Comité pour l'histoire économique et financier de la France, 1993), 15.
3. Mikahil Narinski, "Le Plan Marshall et l'U.R.S.S.," in *Le Plan Marshall et le relèvement économique de l'Europe,* eds. René Girault and Maurice Lévy-Leboyer (Paris: Comité pour l'histoire économique et financier de la France, 1993), 115.
4. John Gillingham, *Coal, Steel, and the Rebirth of Europe, 1945-1955* (Cambridge: Cambridge UP, 1991), 115.
5. Statement of the Foreign Loan Policy of the United States Government by the National Advisory Council on International Monetary and Financial Problems, 21 February 1946, American Foreign Policy Center, Louisiana Tech University (AFPC henceforth), President Harry S. Truman Office Files, 1945-1953.
6. France Policy and Information Statement, Department of State, 15 September 1946, AFPC, President Harry S. Truman Office Files, 1945-1953.
7. Estimated Net Import Requirements of European Countries, 1 October 1947, to 31 March 1948, American Foreign Policy Center, President Harry S. Truman Office Files, 1945-1953.

8. The Immediate Need for Emergency Aid to Europe, 29 September 1947, American Foreign Policy Center, President Harry S. Truman Office Files, 1945-1953; see also Bossuat, *La France, l'aide américaine et la construction européene*, 1: 52.
9. Rapport sur l'evolution de l'économie Française pendant le premier semester de 1948. Secrétaire Général du Comité Interministériel (SGCI henceforth), Archives nationales (AN), F60 *ter* 378.
10. Ibid.
11. Memorandum of Conversations at the White House on 22 August 1945, between the President and General de Gaulle, AFPC, President Harry S. Truman Office Files, 1945-1953.
12. The Immediate Need for Emergency Aid to Europe.
13. France Policy and Information Statement.
14. The Immediate Need for Emergency Aid to Europe.
15. Jean-Pierre Rioux, *The Fourth Republic, 1944-1958,* trans. Godfrey Rodgers (Cambridge: Cambridge University Press, 1987), 110.
16. Letter from A.H. Vandenburg to Paul G. Hoffman, ECA, 24 March 1950, NARA, RG. 469, entry 1193, box 52.
17. Quoted in Maier, "Premises of the European Recovery Program," 16.
18. Irwin Wall, *The United States and the Making of Postwar France, 1944-1954* (Cambridge: Cambridge U.P., 1991), 74–75; William I. Hitchcock, *France Restored: Cold War Diplomacy and the Quest for Leadership in Europe, 1944-1954* (Chapel Hill: University of North Carolina Press, 1998), 207.
19. Maria Höhn concludes that "Germans experienced the 1950s not merely as a process of modernization or Westernization but specifically as a process of Americanization," *GIs and Fräuleins: the German-American Encounter in 1950s West Germany* (Chapel Hill: University of North Carolina Press, 2002), 228.
20. Olivier Pottier, *Les bases américaines en France, 1950-1967* (Paris: L'Harmattan, 2003).
21. Memorandum on Franco-American relations, February 1946, Ministère des Affaires Etrangères, série B, Etats-Unis, 78.
22. Ibid. "Q: Leaving aside for the moment the fact they are our enemies or allies, which one of the following do you like best just as people? A: The French people.....11% The German people......28% The English people.....50% No answer.....11%"
23. Ibid.
24. Comité consultatif, 11 May 1945, Ministère des Affaires Etrangères, relations culturelles, oeuvres divers, 1945-1947.
25. J.G. Sellier, Mission militaire française de liason, Ministère des Affaires Etrangères, relations culturelles, oeuvres divers, 1945-1947.
26. Rapport du 1 Janvier au 31 Juillet 1946, Ministère des Affaires Etrangères, série B, Etats-Unis, 78.
27. Memorandum on Franco-American relations, February 1946, Ministère des Affaires Etrangères, série B, Etats-Unis, 78.
28. Letter from President du conseil to Ministère des Affaires Etrangères, Ministère des Affaires Etrangères, série B, 77.
29. Note pour le President, August 1949, Ministère des Affaires Etrangères, série B, Etats-Unis, 77.
30. Intelligence Report, Factors Adversely Affecting the Acceptance of U.S. Troops in Europe, 11 October 1951, NARA, RG. 469, entry 302, box 10.
31. Information Operational Plan concerning U.S. military forces in Europe, 22 January 1952, NARA, RG. 469, entry 302, box 10.
32. Troop Working Group, 30 October 1952, NARA, RG. 84, entry 2462, box 43.

33. France: policy and information statement, Department of State, 15 September 1946, NARA, central decimal files of the State Department, 711.51.
34. Smith-Mundt Subcommittee: purpose, composition, itinerary, 27 August 1947, National Security Archives at George Washington University, Smith-Mundt group collection, box 1 of 1, volume 1 of 3.
35. Visit by Smith-Mundt group to France, National Security Archives at George Washington University, Smith-Mundt group collection, box 1 of 1, volume 1 of 3.
36. Visit by Smith-Mundt group to France.
37. Frank A. Ninkovich, *The Diplomacy of Ideas: U.S. Foreign Policy and Cultural Relations, 1938-1950* (Cambridge: Cambridge University Press, 1981), 124–128.
38. *Knowledge of the Marshall Plan in France, Report of the Joint Committee on Foreign Economic Cooperation* (Washington, D.C.: G.P.O., 1949), 8–9.
39. *Knowledge of the Marshall Plan in France*, 10.
40. Memorandum for the file, 16 November 1948, *Foreign Relations of the United States* [FRUS henceforth], *The Emergence of the Intelligence Establishment, 1945-1950* (Washington, D.C.: GPO, 1996), 307–308.
41. Irwin Wall, "The American Marshall Plan Mission in France," in René Girault and Maurice Lévy-Leboyer, eds., *Le Plan Marshall et le relèvement économique de l'Europe* (Paris: Comité pour l'histoire économique et financière de la France, 1993), 134.
42. Telegram from Caffery to Secretary of State, 3 March 1949, *F.R.U.S., 1949,* vol. IV, 633.
43. Letter from Harold Kaplan to Georges Elgozy, 1 October 1951, AN, SGCI, F60 *ter* 394.
44. Letter from Donald W. Dresden, Deputy Chief ECA Information, to Helen Kirkpatrick, 17 February 1950, NARA, RG. 469, entry 1193, box 44.
45. Accord de cooperation économique entre la France et les Etats-Unis d'Amerique, Ministère des Affaires Etrangères, série B, questions économiques et financiers, 1944-1952.
46. Les dispositions de l'article VIII de l'accord de cooperation économique entre La France et Les Etats-Unis, 7 July 1950, AN, SGCI, F60 *ter* 393.
47. ECA France, Information Division, Budget, NARA, RG. 469, entry 1193, box 44.
48. Le President du Conseil à le Secrétaire d'Etat chargé de l'Information, 28 décembre 1949, AN, SGCI, F60 *ter* 438.
49. Ibid.
50. Hearings before the Committee on Foreign Relations, House of Representatives, 81st Congress, second session, "Foreign Aid Appropriations for 1951," February 1950.
51. "Remarks of Paul G. Hoffman before OEEC in Paris," AFPC, President Harry S. Truman Office Files, 1945-1953.
52. For an excellent, brief summary of this debate see Irwin Wall, "The Marshall Plan and French Politics," in *The Marshall Plan Fifty Years After,* ed. Martin A. Schain (New York: Palgrave, 2000): 167–183. Reviewing the arguments, Wall concludes that the effects of the Marshall Plan were minimal.
53. Memorandum to all Information officers from Roscoe Drummond, Director of European Information Division, 9 August 1950, NARA, RG. 469, entry 1193, box 44.
54. François David, "Du traité de Versailles à Jean Monnet: John Foster Dulles est-il un père de l'Europe?" in *l'américanisation de l'Europe occidentale au XXe siècle,* eds. Dominique Barjot and Chrisophe Réveillard (Paris: Presses de l'Université de Paris-Sorbonne, 2002), 66.
55. Alessandro Brogi, *A Question of Self-Esteem: the United States and the Cold War Choices in France and Italy, 1944-1958* (Westport: Praeger, 2002), 121–122.

56. Ibid., 145.
57. USIS Semi-Annual Evaluation Report for June 1-November 30, 1952, 13 January 1953, NARA, RG. 84, entry 2462, box 45.
58. Whelan, 336.
59. Review of Information Program, 22 October 1952, NARA, RG. 469, entry 1193, box 51.
60. Richard J. Aldrich, *The Hidden Hand: Britain, America, and Cold War Secret Intelligence* (New York: Overlook Press, 2001), 343.
61. Brogi, 141.
62. Aldrich, 368.
63. Hearings before the Committee on Foreign Relations, House of Representatives, 81st Congress, second session, "Foreign Aid Appropriations for 1951," February 1950.
64. Ibid.
65. Ibid.
66. Memorandum of telephone conversation, 16 December 1949, American Foreign Policy Center, Official Conversations and Meetings of Dean Acheson, 1949-1953.
67. Oral History Interview with Edward W. Barrett, the Harry S. Truman Library.
68. Ninkovich, 137–138.
69. Letter from George F. Kennan to Dean Acheson, 3 January 1949, American Foreign Policy Center, Official Conversations and Meetings of Dean Acheson, 1949–1953.
70. Wagnleitner, 56–57; Hixson, 14–17.
71. Hixson, Chapter 1: "A Campaign of Truth: the Rebirth of Psychological Warfare," 1–27.
72. Psychological Offensive, letter from PAO, Paris, to State Department, 16 October 1950, central decimal files of the State Department, 511.51/10-1650; Wagnleitner discusses the response of the Austrian Mission of the ECA, 77–79.
73. Some notes on the principal obstacles to conducting a cultural program in foreign countries, William R. Tyler, July 1949, NARA, RG. 84, entry 2462, box 4.
74. Official Minutes Initial Meeting of Committee on Books Abroad, 26 February 1952, NARA, RG. 306, entry 1049, box 1.
75. Ninkovich, 5.
76. Areas of World Concern: Priority of Target Areas, Target Groups and Most Effective Media, NARA, RG. 469, entry 924, box 15.
77. Areas of World Concern: Priority of Target Areas, Target Groups and Most Effective Media.
78. Psychological Pressures—Our Global Objectives, 2 June 1950, NARA, RG. 469, entry 924, box 15.
79. The other policy objectives were: "To deter the Soviets from further encroachments" and "To roll back Soviet Power"; "Psychological Pressures—Our Global Objectives."
80. Fourth Quarterly Report, 1950, of Information Division, ECA Mission to France, 2 January 1951, NARA, RG. 469, entry 1193, box 51.
81. Psychological Offensive.
82. Letter to Dr. Ian Fraser, American Library in Paris, 12 December 1950, NARA, RG. 469, entry 1193, box 45.
83. Bingham testified to Congress: "The French are allergic to propaganda. They often confuse what we call information with what they call propaganda, I think that their experience during the German occupation accounts for a good deal of the sentiment on their part." "Foreign Aid Appropriations for 1951" hearings, 28 February 1950.
84. Psychological Offensive.

85. Psychological Offensive.
86. Draft paper for France, William R. Tyler, 6 January 1951, RG. 84, entry 2462, box 13.
87. Memorandum from Roscoe Drummond to all information officers, 9 August 1950, NARA, RG. 469, entry 1193, box 44.
88. Wagnleitner, *Coco-Colonization and the Cold War*, 53.
89. Letter from Robert R. Mullen to Waldemar Nielsen, Deputy Director, Information Division, OSR, 20 June 1950, NARA, RG. 469, entry 302, box 13.
90. Letter from Theodore S. Repplier, President Advertising Council, to Robert R. Mullen, 17 July 1950, NARA, RG. 469, entry 302, box 2.
91. Letter from Jere Patterson, Life International, to Robert R. Mullen, 22 September 1950, NARA, RG. 469, entry 302, box 20.
92. Robert Griffith, "The Selling of America: The Advertising Council and American Politics, 1942-1960," *Business History Review* 57 (Autumn 1983), 391–392.
93. Robert H. Haddow, *Pavilions of Plenty: Exhibiting American Culture Abroad in the 1950s* (Washington: Smithsonian Institution Press, 1997), 4.
94. Hixson, 60.
95. "Advertising: a New Weapon in the World-Wide Fight for Freedom: a Guide for American Business firms Advertising in Foreign Countries Prepared by the Advertising Council in Consultation with the USIS" (New York, 1951).
96. Mullen possessed close links to both the Advertising Council and J. Walter Thompson. His senior consultant in the ECA was a high-ranking official in J. Walter Thompson. Letter from Robert R. Mullen to Waldemar Nielson, Deputy Chief ECA Information Division, 24 July 1950, NARA, RG. 469, entry 302, box 18.
97. Letter from Tyler to Ambassador Bruce, 1 December 1950, RG. 469, entry 1193, box 44.
98. The Foreign Information Activities of the United States, by William R. Tyler, 5 February 1950, NARA, RG. 84, entry 2462, box 4.
99. Letter from Kirkpatrick to Parkman, 2 December 1950, NARA, RG. 469, entry 1193, box 44.
100. Questionnaire on Key Words, 17 June 1952, NARA, RG. 84, entry 2462, box 6.
101. Letter from Hart Preston, OSR Information Division, to Robert R. Mullen, 28 February 1951, NARA, RG. 469, entry 302, box 18.
102. Letter from Thomas W. Wilson, chief Information Division, Mission France, to James R. West, Information Division OSR, NARA, RG. 469, entry 1193, box 49.
103. Letter from Thomas W. Wilson to C.W. Gray, American Embassy, 8 November 1951, NARA, RG. 469, entry 1193, box 44.
104. Letter from Harold Kaplan, acting chief information division, to Eugene Rachlis, 19 August 1952, NARA, RG. 469, entry 1193, box 44.
105. Haddow, 36–37.
106. Ninkovich provides a thorough treatment of this transition, 139–167, but Hixson is also useful, 139–140, 149–150; see also Haddow, 47–53; Serge Guilbaut, *How New York Stole the Idea of Modern Art: Abstract Expressionism, Freedom, and the Cold War* (Chicago: University of Chicago Press, 1983), 204–205; and Naima Prevots, *Dance for Export: Cultural Diplomacy and the Cold War* (Hanover: Wesleyan University Press, 1998), 7–8.
107. Report from France on our International Information Activities, 1 May 1950, NARA, RG. 84, entry 2462, box 4.
108. Report from France on our International Information Activities.
109. Ibid.
110. Sixteenth meeting of the U.S. Advisory Commission on Educational Exchange, official minutes, 13-14 September 1951, NARA, RG. 306, entry 1049, box 1.
111. Ibid.
112. Ibid.

113. Ibid.

114. Ibid.

115. The Ford Foundation official Chester Davis served as a liaison officer between the Foundation and the State Department.

116. Prevots, 8-12. The USIS could, on some occasions, bypass Congress, but in general it did not possess a budget large enough to sponsor large presentations of American art overseas. An exception, of sorts, is the Congress for Cultural Freedom, which used covertly supplied CIA funds to sponsor cultural manifestations.

117. Guilbaut, 177.

118. Prevots, 26.

119. Foreign Aid Appropriations for 1951, Tuesday, 28 February 1950, U.S. Senate Committee on Foreign Relations.

120. Wagnleitner, 208–215.

121. See Haddow, Chapter 6, "Men's Gadgets, Women's Fashions, and the American Way of Life"; Hixson, 203–213; for an examination of Americanization and gender in France see Ellen Furlough's "Selling the American Way in Interwar France: *Prix uniques* and the *Salons des arts ménagers*," *Journal of Social History* 26, no. 3 (1993): 491–519.

122. Whelan, 366; Richard T. Griffiths and Erik Bloemen, "Resisting Revolution in the Netherlands," in *Catching Up with America,* ed. Dominique Barjot, 115–116; Henry B. Wend, "'But the German Manufacturer Doesn't Want Our Advice': West German Labor and Business and the Limits of American Technical Assistance, 1950-1954," in *Catching Up with America,* ed. Dominique Barjot, 123.

123. Bossuat, *La France, l'aide américaine et la construction européene, 1944-1954,* 1: 401.

124. Kuisel, *Seducing the French,* 43–45.

125. *Le Monde,* 17 March 1949.

126. Information Program Meeting, 14 November 1950, NARA, RG. 469, entry 928, box 25.

127. Interview with Hubert Beuve-Méry, 8 February 1951, NARA, RG. 84, entry 2462, box 35.

128. European Neutralism and Third Force-ism, Department of State Policy Advisory Staff, 6 June 1950, NARA, RG. 59, lot file 57D459, box 4.

129. Letter from Robert C. Hickok, State Department Western European Affairs, to William R. Tyler, 2 February 1951, NARA, RG. 84, entry 2462, box 35.

130. Aldrich, 140.

131. Minutes of meeting Schweitzer, Robert Mitterand, Elgozy, Chouraqui, 5 December 1948, AN, SGCI, F60 *ter* 393.

132. Ibid.

133. Letter from John L. Brown to Maurice Chouraqui, 14 March 1949, AN, SGCI, F60, SGCI F60 *ter* 393.

134. La verité sur l'Union Sovietique, Tribune de Paris, 11 February 1949, enregistrement sonore, Bibliotheque nationale, François Mitterand.

135. Groupes sociaux en France, 20, 27 August, 3 September, 1948, Tribune de Paris, enregisterement sonore, Bibliotheque nationale, François Mitterand.

136. La condition des travailleurs en l'an 2000, Tribune de Paris, 13 April 1949, enregisterement sonore, Bibliotheque nationale, François Mitterand.

137. Note, Information, 15 March 1949, AN, SGCI, F60 *ter* 393.

138. Ibid.

139. Note pour le Ministre des Finances et des Affaires économiques, 7 April 1949, AN, SGCI, F60 *ter* 381; Letter from Robert Schuman, Ministre des Affaires Etrangères, to le Vice-President du conseil, chargé de l'information, 1 December 1949, AN, SGCI, F60 *ter* 438.

140. Exécution des clauses de l'accord bilateral relatives à l'information, 12 November 1948, AN, SGCI, F60 *ter* 381.

141. Schweitzer to Brown, 23 May 1949, F60 *ter* 393.

142. Letter from Horace G. Reed, acting chief of Mission France, to Schweitzer, SGCI, 11 May 1949, AN, SGCI, F60 *ter* 393.

143. Letter from SGCI to Schuman, 9 February 1949, AN, SGCI, F60 *ter* 393.

144. Les dispositions de l'article VIII de l'accord de cooperation économique entre La France et Les Etats-Unis, 7 July 1950, AN, SGCI, F60 *ter* 393.

145. Ibid.

146. Note pour le ministre des Finances et Affaires économiques, 7 April 1949, AN, SGCI, F60 *ter* 381.

147. Notes sur quelques formes de la diffusion et la vulgarisation des informations relatives au Plan Marshall en France, notes diverses Fevrier-Avril 1949, AN, SGCI, F60 *ter* 438.

148. Les dispositions de l'article VIII de l'accord de cooperation économique entre La France et Les Etats-Unis, 7 July 1950, AN, SGCI, F60 *ter* 393.

149. Checklist, NARA, RG. 469, entry 353, box 16.

150. Ibid.

151. Sallie Pisani, *The CIA and the Marshall Plan* (Lawrence: University Press of Kansas, 1991), 104.

152. Paix et Liberté, embassy telegram, 9 October 1950, NARA, RG. 84, entry 2462, box 37.

153. Note sur le credit special destine a la diffusion des informations relatives au Plan de relevement Europeen, 2 December 1952, AN, SGCI, F60 *ter* 393.

154. De la propagande américaine en France, J. Constant, 15 January 1952, Archives du Ministère des Affaires Etrangères, série B, 511.

155. Ibid.

156. Ibid.

157. Ibid.

158. Letter from Harry Martin to Merrill Cody, Chief Department of State Liaison with OSR, 11 December 1950, NARA, RG 469, entry 1193, box 44.

159. De la propagande américaine en France.

160. Ibid.

161. Ibid.

162. Manifeste de Robert Geffroy, 5 October 1945, Salle Pleyel, Paris; "*France–Etats-Unis* Request for approval of counterpart funds," 30 June 1950, Mission France Information Division; NARA, RG. 84, entry 2462, box 28.

163. Letter from Willard Hill to George Rehm, USIS Marseille, 2 May 1947; Letter from Douglas Schneider, USIS director, Paris, to George Rhem, 22 May 1947; NARA, RG. 84, entry 2462, box 28.

164. Ninkovich, 157.

165. Kuisel, *Seducing the French*, 55.

166. "France–Etats-Unis Request for approval of counterpart funds," the outlay prior to 1950 was 7.2 million francs per year, or $23,684 at the official 1948 exchange rate.

167. Ibid.

168. Letter from Kirkpatrick to Elgozy, 18 November 1949, AN, SGCI, F60 *ter* 438.

169. Ibid.

170. American officials were shocked by the candor of Elgozy, head of the SGCI, but it merely confirmed French behavior to date; Letter from Donald W. Dresden, Deputy Chief ECA Information, to Helen Kirkpatrick, 17 February 1950; Letter from Donald W. Dresden to Horace Reed and Helen Kirkpatrick, 17 February 1950; NARA, RG. 469, entry 1193, box 44.

171. Letter from Donald W. Dresden to Horace Reed and Helen Kirkpatrick, 17 February 1950.
172. Letter from Kirkpatrick to Makinsky, 12 September 1950; Letter from Makinsky to Kirkpatrick, 8 September 1950; NARA, RG. 84, entry 2462, box 28.
173. Telegraph from Paris embassy (Tyler) to State Department, 15 December 1950, NARA, central decimal files of the State Department, 511.51/12-2951; "*France–Etats-Unis* Request for approval of counterpart funds."
174. Inauguration of Section Lafayette of France–Etats-Unis at Le Puy, 10 February 1950, State Department Decimal Files, France Foreign Affairs, American Foreign Policy Center.
175. Anticipated Financial Problems of France–Etats-Unis, 23 November 1951, State Department Confidential Files, France Internal Affairs, American Foreign Policy Center.
176. Publication entitled *Amitié Franco-Américaine,* 8 November 1951, State Department Confidential Files, France Foreign Affairs, American Foreign Policy Center.
177. Ibid.
178. Letter from Philip Dur to Davis O. Harrington, Assistant Public Affairs Officer, Paris, 18 September 1950, NARA, RG. 84, entry 2462, box 28.
179. Letter from Davis O. Harrington to Abram Manell, 14 December 1950, NARA, RG. 84, entry 2462, box 28.
180. Letter from Ted Arthur, Public Affairs Officer, Bordeaux, to Davis Harrington, 6 October 1950, NARA, RG. 84, entry 2462, box 28.
181. Ibid.
182. Letter from Davis O. Harrington to Ted Arthur, 6 October 1950, NARA, RG. 84, entry 2462, box 28.
183. Letter from G. Martin to Kirkpatrick, 15 May 1950, NARA, RG. 469, entry 1193, box 45.
184. Ibid.
185. France–Etats-Unis activities in the Lyon area, 27 May 1950, NARA, RG. 84, entry 2462, box 28.
186. Ibid.
187. Letter from Ted Arthur, Public Affairs Officer, Bordeaux, to Davis Harrington, 6 October 1950.
188. Telegram from PAO Lyon to Department of State, 9 November 1950; Telegram for PAO Lyon to Department of State, 20 November 1950; Telegram from PAO Lyon to Department of State, 6 December 1950; NARA, central decimal files of the State Department, 511.51/10-1350–511.51/12-2951.
189. *Dépêches et Espoir de St. Etienne,* 15 November 1950.
190. *La République* (territoire de Belfort), 6 November 1950.
191. Projet action France–Etats-Unis, Octobre à Decembre 1950, 25 July 1950; Letter from Makinsky to D.O. Harrington, 6 September 1950; NARA, RG. 84, entry 2462, box 28.
192. Letter from Makinsky to M. Serge Cohen, 14 September 1950, NARA, RG. 84, entry 2462, box 28.
193. Ibid.
194. Letter from D.O. Harrington to Dur, 13 September 1950, NARA, RG. 84, entry 2462, box 28.
195. *Le Voix du peuple,* 7 September 1950.
196. Letter for Dur to Harrington, 18 September 1950, NARA, RG. 84, entry 2462, box 28; Letter from Kirkpatrick to White, 17 November 1950, NARA, RG. 84, entry 2462, box 37.
197. Rapport moral 1952, NARA, RG. 469, entry 1193, box 51.

198. Letter from Mary Vance Trent, Foreign Affairs Office Western Europe, State Department, to Charles K. Moffly, PAO Paris, 29 July 1953, NARA, RG. 469, entry 1193, box 45.

199. Letter from John L. Brown, USIS, to Max Gluck, Mission France, 8 June 1951, NARA, RG. 84, entry 2462, box 16.

200. Anticipated Financial Problems of France–Etats-Unis, 23 November 1951, State Department Confidential Files, France Internal Affairs, American Foreign Policy Center.

201. Contract France–Etats-Unis fiscal year 1953, RG. 84, entry 2462, box 16.

202. Quoted in letter from Mary Vance Trent, Foreign Affairs Office Western Europe, State Department, to Charles K. Moffly, PAO Paris, 29 July 1953.

203. Compte rendu, 1946, Ministère des Affaires Etrangères, relations culturelle, 1945-1947.

204. John Trumpbour, *Selling Hollywood to the World: U.S. and European Struggles for Mastery of the Global Film Industry, 1920-1950* (Cambridge: Cambridge University Press, 2002), 266–267.

205. Jean-Pierre Jeancolas, "L'arrangement Blum-Byrnes à l'épreuve des faits: Les relations (cinématographiques) franco-américaines de 1944 à 1948," *Bulletin de l'Association française de recherches sur l'histoire du cinema* 13 (1992), 24; Laurent Creton, *Histoire économique du cinema français* (Paris: CNRS Editions, 2004), 184.

206. Simone de Beauvoir, *After the War: Force of Circumstance, Vol I: the autobiography of Simone de Beauvoir*, trans. Richard Howard (New York: Paragon, 1992), 13.

207. Ibid., 29.

208. Renegotiation of Franco-American Accord on Motion Pictures, 15 February 1952, NARA, Central Decimal Files of the State Department, 851.452/2-1552.

209. Franco-American Motion Picture Agreement: Conversation with French Officials, 13 February 1952, NARA, Central Decimal Files of the State Department, 851.452/2-1352.

210. Entertainment motion picture—35 mm. France, State Department, Central Decimal Files of the State Department, 851.452/2-251.

211. Telegram from Paris to Secretary of State, 19 June 1952 NARA, RG. 469, entry 236, box 96.

212. Patricia Hubert-Lacombe, *Le Cinema Français dans La Guerre Froide, 1946-1956* (Paris: L'Harmattan, 1996), 181.

213. Desson's report on the Cinema Industry, Embassy translation, 8 May 1952, NARA, Central Decimal Files of the State Department, 851.452/5-852.

214. Ibid.

215. Creton, 291.

216. Guy Desson, "Après le vote de la Loi d'Aide: la leçon des chiffres," *Le Film Français,* 31 Juillet 1953.

217. Compte rendu, 1946, Ministère des Affaires Etrangères, relations culturelle, 1945-1947.

218. Compte rendu, 1946, Ministère des Affaires Etrangères, relations culturelle, 1945-1947.

219. Bernard Piniau, *L'action artistique de la France dans le monde: histoire de l'Association française d'action artistique (AFAA) de 1922 à nos jours* (Paris: L'Harmattan, 1998), 105.

220. Ibid.

221. Note pour le Cabinet du Ministre, 29 Avril 1955, Ministère des Affaires Etrangères, Cabinet du Ministre Antoine Pinay 1955-1956, relations culturelles.

222. Comité d'organisation séance, 12 November 1946, Ministère des Affaires Etrangères, relations culturelles, 1945-1947.
223. Highlights and Significance of the IVth International Cannes Film Festival, NARA, Central Decimal Files of the State Department, 851.191/5-1751. This report contains an overview of the Festivals since 1946.
224. Note pour le cabinet du Ministre, 17 April 1947, Ministère des Affaires Etrangères, relations culturelles, 1945-1947.
225. Comité d'organisation séance, 1 July 1946, Ministère des Affaires Etrangères, relations culturelles 1945-1947, carton 3.
226. Note pour le Cabinet du Ministre, signe: Seydoux, Ministère des Affaires Etrangères, Direction générale des Relations Culturelles, echanges culturelles, Carton 225.
227. "La foi qui sauve: Cannes 1952," *Cahiers du cinema*, Juin 1952.
228. Highlights and Significance of the IVth International Cannes Film Festival, NARA, Central Decimal Files of the State Department, 851.191/5-1751.
229. *L'Humanité*, 15 April 1951.
230. Highlights and Significance of the IVth International Cannes Film Festival, NARA, Central Decimal Files of the State Department, 851.191/5-1751.
231. Ibid.
232. Ibid.
233. Ibid.
234. Letter from B.E.L. Timmons to Pierre Charpentier, Ministère des Affaires Etrangères, 18 September 1952, NARA, RG. 469, entry 1193, box 52.
235. Telegram from State Department to Paris, Tokyo, 31 January 1953, NARA, RG. 469, entry 1193, box 45.
236. Memorandum of conversation: Terrill, Mayer, Fourre-Cormeray, Gompel, Weil-Laurac, NARA, Central Decimal Files of the State Department, 851.452/2-251.
237. Circular to all ERP countries from Minister of Foreign Affairs, 21 January 1949, Ministère des Affaires Etrangères, série B-Amérique 53 "Propaganda politique des Etats-Unis à l'étranger."
238. Telegram from foreign minister to French ambassador in Washington, 16 February 1949, Ministère des Affaires Etrangères, série B-Amérique 53 "Propaganda politique des Etats-Unis à l'étranger."

Chapter 2

"THE TRUE FACE OF THE UNITED STATES" AMERICAN EXHIBITS IN FRANCE, 1948–1952

The exhibits of Mission France were one of the most visible signs of the increased cultural presence of the United States in France. Focusing on American exhibits and American participation in French fairs, this chapter examines the efforts of the French Mission of the ECA and the USIS to promote the American Way of life in France. The participation of the United States in regional fairs and the traveling exhibits, which reached the heart of *La France profonde,* were unprecedented interventions by the U.S. in the French public sphere. American exhibits were prescriptive, normative, and informed by anti-Communist political imperatives. Furthermore, they reflected rigid, even stereotyped perceptions of France.

Robert H. Haddow argues that during the 1950s exhibiting American culture reflected a desire by U.S. corporate interests, designers, and the American government to promote an anti-Communist Internationalism predicated on the globalization of the American model of consumption."[1] This argument is particularly germane to Marshall Plan exhibits, which represented modernity as intrinsically American. Reports from the field staffs of the exhibits suggest that individual French reactions can be read as part of a broader narrative about modernization, consumption, and the United States. American exhibits in France strengthened the symbolic link between the United States and modernity. However, French criticism of Americanization did not reflect an inability to perceive the "real" culprit, modernization, behind the changes occurring in French society. French reactions illustrated the strength of a hegemonic narrative: to be modern was to be American.

Then there was politics. One visible political effect of the American presence was to provide an opportunity for local notables and other groups to demonstrate against the French Communist Party (PCF). Conservative politicians used American exhibits as a stick to beat the Communists with, a reward to loyal followers, and a means to consolidate support. Conversely, the PCF often mobilized against the American presence. Thus, local politics mirrored national political divides. In some cases French mayors feared the appearance of these provocative exhibits and asked that their town be bypassed. The American exhibits thus contributed to and exacerbated the political strains within the Fourth Republic.

The American experience in France provided valuable lessons for American public diplomacy, and this chapter illustrates the evolution of American exhibits. The United States deployed three major traveling exhibits during the Marshall Plan. *Le vrai visage des Etats-Unis* ("The true face of the United States"), *La productivité agricole* ("agricultural productivity"), and *D'homme à homme* ("From man to man"). The latter targeted the working class, while the agricultural exhibit visited small farming communities throughout France. The United States also participated in a number of regional fairs. Finally, the United States hosted several exhibitions meant to highlight its cultural achievements.

The Traveling Agricultural Exhibit of Mission France

Given the food shortages that had plagued France in the immediate postwar years, it is not surprising that agriculture was the topic of the first American traveling exhibit. Planning for it began in late 1948. As was the case with other exhibits, it was the creation of Mission France information specialists working with French nationals. At the request of Mission France Pierre Ladune, a French consultant, provided a formal proposal for the exhibit.[2] Ladune argued that an agricultural exhibit was needed in order to overcome the relative isolation of the rural population, remedy the lack of knowledge about the Marshall Plan in rural France, and challenge the strength of the PCF among farmers and agricultural workers. Ladune pointed out that while the ERP enjoyed a relatively high level of attention in the large Parisian and regional dailies, it received virtually no mention in small papers with circulation limited to a department. According to Ladune, such papers, which appeared only once or twice a week and on market days, exercised a "deep and direct" influence on farmers and "peasants."[3] Previous attempts to reach such papers by adding them to the USIS and Mission France press release distribution list had proved fruitless. The character of the releases was simply too general for inclusion in a two to four page rural paper. For U.S. planners, the silence of small papers was especially regrettable because many were clearly sympathetic to the United States.

Local Communist papers, on the other hand, frequently made reference to the Marshall Plan. The lack of information about the Marshall Plan allowed small Communist papers to use it as a scapegoat. Anything and everything that went wrong could be blamed on the Marshall Plan. The success of this tactic, according to Ladune, was evidenced by the fact that similar perceptions appeared in non-Communist newspapers. Ladune stated, "It is difficult, indeed impossible, to fix this situation from Paris."[4]

The agricultural exhibit offered the opportunity for direct, local intervention. Ladune provided a hypothetical chronology of a visit by the agricultural exhibit. The arrival of the traveling exhibit would create a local spectacle. The local press would announce the arrival of the exhibit and provide a summary of its information. The mayor of the village would add legitimacy and importance to the event by making an inaugural speech. Most importantly, the peasants of the region would visit the exhibit and, as a result, understand the significance of the Marshall Plan. As the exhibit left town, contacts with local newspapers would be solidified. The rural population, now more interested in the Marshall Plan, would be happy to see articles about it appear in their local paper, thus overcoming the resistance of the editors to print general USIS and Mission France press releases.

Ladune attached two important qualifications to this cheery scenario. Indeed, he insisted that the American effort would fail if it did not heed his warnings. The first was that the exhibit and American propaganda in general, must not give the impression of meddling in domestic French politics. Instead, the exhibit should be presented in terms of European economic cooperation, portraying France as a vital link. Secondly, Ladune was quick to point out that if the economic aspect was to be stressed the Americans needed to avoid creating the impression that the Marshall Plan favored American material, particularly farm equipment, to the detriment of French manufacturers.

In December 1948, David Bruce, the head of Mission France, was ready to approach the French government with the proposal. Writing to the French Minister of Agriculture, Pierre Pflimlin, Bruce stated: "It has been brought to the attention of this Mission on several occasions, that the French rural population has comparatively little knowledge of the aims, advantages, and methods of application of the European Recovery Program."[5] Bruce went on to suggest the creation of the traveling exhibition and he outlined its three purposes: telling farmers about the Marshall Plan, showing how it could help them, and, most importantly, explaining "how they can cooperate with it by raising their level of production." Bruce made the modernizing intentions clear when he declared that the exhibit would "awaken interest" in the rural population and provide a positive influence on "rural thought and action."[6] Similarly, Mission France's newsletter, *L'aide Américain à la France*, declared: "The traveling agricultural exhibition has been created in a spirit completely different from previous spectacles that French farmers are used to, and its power of suggestion can only be that much greater."[7] Bruce assured Pflimlin: "This exhibit will be completely unpolitical in character."[8]

The French acceded to the American request almost immediately. Pflimlin told Bruce that he agreed it was important to show peasants the importance of agriculture in French recovery.[9] Yet he pointed out that the American effort would be redundant because his administration had already undertaken such a program. Nevertheless, Pflimlin offered the services of his department and assigned a staff member to follow and assist the American effort by organizing contact with local representatives of the Confédération Générale de l'Agriculture (CGA, a national confederation of agricultural trade unions and associations).

Having gained French acceptance, the exhibit's planning entered the final stage. The inauguration date was set for 6 June 1949, the fifth anniversary of the American landings at Normandy. The location chosen, the village Sainte-Marie-du-Mont, was near the beaches where American troops had landed. From there the exhibit would follow the *voie de la liberté,* the path taken by American troops to Paris. This path was chosen to emphasize that in 1944 American military assistance had helped rid France of Nazi rule, while in 1949 American economic assistance was helping France with recovery efforts.[10] During the exhibit's six month itinerary it was to cross the departments from Normandy to Alsace, after which it would be refitted and begin another tour in early 1950.

The development of the exhibit proceeded smoothly. Pflimlin provided the assistance of a French architect who had studied under Le Corbusier to help with the design.[11] The final design comprised three components. The first was over a hundred panels containing diagrams, montages, and text that explained the functioning of the Marshall Plan. General information about its financial mechanism, counterpart funds, and the history of the American "offer" were shown alongside panels specific to France. The latter detailed how much France received and some of the projects funded by counterpart funds. The panels explained the importance of French agriculture in French re-covery. The ERP urged farmers to increase agricultural productivity to reach the goal of the Monnet Plan (the general postwar French plan for recovery and reconstruction) of making French farm prod-ucts twenty-five percent of total exports.[12] By 1950 the message of recovery in the exhibit also encompassed the idea of "defense" in addition to material prosperity.

The second component was a display of modern farming equip-ment: a high volume water pump, French-made mechanical grape-crushing devices, milking machines, and other labor-saving devices. Several American tractors were also included in the exhibit. The pan-els explained that American agricultural productivity was high due to mechanization, and that French farmers could increase their pro-ductivity by adopting American techniques. Interspersed in this display of farm equipment were consumer goods such as a vacuum cleaner and a washing machine. These items underscored the na-ture of material prosperity that Americans enjoyed as a result of high productivity. The final component was a portable cinema that showed American newsreels and documentaries about the Marshall Plan. All of this material was loaded on four Renault trucks (three seven-ton trucks and one two and a half ton truck) and a 15CV Citroën.[13]

Another function of the exhibit was to distribute printed material. Mission France created a pamphlet specifically for the use of the agri-cultural exhibit entitled *La France agricole*. The exhibit also distributed the pamphlet *Le Plan Marshall cet inconnu* and the Mission France publication *Rapports France–Etats-Unis*. Each of these contained small cards at the back that the reader could use to request more informa-tion: "You can be objectively informed about American aid to France by asking for the complimentary information bulletin of the Mar-shall Plan." Beginning in 1948 the Embassy began to accumulate a large record of names and addresses from such cards.

La France agricole was a brightly colored twenty-eight-page pam-phlet. It contained dozens of photographs and numerous diagrams. The high quality and expensive nature of American pamphlets imme-diately set them apart from anything the Communists (or the French government for that matter) could afford. A key theme of the pam-phlet was that increased productivity by French farmers was essen-tial for the success of not only the Marshall Plan but also the Four Year plan (*Plan de modernisation et d'équipement de l'agriculture*). *La France agricole* began "Agricultural France will be prosperous thanks to the Marshall Plan, the Four Year plan, and your efforts."[14] The pamphlet listed production targets for wheat, corn, potatoes, turnips, milk, butter, and cheese. It called for an increase in the head of cat-

Figure 2.1
The traveling agricultural exhibit (NARA, RG. 469, entry 1193, box 52)

tle from fifteen million to seventeen million, primarily cows to supply
dairy products. According to the pamphlet, sheep needed to increase
by a million head and pigs by over three million. Only by meeting these
figures, the pamphlet explained, could France supply its own needs
and export enough to "recover its past prosperity." *La France agricole* stated that in order to meet these goals French agriculture needed
to undergo a modernizing transformation. "Yet this transformation
especially depends on you," the pamphlet explained, "It's you who
will make it effective. Give your support to the Plan and the Plan will
help you."

The changes envisioned by *La France agricole* were indeed transformative. According to the pamphlet, the entire "physiognomy of
French agriculture" needed to be changed along three lines: the acquisition and use of modern equipment, including land improvements

and construction projects; intensive use of fertilizers; and improved farming techniques. "Cut your meadows and alfalfa early," the pamphlet recommended, "turning the hay quickly to avoid losing its richest parts. Store in silos what you cannot turn. Partition pastures into compartments where livestock will graze successively on young, nourishing grass."

The second half of *La France agricole* was devoted to the Marshall Plan. It explained, "The Four Year plan could not be achieved were it not for the Marshall Plan." A series of diagrams followed illustrating the functioning of counterpart funds, beginning with the "sacrifices consented to by each American citizen" (Step 1) and ending with the transfer of French francs into a reserve (Step 7). Other illustrations showed how this reserve was then used for the modernization of factories, the creation of hydroelectric stations, and investment in agricultural programs. The Crédit Agricole, a government bank, received a large amount of these funds, which were available to farmers and cooperatives in the form of loans.

The concluding section of *La France agricole* contained a propaganda Achilles' heel. One picture showed a shiny new tractor being unloaded from a ship, another a large stockpile of grain (to the ceiling!) in a warehouse. A table listed the amount of material that France had received from the United States. This included six thousand tractors, twenty thousand tons of condensed milk, and a half-billion kilograms of wheat and flour. To be sure, such aid had been critical during the winters of 1946–1947 and 1947–1948. Yet by the time the American exhibit was being created French farmers, particularly small holders, were reducing production due to a slump in farm prices.[15] It was all too easy for the Communists to argue that the drop in price was due to the flooding of the market with surplus American wheat, regardless of the low production of French agriculture or the need to increase French agricultural exports. Finally, the emphasis on the manufactured goods imported on behalf of the Marshall Plan allowed the Communists to argue that the Marshall Plan cost France manufacturing jobs.

Le Plan Marshall ... cet inconnu was another pamphlet distributed by the tens of thousands. As the title suggests, its purpose was to impart a rudimentary knowledge of the Marshall Plan. Yet the pamphlet was also explicitly anti-Communist. According to the pamphlet, the countries that had accepted the "generous American proposition" were no longer threatened by "hunger, misery, or chaos." Interspersed in the text were drawings of Uncle Sam amid destroyed buildings handing out bags of dollars ("$") to beret-wearing Frenchmen. The next section sought to counter criticisms that the Marshall Plan violated the sovereignty of participating countries: "Their independence is protected and, contrary to what those opposed to this grand, unprecedented undertaking declare, their sovereignty has not been undermined. Every objective mind cannot help but recognize the beneficial effects of the Marshall Plan." Yet the presence of the pamphlet and the agricultural exhibit—requirements dictated as a condition of economic aid—was a clear indication that the Marshall Plan had compromised French sovereignty.

La France agricole and *Le Plan Marshall ... cet inconnu* were the two primary publications carried and distributed by the traveling agricultural exhibit. These were some of the earliest public diplomacy efforts by Mission France and their weaknesses were manifest. *La France agricole*'s flawed design reinforced Communist criticisms of the Marshall Plan. *Le Plan Marshall ... cet inconnu* was heavy-handed political propaganda. The exhibit had not even begun its tour and it had already violated Ladune's two principles of not entering French politics or giving the impression that the Marshall Plan favored American industry.

The inauguration of the exhibit occurred as scheduled, on 6 June 1949, in the small village of Sainte-Marie-du-Mont, only a few kilometers from Utah Beach. Franco-American amity ruled the day.[16] The exhibit's inauguration occurred simultaneously with commemorative ceremonies on the Normandy beaches. The American consul at Cherbourg and the head information officer for Mission France attended the opening of the exhibit for the American side while the Viscount René de Tocqueville (in his capacity as department head of the CGA) and a representative of the Agriculture Ministry represented the French. Higher-ranking officials attended the beach ceremonies. At Sainte-Marie-du-Mont a small girl clad in a star-spangled dress presented the American officials with a white rooster, the Gallic symbol of France.[17] Jacques Bauche, the chief of the exhibit, then conducted the gathered crowd on a tour of the exhibit. Some four thousand people visited the exhibit that day.[18]

The exhibit then traveled to Coutances, Saint-Lô, and Bayeux.[19] During these first stages the exhibit staff familiarized themselves with the equipment and tried to establish a routine for entering each village, setting up the exhibit, and leaving. The Citroën was equipped with a loudspeaker and in the days preceding the exhibit's entrance this vehicle circled the target village in a twelve-kilometer radius announcing its arrival. Typically two to three days before the opening date Bauche, acting as a vanguard of sorts, would arrive in the village and inform the mayor of the exhibit's imminent arrival. Bauche would then contact local papers and place posters around the village.

David Bruce, now promoted from head of the French Mission to American ambassador to France, participated in the Saint-Lô showing. He made a brief speech, stating that a genealogical researcher had told him that he had relatives from Normandy. This was no surprise, he said, as his love of the local cuisine clearly illustrated his affinity with the region.[20] Bruce went on to thank the French farmers for their efforts to speed French recovery. The French minister of Agriculture also delivered a speech, as did the head of the French Mission, Barry Bingham.[21]

Local French reaction was generally favorable, but the most positive remarks concerned Bruce's excellent French. *L'Epoque* declared: "The representative of the Grand Republic expressed himself in excellent French. His speech was subtle, sparkled with humor yet serious, even moving." In fact, a general proposition concerning American exhibits was that French commentary was never more positive than when an American addressed the crowd in excellent French. Language and dialogue were not often the strengths of U.S. public diplomacy.

The attendance figures for these stops, although most likely inflated, provide an indication of the exhibit's impact. The combined population for Coutance, Saint-Lô, and Bayeux totaled 18,600. The exhibit split five days between the locations (two days at Coutance and Bayeux, and one at Saint-Lô) with a total attendance of 9,800, well over half of the population.[22] These figures represented the success of Ladune's method of creating local spectacles. The presence of high officials, and other ceremonies contributed to the large attendance figures. The head of the information division of Mission France reported to the ECA:

> [The agricultural exhibit] touches areas of French rural life which are not easily reached by usual informational media.... It is doing valuable work in spreading knowledge of the Marshall Plan among rural populations who do not ordinarily read newspapers or listen to radios, and who rarely attend movies.[23]

The film showings held at the exhibit were also popular. For the three presentations above, the total film audience was 3,960, an impressive figure.[24] In a few cases the films were shown at a local theater. On many occasions the amount of time for showings and the number of seats were the only limits on audience size. One full audience after another would fill the tent or rented hall while the films were rewound. At Cherbourg, and in a few other locations, films could not be shown because the theater's roof was bombed-out.[25] The films were also presented to schoolchildren, earning some compulsory attendance figures.[26]

During the first few weeks on the road the staff tried to work the kinks out of the exhibit. In particular, the staff claimed that the seven-ton Renaults were too difficult to work with and that the loudspeaker was too fragile for the rural roads.[27] The staff also suggested that publicity efforts be increased. Rather than a three-day advance arrival, an eight-day advance notice would bring better results. Three days was simply not enough time to coordinate matters with local officials and newspapers. This would require the addition of another vehicle, but this was also necessary due to the reoccurring need to drive to print shops to obtain more pamphlets and posters.[28]

The exhibit enjoyed successes in early July. A stop in Avranches coincided with the passage of the Tour de France. As crowds gathered to view the Italian Fausto Coppi on his way to victory, Mission France used an airplane to drop pamphlets along the route.[29] The exhibit lingered for three days, taking in over eight thousand visitors. The following year Mission France sought to develop a board game for distribution during the Tour de France. The ERP mission in Italy had developed one for the Giro d'Italia. The game was similar to "Chutes and Ladders." The playing board represented Italy and players followed a path similar to that year's Giro. Landing on some squares allowed an advance: "Bridge reconstructed by the Marshall Plan, gain five hours and advance to square 33" or "The rider advances to square 61 on a magnificent road reconstructed with counterpart funds from the Marshall Plan." Other squares sent the rider back: "The level-crossing is closed, return to square 41 where the Marshall Plan has reconstructed the crossing over the road." The reverse side of the playing board contained information such as stage profiles and previous winners, alongside information about ERP projects. "The goal of this game," explained the head of Mission France's information division to French officials, "is to teach the numerous amateurs of the Tour de France about the works of the Marshall Plan, while at the same time providing them with an innocent and rather amusing past-time."[30] French officials judged the moment "inopportune" for such a game.[31] Nevertheless, French officials at the Ministry of Foreign Affairs clearly understood the public diplomacy potential afforded by the Tour. They saw, for example, French support for Italian riders as evidence of a Franco-Italian rapprochement.[32]

In Vitre, Bauche, the exhibit's chief, arranged for a local dairy cooperative to display its most advanced equipment with the exhibit. Incorporating equipment from local manufacturers generally improved audience reaction.[33] Over two thousand people, nearly a quarter of the town's population, visited the exhibit. From Vitre the exhibit proceeded to Angers, Saumur, Segré, Cholet, and Baugé before stopping to rest for a week. Angers, with a population in excess of eighty thousand, proved to be the most difficult stop. Bauche reported that "the number of agricultural visitors is inversely proportional to the number of inhabitants of the town visited."[34] Only five hundred people visited the exhibit at Angers. It simply failed to generate interest in large towns and cities.

By the beginning of August the exhibit had visited thirteen locations without encountering much difficulty or public opposition. This changed at Le Mans. The troubles began when local officials failed to cooperate with Bauche. The hall originally booked for the exhibit was no longer available. According to Bauche, the replacement hall was unsuitable. It was in a "poor neighborhood" and close to the offices of the Confédération général du travail.[35] Bauche briefly considered canceling the exhibit but decided to go forward because the trucks were already in the town. Yet, as Bauche began to organize the installation of the exhibit town officials informed him that he would not be allowed to proceed with the exhibit. Knowledge of a counterdemonstration by the Communist Party had been leaked to a local paper and the prefect did not have enough police to guarantee the safety of the exhibit's staff.

The prefect told Bauche the Marshall Plan exhibit was not welcome in Le Mans for two reasons. First, the main crop of local farmers was hemp and the government had just ordered a large foreign shipment of it. Farmers blamed the Marshall Plan for the government's decision. The second reason concerned workers. A local tractor-producing Renault factory was on the verge of laying off employees. The CGT had made widely publicized claims that this slump was due to the importation of foreign tractors. Both of these charges were inadvertently reinforced by the American pamphlet *La France agricole*. Bauche, heeding the advice of the officials, ordered the exhibit to quit the town immediately. Mission France reacted poorly to Bauche's report from Le Mans. The Mission's chief information officer wrote Bauche to demand a detailed explanation. The Le Mans visit made clear that Bauche's staid presentation of attendance figures belied deeper reactions.

After a few months on the road Bauche provided a general assessment of the exhibit. He classified visitors to the exhibit into three groups: officials and industrialists; merchants and well-to-do farmers; industrial and agricultural workers.[36] Bauche explained that the first group was the smallest in number but the most favorable to the Marshall Plan and the exhibit. The second group constituted the majority of the visitors to the exhibit. This was a taciturn group. According to Bauche, although they said little it was clear they studied the exhibit closely, and they never left without taking the available documentation. The third group made an "honest effort to understand the panels" and was not afraid to ask difficult questions. Bauche provided the following "typical" comments from visitors:

At the entrance:
—What does this exhibit have to say?
—Here are the Americans selling their equipment!
—Me, I don't benefit from the Marshall Plan. The Americans haven't given me a thing!
In the exhibit:
—Yes, they are helping us, but they send us what they have too much of or what no longer is of use to them.
—Without question their equipment is excellent, but it will create unemployment in France.
—Mechanization is quite nice, but if the machine replaces the man what will become of the man?
—We are convinced about the advice they give, but it takes a fortune to buy this modern equipment.
At the exit:
—An interesting exhibit, but all this costs too much.
—We think that the goals of the Four Year plan concerning rural roads, electricity, and irrigation will not be achieved.
—The production goals of the Four Year plan risk creating a surplus and that would be catastrophic for peasants.
—The Marshall Plan is a generous and ingenious idea, but the French government makes poor use of it. It orders material from the U.S. that does not correspond to French needs, for example tractors.

Mission France concluded that the exhibit could be improved if more attention was given to its setup and presentation. After visiting the exhibit at Saumur an American official described it as "dull and lifeless."[37] He suggested that the tractors be arranged in a "V," acting as a funnel to the entrance of the exhibit. He also criticized Bauche for placing the panels against walls; instead they should be placed at right angles to the walls to form alcoves. A final suggestion was to include an electrical map of France with buttons and lights corresponding to ERP projects in France. Yet the only modification that appears to have been made on the exhibit was an effort to create at least three panels listing the specific benefits of the Marshall Plan to the department the exhibit was touring. Bauche also adjusted the presentation of the exhibit to render it more "three-dimensional."

The exhibit enjoyed a number of successes in August. In many cases its arrival coincided nicely with festivals celebrating the fifth anniversary of a town's liberation.[38] Nearly twenty thousand people visited the exhibit during the second half of August.[39] Local press reaction was generally favorable. *L'Informateur Rouennais* declared that the Marshall Plan "contributed to the necessary modernization of agricultural techniques, an essential condition for French prosperity."[40] *Ouest-France* declared that the exhibit showed the Marshall Plan was not merely a program to help industry.[41] Yet sometimes even the most positive presentations also reinforced negative assumptions about the Marshall Plan. For example, *Paris-Normandie* congratulated the Americans for the attractive and well thought-out exhibit. However, the article included a large photograph of a tractor surrounded by a group of French farmers. The caption read: "Two-hundred and nine American tractors have been brought to France."[42] Bauche reported that it was increasingly common for visitors to criticize the French government for misuse of Marshall Plan aid (i.e., not purchasing from national manufacturers).[43]

Beginning in September references to "police protection" became more frequent in Bauche's reports. This was necessary in Le Heubourg (population two thousand) as well as Chartres. The reports also indicated a growing reticence on the part of town officials to either participate with the exhibit or provide assistance. Officials in Evreux, for example, were "too busy" to assist the exhibit. Other officials were simply not *au courant,* according to Bauche, and responded indifferently.[44] Attendance figures remained high, however. This was due, in part, to the timing of the exhibit, which continued to appear on market days. American newsreels also remained a popular draw. A further development in the exhibit was the increasing cooperation of the CGA.

At Chartres, an agricultural engineer from the CGA delivered a long, detailed speech spanning a number of topics: artificial insemination; the diminution of livestock herds during the past fifty years; the creation of regional abattoirs and the need to stop slaughtering on farms; the need to protect cereal crops against disease; the goal of irrigation and land regrouping. This CGA representative also saluted the Marshall Plan for its support of the Four Year plan "which made all of these advances possible."[45] Under the auspices of the exhibit CGA officials delivered similar addresses in Le Heubourg, Evreux, and Chateauneuf-en-Thymerais.[46]

After a four-week respite, the exhibit began another round of showings in mid-October. Continuing a trend first noted in September, the presentations closing out 1949 were marked by increased hostility to the exhibit. It had two sources. The first was a policy of opposition by the PCF. During 1947 and 1948 the PCF led strikes across the nation. The most important strike occurred in the major French coal mines. The government, declaring the coal mines as essential to national security, used the military to break the miners' strike. In Marseille PCF dockworkers had thrown military material in the harbor.

Violent opposition by the PCF to American exhibits remained a constant concern for French and American officials. The other source of hostility was growing public resentment at American tactics. On a number of occasions French officials prohibited the use of the loudspeaker.[47] Sensitive observers had warned Mission France that such techniques were reminiscent of Nazi propaganda during the occupation.[48] In Nemours the exhibit's posters were ripped down during the night. At Coulommiers Bauche noticed a quiet hostility in many of the visitors as they looked at the level of aid given to French agriculture: "One can tell by the look on their faces," he reported, "that they feel that they have been wronged."[49] Clearly U.S. aid was substantial, but these French farmers had not benefited from it.[50]

Yet if the exhibit failed to attain public support in some showings, support from non-Communist local notables remained constant. At Châlons-sur-Marne the prefect forbade the use of the loudspeaker for "political reasons."[51] Despite this interdiction the prefect was helpful in securing representation from the local bishop, the general of a nearby military training facility, representatives of the CGA, and various municipal councilors. Bauche reported that attendance to the exhibit gained in quality what it lost in quantity.[52] Presentations of the exhibit followed a similar pattern in Reims, Bar-le-Duc, Toul, and Commercy.[53] In Vitry-le-François the attendance of eighty notables on the first day of the exhibit was almost greater than the number of regular visitors.[54]

The village Vezelise was the last stop for 1949. "The farmers of this region, like many others," reported Bauche, "have never heard of the Marshall Plan." Nevertheless, the majority of the visitors appeared quite sympathetic to the exhibit. According to Bauche they were eager to learn about the Marshall Plan. They were "attentive" spectators for the showing of documentaries. The speech of the local representative of the CGA was likewise well received.

Bauche presented the *compte-rendu* for 1949 shortly after leaving Vezelise. The American exhibit had visited seventeen locations in six departments, covering over 2,300 kilometers.[55] Bauche claimed the exhibit received some fifty-four thousand visitors, an average of over three thousand per stop. Twenty-two thousand individuals, according to Bauche, watched the exhibit's films.[56] Perhaps more telling, however, were the populations of the locations visited. The median population figure for the seventeen stops was nine thousand, the average of eighteen thousand due only to the inclusion of the city Reims.[57]

The distribution of pamphlets and the coverage of the exhibit in the local press provide another way of measuring the impact of the exhibit. The exhibit's printed material virtually blanketed each village visited. Bauche reported "distributing" between ten and twenty thousand pamphlets (primarily *La France agricole* and *Le Plan Marshall ... cet inconnu*) per stop.[58] Some twenty-four regional newspapers carried over one hundred articles about the exhibit.[59] The loudspeaker-bearing Citroën further increased the presence of the American exhibit even among those who did not visit it. Thus, even if we take only the film spectators as an accurate representation of the visitors to the exhibit the impact on *La France profonde* was still notable. It is not surprising, therefore, that at the end of 1949 the head of information for Mission France reported that the exhibit was "the single most important media employed by this Mission to tell the story of the Marshall Plan in France."[60]

Although the presence of the exhibit was demonstrable, its reception was less clear. As we saw, Bauche reported that many visitors were surprised by the amount of aid France received and, in light of the negligible effect of the plan on their lives, concluded that the government was misusing the funds. The composition of the visitors suggests that those who were sympathetic to U.S. policy were more likely to visit the exhibit. According to Bauche, farmers and agricultural workers were underrepresented while a good showing by professionals and clergy was typical.[61] As the exhibit refit for the 1950 tour the staff reduced the amount of technical agricultural information to increase its appeal to a general audience.[62]

The Korean War and the deteriorating international situation affected exhibit showings in 1950. In a provocative move, the agricultural exhibit made sorties into towns and regions sympathetic to Communist criticisms of the Marshall Plan. PCF opposition also became more organized. Another phenomenon, already seen in 1949, was the growing support of the exhibit by rural notables. Finally, Bauche's reports for 1950 indicated that French reaction to the exhibit was increasingly expressed in language that reflected stereotypical French perceptions of American society and culture.

In January the exhibit entered Alsace. Bauche reported that the region was pro-American, but that the farmers were rather traditional. One group protested when shown a documentary about artificial insemination, a form of progress they deemed unchristian.[63] This was the worst reaction the exhibit received in Alsace. During January and February the exhibit made ten presentations in the departments of Bas Rhin and Haut Rhin. Bauche reported that the showings were a success. Indeed, many were characterized by displays of goodwill. The exhibit arrived in Thann (population 5,700) to find the main street covered with ERP banners and flags.[64] Mission France reported that

31,500 people visited the exhibit during its two-month presentation in the region.[65]

In March the exhibit cancelled showings at Maiche and Pierrefontaine due to an outbreak of foot-and-mouth disease among local livestock.[66] The French *Services Agricoles* had requested both the presentations. A minor public relations crisis ensued when staff members of Mission France traveled to Pierrefontaine to update the exhibit's material and supplies. To their frustration, the exhibit's crew had taken one of the vehicles to Paris. The outbreak had abated, the livestock had been vaccinated, and the town was holding its market days as usual. "A whole group of important people in the district," one American reported, "are discontented and possibly prejudiced against the Marshall Plan, which doesn't keep its engagements."[67] As a consequence of the Pierrefontaine cancellation, Mission France increased the coordination between the exhibit and local American officials.[68]

When the exhibit entered the department of Jura the USIS attaché in Lyon, Philip Dur, established contact. He helped coordinate the next seven showings and provided an American presence, which had been lacking since the earliest presentations of the exhibit in 1949. Dur, the son of French immigrants to the United States, spoke French fluently without accent. According to Bauche, Dur's presence improved the reception of the exhibit at virtually every showing he attended. [69]

Dur first appeared with the exhibit in the village of Saint-Amour. He addressed about fifty notables (municipal councilors, the mayor, mayors of neighboring villages) at a ceremonial *vin d'honneur*.[70] A few days later at Bletterans the local notables also provided a strong showing. Bauche was especially pleased to see large numbers of local industrialists, clergy, and merchants.[71] The vicar of the diocese and a colonel in the French army were official guests at Autun.[72] At another showing a group of *patrons* volunteered to give their workers a two-hour break to attend the exhibit.[73] The mayor of Mâcon was so impressed by the exhibit that he reportedly exclaimed: "Why can't France be made the forty-ninth state?"[74] The exhibit's staff used the presence of Dur to provoke local chauvinism among notables to see which village could give the best reception to this high-ranking American official.[75] On at least two occasions (Le Mans and Saint Pourçain) the local government was divided between non-Communist and Communist factions.[76] Presentations at Lons-le-Saunier, Dole, and Verdun-sur-Doubs were marked by ceremonial *vin d'honneurs* and receptions for the American attaché.[77]

Although Dur's presence created a stir among local figures, any other effect was less evident. Reports from the field indicated that arguments with Communists were frequent, but the staff also spent a considerable amount of time with non-Communists explaining that the Marshall Plan was not merely a means to dispose of American surpluses.[78] Other visitors to the exhibit questioned the adoption of American methods; one suggested that methods devoted to high productivity had transformed the American worker into a "homme-robot."[79]

The exhibit encountered organized opposition by the PCF in May. At Le Mans, Toul, Metz, Chalon-sur-Soane, and Vezelise the PCF distributed handbills blaming the Marshall Plan for unemployment, "the colonization of France," and "war."[80] The handbill also blamed the U.S. for dumping surpluses: "Seven hundred French tractors sit idle in the SNECMA factory on the outskirts of Paris. At the same time American tractors too expensive for French peasants are imported."[81] In Toul PCF pamphlets warned: "No sector of agricultural production can escape the Marshall Plan."[82] According to the PCF, Marshall Plan imports hurt French producers of grains, vegetables, wine, fruit, and dairy.

The regional daily *Le Patriot* (Cluny) urged farmers to avoid the exhibit. The PCF hosted speakers and held meetings on one side of town while the exhibit was presented at the other.[83] "The Marshallization of France and occidental Europe," warned *Le Patriot*, "is the export to us of our American brothers' misery; as soon as we have been subjugated by the Marshall Plan we will be ripe for war against our Russian brothers at the bidding of Yankee capitalists!" The paper further urged farmers to familiarize themselves with Steinbeck's *The Grapes of Wrath* in order to see how American farmers really lived.

With the onset of the Korean War in June Mission France reported that Communist activity had increased.[84] Two PCF pamphlets were examples of so-called "black propaganda." The PCF copied two American pamphlets and altered the text to reflect the Communist line. According to Mission France the Communists had successfully inserted some of these copies with the pamphlet stock of the exhibit. For a time the exhibit's staff distributed the bogus pamphlets as ECA material.[85] The language used by the Communists to critique the ERP's presence in rural France resembled centuries-old peasant critiques of nobles and landlords. One pamphlet quoted a farmer's anger at the American presence in France:

> The U.S. sticks its nose into everything we do ... just listen to the radio and read the papers, they're everywhere. It's as though there were someone behind my back when I clean out the barn, or someone following me in the fields to check if my furrow is good and straight.[86]

A picture showed a cow marked "France" eating from a bucket labeled "250 billion francs of aid" while Uncle Sam milked coins from "France" into a sack marked "600 billion in armaments."

The Communists' success with this ploy did not last long, however. They had chosen two little-used American pamphlets to duplicate. After their initial success the exhibit's staff was able to identify and remove them. The exhibit staff explained that Communist oppo-

Table 2.1 Exhibits Program 1951: La productivité agricole[90]

	Agricultural Exhibit	Agricultural Train Exhibit Etapes
January	Seine et Oise: 3 shows	
February	Loiret: 15 shows Paris 27–4	
March	Brignoles 10–18 Salon 21 Toulouse 27–1	Paris 28–30
April	Lyon 1–9 Orléans 13–15 Connerré 18 Château-du-loir 21–22 Loué 24	14 stops
May	Rennes 28–7 Poiters 21–21	18 stops
June	Toulon 2–17 Bourges 23–1	16 stops
July	Montluçon 7–15	
August		
September	Fresnay 2 Sillé 8–9 Le Mans 15–16 St. Sauveur Toucy Vermenton Courson Villeneuve l'archevêque	Arpajon
October	Villeneuve sur Yonne Avallon Charney Villeneuve la Guyard Tonnerre St. Florentin Joigny St. Valérien Chablis Auxerre Séné	Bretagne
November		Normandie
December		Nord

sition had been on the rise since the showing at Lons-le Saunier in April.[87] Despite this, the staff stressed, the exhibit was creating a climate "more and more favorable to the realization of the Marshall Plan's goals." The evidence of this, according to the report, was the increased volume of propaganda attacks against the exhibit. Such indirect means of measuring influence were common.

At the end of May 1950 the traveling agricultural exhibit made its final presentation of the year. Mission France claimed that the increased opposition was not a factor in this decision. Rather, a combination of other factors led to the decision: material degradation, staffing problems, and a desire to update and revise the exhibit.[88] However, it seems probable that the outbreak of the Korean War and French participation in NATO created an unfavorable or unpredictable climate for the American exhibit in rural France. The exhibit was refurbished and reappeared in 1951 and 1952 under the aegis of the Minister of Agriculture.[89] In addition, Mission France launched a train version of the exhibit.

Despite the difficulties in assessing the influence of the exhibit, its presence among populations previously unexposed to American propaganda was significant. From June 1949 to May 1950 the exhibit visited a total of seventy-two towns and villages in nineteen departments. The majority of villages visited had less than five thousand inhabitants. Eight villages visited during 1950, for example, had populations of two thousand or less. Bauche claimed to have received 234,000 visitors and distributed on average three pamphlets per visitor.[91] Bauche reported, "We are confident that in the small and medium-sized villages the passage of the traveling agricultural exhibit was a major event."[92] Mission France concluded the exhibit was a success.[93] Cooperation with the French government was never easy to attain, but the aid of the Ministry of Agriculture had exceeded any previous assistance.[94] In part this was due to the local representatives of the CGA.

"The true face of the United States" differed greatly in intent and design from the agricultural exhibit. The purpose of the latter had been, at least ostensibly, to provide technical information to French farmers. "The true face," in contrast, attempted to refute criticisms of the American way of life. Mission France fielded three of these exhibits, and their showings occurred primarily in towns and cities.[95] It was also developed later than the agricultural exhibit, its first showings in 1951. The first component of the exhibit was a marquee that automatically rotated different posters. Its purpose was to introduce the themes of the exhibit and present visitors with a series of questions they could expect the exhibit to address.[96] *"Bluff ou réalité?"* showed an interstate exchange and a barge carrying hundreds of automobiles. Others focused on labor: *"Esclave ou homme libre?"* showed a "typical" American worker, while *"Adversaires ou allies?"* pictured workers and managers in conversation. *"Propagande ou vérité"* juxtaposed a picture of the Statue of Liberty with Picasso's Dove of Peace. Like the agricultural exhibit, "the true face" units possessed mobile cinema units.

The exhibit's panels were awash with statistics illustrating the high standard of living in the U.S. The caption accompanying a picture of American miners read:

Today in the United States:
    National minimum wage: 262 frs. per hour
    Sliding pay scale
    An unemployed worker receives 6,500 frs. each week
    Each worker can retire at age 65 with:
        28,000 frs. per month
        14,000 frs. per month to his spouse

Table 2.2 Exhibits Program 1951: Le vrai visage des Etats Unis[97]

	Unit 1	Unit 2	Unit 3
January			
February			
March			
April	Le Havre 14–29	Vesoul [sic] 7–15	Nantes 12–17 Melun 21–30
May	Tours 5–14 Quimper 19–28	Paris (Rossini) 28–14 Limoges 19–3	Nevers 5–13 Blois 19–28
June	Rouen 2–17 Lille 23–8	Bordeaux 10–25	Reims 3–17 Fontenay 21–25
July	Sables-d'Olonne 13–26	Meaux 30–8 Nancy 14–29	Abbeville 30–9 Aix les Bains 13–30
August	Ile d'Oleron 1–5	Châlons 25–2	
September	Grenoble 1–10 St. Brieuc 8–16 Marseille 15–1	Vannes 1–16 Caen 20–24 Lens 29-8	Strausbourg 1–16 St. Etienne 20–1
October	Montpellier 6–21	Salon Auto-Paris 4–14 Tourcoing 13–22	Roanne 6–15
November			
December			

"The true face" explained that the secret of American prosperity was quite simple, as expressed in the following formula: "Increasing production=lower prices=increased sales=higher salaries and more numerous jobs." The section of the exhibit "Is he a slave?" was also awash with statistics. The exhibit's designers felt compelled to answer the question for the audience: "No." The American worker possessed both time and money for leisure. The latter was broken into three categories: family ("1 television per 6 families"), sport ("20 million Americans are bowling enthusiasts"), cultural ("one free library for every 2,000 inhabitants"). "Does the American worker support the economic system of the United States?" asked another panel. "Evidently," came the answer:

> Because he has the highest salary in the world in a country where
> - production is the highest in the world and where
> - the majority of costs, proportional to the work necessary to pay them, are the lowest in the world.
>
> He possesses the highest purchasing power in the world.
> He enjoys excellent working conditions.
> The right to strike in order to defend his benefits or to gain new ones is guaranteed by law.

Comparisons demonstrating the superiority of the United States were at the heart of the exhibit. A caption under a picture of an electrical plant and industrial tools and machinery read: "Each worker uses three times more mechanical energy than in Europe." A whole series of panels compared the number of work hours necessary to purchase consumer goods in the U.S. with the amount necessary to purchase the same item in the Soviet Union, France, Italy, Norway, and other European countries.

French and U.S. archives contain few reports that indicate how French audiences received "the true face." The photographs showing crowds outside the portable cinema indicate that, as with other exhibits, the cinema was a primary attraction. What of the rest of the exhibit? The veracity of the statistics was no doubt an issue for some visitors habituated to propaganda. Claims about "the right to strike" may also have raised eyebrows among French visitors who had followed the passage of the Taft-Hartley act in the French press. One wonders too if the emphasis on American superiority vis-à-vis other European nations rubbed visitors the wrong way. Finally, as a piece of anti-Communist propaganda the exhibit certainly must have provoked strong reactions from the PCF.

A report from February 1952 details the exhibit's reception in one town.[98] Le vrai visage arrived in Vierzon (south of Orléans) on the 22nd. The CGT distributed handbills at factory exits calling for a demonstration on the evening of the 28th. According to the prefect, the exhibit's director refused police protection "in order to avoid the impression of being placed under the protection of the police." Against his wishes, however, the chief of police deployed twenty-nine officers to the exhibit site. At 6:30 p.m. a crowd of about three hundred assembled at the exhibit. The local secretary of the CGT gave a speech criticizing the American presence in France. The crowd had grown to five hundred when he finished speaking. At 7:10 p.m., with darkness descended, demonstrators started pelting the exhibit trucks with projectiles. Amid the resulting disorder protestors also destroyed the supports holding up the tent for the portable cinema. The situation could have developed into something more serious, but a Communist official urged the protestors to disperse. The exhibit's curator was unwilling to concede the field, however. The next day he told the departmental prefect that he intended to continue with the exhibit for three more days. This prompted the prefect to demand emergency troops from the interior ministry. The request was cancelled, however, when the mayor of Vierzon revoked the exhibit's permit and asked that it leave forthwith.

Although it is difficult to assess the impact of these exhibits, a 1950 report by the advertising firm J. Walter Thompson does shed some light on their ability to increase French awareness of the United States and the Marshall Plan. The report's author, Vergil D. Reed, concluded that the French rural population did possess a basic knowledge of the Marshall Plan: only 13 percent of the rural population had not heard of it.[99] Reed based his conclusions on a Europe-wide survey taken at the end of 1949 and thus these figures did not reflect the work of the exhibit during 1950. Nevertheless, Reed's assessment showed that any measure of the exhibit's "success" would have to move beyond the mere quantitative measurement of visitors. When asked to choose between "the Marshall Plan is good for France; the Marshall Plan is bad for France; don't know if the Marshall Plan is either good or bad for France," the French rural population had the highest "undecided" response rate of any group that had "heard of it" in all of Europe: 51 percent. Indeed, Reed concluded that even though the majority of the population had heard of the Marshall Plan, 78 percent of the rural population stated they did not receive enough information about it. Thirty-seven percent of the rural population thought the Marshall Plan "good" for France while 12 percent considered it "bad" for France.

Reed's conclusions do not, however, move us any closer to assessing the impact of the agricultural exhibit. The report did not specifically address the role of the traveling agricultural exhibit in contributing to the rural population's knowledge of the Marshall Plan. The uninspiring conclusion that the exhibit accomplished its primary objective of acquainting sections of the rural population with the Marshall Plan is tenable, but we are less able to judge the nature of French reception. Bauche's reports indicate that the exhibit did provoke reactions, both good and bad. What is clear is that the exhibit did reach a demographic group which had less contact with newspapers or radios than any other, and that the exhibit inserted national, indeed global, politics into the local political scene.

French Fairs and American Exhibits

By late 1950 Mission France had supplemented the traveling exhibits with other projects. One early addition was an exhibit entitled *L'Avenir est à vous* ("the future is yours").[100] This exhibit was intended for use at important regional fairs. Its basis was a series of articles from a hypothetical 1960 newspaper, *France-Avenir,* which illustrated the manner of life that "could be" if French recovery proceeded apace. The exhibit possessed four components. The first was a series of imaginary newspaper articles from 1960 that represented how France would look having accomplished the objectives of the Marshall Plan. The second part of the exhibit explained how these goals could be accomplished. The third depicted the benefits to individuals as a result of obtaining these goals, and the fourth component provided specific information about the financial mechanism behind the Marshall Plan. Finally, at each showing Mission France worked with the USIS to establish a temporary movie cinema adjacent to the exhibit.

"The future is yours" was as an American projection, a normative vision, for France's course of development. The hypothetical news items in *France-Avenir* included a report on the transatlantic tourism boom in France, the exchangeability of the franc on the world market ("even in the Philippines"), and the inauguration of a Paris-Nice express train.[101] Advertisements sold weekend trips to New York and television sets: "Two million television sets in French homes—why not yours?" *France-Avenir* devoted other articles to the United Nations ("Longest period without a war anywhere in the world") and the richness of the French diet as a result of free trade. In an attempt to appeal to Gallic humor and pride, the American staff included a story that read: "France lends U.S.A. three billion francs for cultural improvement."[102]

Figure 2.2
Miss Exposition at a fair in Lille (NARA, RG. 469, entry 1193, 47)

Themes relating to gender and domesticity were an important component of *France-Avenir*. This exhibit, like other instances of U.S. public diplomacy, sought to allay concerns that Americanization would challenge traditional gender roles. The exhibit displayed pictures of kitchens replete with appliances. One story told of a women's club in a working-class neighborhood that had polled its members and discovered that mechanical aids allowed them to clean a four-room flat in only half a day. [103] Another article explained that French tailors were demanding that the finance minister issue larger denominations of currency because "men now have so much money it bulges their suits." Another advertisement read: "Interesting foreign

jobs—men wanted to work in Switzerland, Belgium, Sweden, U.S.A.—
no formalities or papers required."[104]

The next series of panels informed visitors that increasing productivity was the key to creating the France of *France-Avenir*. Just as
mechanization could make women more efficient housewives, so too
could it increase the output of French industry. As one U.S. film documentary explained, productivity was the "key to plenty." *France-
Avenir* detailed the benefits high productivity had brought France
by 1960: plentiful jobs, low prices, high wages. These factors combined to make the French standard of living one of the highest in the
world. The French suburbs portrayed in this exhibit resembled
American suburbs both physically and economically.

During 1950 "the future is yours" showed at nine regional fairs:
Lyons, Tours, Limoges, Lille, Amiens, Strasbourg, Marseille, Montpellier, and Metz.[105] Although the economic importance of these fairs
had waned since the nineteenth century, they remained important
features of provincial culture. Mission France was thus assured of a
large audience for its exhibits. Each fair generally secured an opening address by a ranking French official. The head of Mission France,
Henry Parkman, participated in several. Jacques Bauche, on loan from
the agricultural exhibit, was the curator for the American exhibit.

Figure 2.3
The future is yours (NARA, RG. 469, entry 1193, box 47)

The Strasbourg exposition occurred during the first two weeks of September. As was the case with most showings of "the future is yours," the American exhibit was one of the biggest at the fair. Bauche reported that seventy-five thousand people had visited the exhibit.[106] The cinema was also quite popular, taking in just under ten thousand spectators. Bauche reported that the exhibit's staff distributed three hundred thousand brochures, pamphlets, Marshall Plan book covers, and Marshall Plan ink blotters. However, according to Bauche few of the visitors actually studied the exhibit's panels. He suggested that the exhibit add a panel at the entrance entitled "Work completed in France thanks in part to the Marshall Plan." In Bauche's judgment this would be more interesting than panels describing a hypothetical state of affairs.

The showing at Metz achieved similar results. Fifty-four thousand people visited the exhibit taking away tens of thousands of pamphlets.[107] The president of the fair (a local notable, M. Weydert) and Minister Guillant, the undersecretary for commerce and industry, declared September 26 "Marshall Plan day." In a speech celebrating Franco-American amity Weydert declared,

> The citizens of Metz and the department of the Moselle have not forgotten the autumn of 1944 and their liberation thanks to the heroism of General Patton's valiant soldiers. They are fully aware of the benefits derived from another, different kind of liberation made possible by another great American, General Marshall.[108]

Bauche reported that the exhibit was a success. Visitors spent a lot of time looking over the panels and seemed generally pleased with the content.[109]

Significantly, the exhibit also appeared in Algeria at Oran and Algiers. In October Henry Parkman, the head of Mission France, flew to Oran to open it. During the showing the exhibit attracted thousands of visitors. Photographs sent to Paris showed crowds of children waiting to get in to the USIS cinema. Jeanne Blanc, the curator of the exhibit in Oran and Algiers, reported that the population was in "total ignorance" of the Marshall Plan.[110] "People know nothing," she reported, "understand nothing—the *colons* no more than the others." Blanc noted that Communist propaganda was widespread among the Arab population. This could not be countered, however, because the ERP did not possess any Arabic pamphlets. Nevertheless, the pamphlets in French were extremely popular. Blanc reported that Arab children were fascinated with the United States but cared little about the Marshall Plan. She observed that groups of men "from the interior" had arrived with nothing but left with handfuls of pamphlets. "It is fair to say," concluded Blanc, "that the fair was attractive, well-organized, and brought good results."[111]

Mission France began planning for the Marseille fair in August. French officials worried that the participation of the United States would prompt the Communists to demand representation in the fair, or to physically attack the exhibit itself. "Because our exhibits have necessarily been pretty straight propaganda," explained Helen Kirkpatrick, "the fair authorities are always somewhat worried for fear our presence will incite the Communists to demand representation."[112] Officials in Marseille stated that although hostility to the U.S. was latent, the Marshall Plan exhibit was sure to provoke negative reactions.[113] They requested that "Plan Marshall" not appear in the title of the exhibit, or on any banners and placards.

One French staff member of the visual information unit (which oversaw the setting up and operation of film projectors and slide shows) of Mission France did his best to explain such reticence by explaining that the Marshall Plan heightened fears of Americanization: "Non-Communist French do not want to be 'Americanized,' and I am also sure that the French Communists do no want to be Rus-

Figure 2.4
Local officials visit a Marshall Plan exhibit in Lille (NARA, RG. 469, entry 1193, box 47).

sians."[114] Concerns about French independence were also at the root of resistance to the ERP. "The Marshall Plan," he concluded, "for the majority of people, is business, American business."[115]

The Marseille fair opened in mid-September. The American exhibit, having removed "Plan Marshall" from the title, was one of the centerpieces of the fairgrounds. Mission France secured wide coverage of the American display from four sympathetic newspapers: *Le Soir, Le Meridional, La France, Le Provençal.* September 26 was "Franco-American day" at the fair. Parkman delivered a well-attended speech at the chamber of commerce. He stressed the need to increase French industrial productivity and he blamed "Stalinists" for weakening the position of the working class. "Misery is the breeding ground of fanaticism," he proclaimed.[116]

Despite official anxiety, Communist opposition to the exhibit took no form harsher than pamphlets and articles in *La Marseillaise.* The police presence around the exhibit was constant, and two undercover officers monitored the interior.[117] The forces of order could also take comfort in the eight-inch guns of the heavy cruiser *U.S.S. Salem,* the flagship of the American sixth fleet. It arrived in port for "Franco-American day" and hosted a reception for local dignitaries.[118] *Le Provençal* explained that the seventeen-thousand–ton cruiser was uniquely American because it was one of two air-conditioned warships in the world.[119] The head of the exhibit, Jeanne Blanc, reported a large turnout by the bourgeoisie of Marseille.[120] She reported that women had an "insatiable appetite" for the pamphlets, but in general everyone accepted them. "No body refuses our pamphlets," she explained, "but that does not necessarily indicate genuine interest."[121] Although many workers came to ask for documentation, few entered the exhibit. Blanc suspected that they were gathering pamphlets for review by Communist officials.

Mission France reported that 1950 was a successful year for American propaganda in France. According to the annual report, ten million French had visited Marshall Plan exhibits. "Judging by our own counts," the report stated, "and the tons of literature they carried away with them, the visitors made the most of that chance."[122] Like the reports for individual exhibit reports, this report illustrated that Mission France measured success in quantitative terms: the number of visitors, the number of pamphlets distributed, and the column-inches of newspaper coverage. There were a number of reasons for this. First, the information division of Mission France operated under the guidelines of the Smith-Mundt Act of 1948, which stressed the need to increase Europeans' understanding of the United States and combat Communist misrepresentations. Mission France argued

Figure 2.5
Distributing pamphlets at a Marshall Plan exhibit (NARA, RG. 469, entry 1193, box 46).

the distribution figures represented exposure of the French to the Marshall Plan and the "truth" about the United States. Quantitative figures also satisfied the need of Congress for clear indicators of successful propaganda. The public relations adage that "half of PR budgets are wasted; the question is, which half?" was unsatisfactory for congressional leaders.[123]

The Cultural Offensive

Beginning in 1950 the cultural attaché in Paris and Mission France began to organize several important showings of American art in France for the closing years of the Marshall Plan. These supplemented exhibits of a lesser scale sponsored by the embassy. For example, in 1950 the embassy sponsored a traveling exhibit of American artists living in France. Most of the paintings were derivative of modern French style, but according to embassy personnel French critics responded positively to such flattery whatever the merits of the actual paintings.[124] Nevertheless, the imitative nature of the American paintings may also have reinforced the impression that the United States possessed no indigenous school.

Larger artistic showings occurred in 1951. A showing of etchings, lithographs, and engravings by American artists was well received in Paris.[125] The USIS library in Paris presented an exhibit entitled "The Best American Books of the Year." The report summarizing these activities contained a section, as required, entitled "Evidence of Effectiveness." While previous reports from France had provided attendance figures and distribution numbers, this one now stated: "Evaluation of effectiveness is almost impossible to obtain. There appears to be no valid way of measuring states of mind change by such methods as are used by this Section."[126]

At the end of 1951 the cultural section of the Embassy organized a showing of sixty-eight prints from the permanent collection of the Museum of Modern Art in New York with the assistance of the Rockefeller Foundation.[127] The publicity for the showing was discrete and professional: two hundred posters were distributed to bookstores, galleries, hotels, and cafés. The embassy also conducted a specialized mailing for lycées, art schools, and publishers. The official opening and reception attracted a crowd of French art critics, artists, and officials from the cultural relations bureau of the Foreign Ministry. About half the prints were semiabstract. David Bruce, the American ambassador, argued that the inclusion of such works was important because the style was "banned" in the Soviet Union. According to Bruce, abstract art was a "salutary antidote" to the "Communist poison" of social realism.[128]

French reaction to the exhibit was mixed, but also stereotypical. *Carrefour* praised the "remarkable technique" of the artists, but stated that "skill and application" prevailed over "instinct and sensibility."[129] *Age Nouveau* also commented on the "faultless technique" of the artists, animated, like the United States itself, by a "healthy, vigorous youth." [130] *Le Monde* described the assembled works as "prints of importance" and praised their variety and the complexity of the media.[131] Almost two thousand people visited the show. According to the embassy, the exhibit's popularity necessitated a one-week extension.[132] The exhibit was immediately followed by a show of American oil paintings on loan from the Corcoran Gallery in Washington, D.C. The Ambassador reported that these showings were "effective in combating vicious anti-American propaganda by Communists."[133]

The next year, 1952, saw a continuation of the high culture offensive by the United States in France, but with a qualitative improvement. Two events, in particular, stood out. The first was the visit of

Frank Lloyd Wright and a large display of his work at the *Ecole Nationale des Beaux-Arts.* The second, in May, was the festival *L'oeuvre du XXe siècle* ("masterpieces of the twentieth century") organized by the Congress for Cultural Freedom. Both presented material not previously seen in France. French critics could—and did—criticize the performances of "masterpieces of the twentieth century" and the vision of Wright, but in doing so they risked assuming the role of defenders of the status quo. This was one way in which the United States "stole the idea of modern art."[134]

The Wright exhibit was notable for the presence of the architect himself. The eighty-three-year-old Wright crossed the Atlantic in April to open the month-long exhibit. He delivered several lectures and was, by most accounts, a forceful presence in Paris. His first week was filled with official receptions. He met a group of three hundred architectural students who, according to reports, greeted him with songs and cheers.[135] Wright spent hours with the students discussing his work. When the time came for Wright to leave—his schedule carefully planned to achieve maximum exposure—a spontaneous demonstration occurred. Students cheered, stamped their feet, and sang the school anthem. It moved Wright to tears. The American cultural attaché, noting the weight of tradition at *Beaux-Arts,* thought the support of the students was a clear indication that the American emphasis on high culture was worthwhile.[136]

Indeed, the Wright exhibit was particularly suited to Paris and France. To a population that was suffering the worst housing shortage in decades, the display of large American homes was a forceful argument for the American way of life. The exhibit contained Wright's model city, the decentralized Broad Acre, as well as dozens of sketches, diagrams, and pictures of Wright homes. At receptions Wright spoke of plans for an inexpensive home composed of interchangeable parts that could be assembled without expert skill. He pointed out that Broad Acre was premised on the human need for light and air, the freshness of trees and lawns, and a hearth of one's own. Such a city, he argued, could only exist in "free," democratic societies.[137]

French reaction to the exhibit was generally positive. Even the Communist *Les Lettres françaises* begrudgingly offered some compliments. Writing in *Les Lettres françaises,* Marcel Cornu acknowledged Wright's "authenticity."[138] Yet the reaction of major French newspapers shared a common feature. They praised his work, but they also made it clear that as far as American culture was concerned, Wright was an anomaly, perhaps even the exception that proved the rule that the U.S. had no high culture. *Le Monde* stated that his visit was a "triumph."[139] The article declared that "Wright's inspiration is the

- boldest and richest of the twentieth century." *Le Figaro littéraire* called him a prophet and compared his devotion to nature and the individual with that of Rousseau.[140] *Carrefour* stated that Wright was "probably the greatest" architect of the century.[141]

The French press portrayed Wright's architecture as un-American. *Le Monde, Les Lettres françaises, Le Figaro littéraire,* and *Carrefour* all devoted at least a paragraph to Wright's dislike of skyscrapers. "As early as 1900," declared *Le Monde,* "he protested against skyscrapers.... In a country which seems endowed with enormous chaotic cities he has denied their inevitability and even their usefulness."[142] *Le Figaro littéraire* headlined the article: "Frank Lloyd Wright has come to Paris to preach the crusade against the skyscrapers."[143] *Les Lettres françaises* explained that the policies of the United States were trying to accustom the world to the type of architecture opposed by Wright.[144]

Both *Les Lettres françaises* and *Le Figaro littéraire* criticized Wright's houses as being out of reach for average people. The latter described his designs as "extravagant and costly villas."[145] *Les Lettres françaises* lamented the evolution of his work from Prairie House, which it praised, to Falling Waters and other "sensational creations designed to serve as residences for millionaires." *Le Figaro littéraire* thought Wright's gift of incorporating the countryside into the dwelling was immoderate. The article's author, Bernard Champigneulle, explained:

> I know many men who love nature and yet not this concept of "at home," who prefer to retreat to less transparent rooms and who take pleasure in seeing a charming countryside framed in an average-sized window as in the paintings of old masters.

Although *Les Lettres françaises* criticized Wright's style ("This feast of formalism creates a tyrannical architecture"), its most trenchant criticisms were political. The Communists clearly recognized the new tactic employed by the embassy and Mission France. Cornu declared that the exhibit was a product of the "American propaganda service," and he warned potential visitors that the organizers were the same who had advertised the praises of the Marshall Plan and NATO. The showing of Wright's work was not altogether different from the cultural invasion of France by *Reader's Digest,* or the physical presence of U.S. troops. The Americans aimed at achieving the same objectives with Wright's work, but with "a nobler weapon, art." "Everything changes color and lends itself to suspicion," he warned, "The exhibition although itself pacific, forms part of a link with others which were scarcely so."[146]

The embassy and Mission France expected such criticism from the Communists, to be sure, and they deemed the exhibit a resounding success. The cultural attaché reported: "The impact of the show, in terms of target groups reached and psychological objectives achieved, exceeded the expectations of the Embassy."[147] He claimed the exhibit received over a thousand visitors per day throughout the month. State Department officials in Washington were also pleased with the results of the exhibit. Its success assuaged any fears about the upcoming festival "masterpieces of the twentieth century."[148]

This festival has received little treatment by historians. Those who do discuss it treat it in the context of the Congress for Cultural Freedom, which organized the event. Yet even here the neglect is surprising. Pierre Grémion describes it as "the first artistic festival of its kind organized by the United States on the European continent."[149] Yet he devotes scarcely more than one page to it in his six hundred–page tome. Peter Coleman, who states that the festival "put the Congress on the map," devotes two pages to it.[150] Frances Stoner Saunder's discussion of the festival, focusing on the pipeline of covert CIA aid, helps to the fill the lacuna.[151] It is also possible to understand the festival in the context of American public diplomacy in France. It was, in this sense, the loudest, largest broadside yet fired in the Cold War at a difficult target: French intellectuals.

Planning for the festival began in early 1951. The Congress for Cultural Freedom received the active support of the State Department in addition to CIA funds.[152] The President of the Fairfield Foundation, the primary conduit for CIA funds to the Congress, played an active role in raising funds for the festival.[153] Information specialist Edward Barret of the Office of International and Cultural Affairs in the State Department wrote the president of the American Express Company to raise money. He described the festival as "a potent weapon in reaching many of the straddlers and doubters in Europe."[154] Barrett was also excited about the chance "to strike some blows for American culture." For Barrett and other American officials the Congress for Cultural Freedom represented an ideal tool for reaching European intellectuals. The group's potential efficacy was based on its strong composition of European intellectuals. André Malraux, François Mauriac, Bertrand Russell, Raymond Aron, Benedetto Croce, and Jacques Maritain were all affiliated at one time or another. "They have an assorted background," explained Barrett, "which is one of the things that makes it possible for them to reach into the opposition."[155] "We are lucky to have them on our side," he concluded.

Five months before the opening of the exhibit *The New York Times* rebuked the American government for not funding the effort. The editorial stressed the support given the arts by the Soviet State and argued that Europe was in need of "more examples of America's impressive cultural life."[156] The festival was one such effort, and the editors suggested that the United States was missing a "golden opportunity" by not providing funds. State Department officials bristled at the editorial. The Congress chose to use private funds to avoid any "official" label. In any event, the U.S. could hardly be forthcoming with the assistance it did supply.[157]

The Congress began planning the festival in earnest in May 1951. As its title suggests, "masterpieces of the twentieth century" was an effort by the Congress for Cultural Freedom, as a U.S. proxy, to co-opt some of the finest art of the century. The festival was massive. At the Musée d'Art moderne one hundred and fifty pieces were shown representing fifty-five painters and a dozen sculptors. Nine orchestras (including the Boston Symphony) and the New York Ballet performed at a half-dozen venues throughout Paris. Just as Bertrand Russell and other European intellectuals were unknowingly involved in a CIA operation, so too were the works of Stravinsky, Chagall, Giacometti, and dozens of other artists mustered in support of "Freedom" and "Western Civilization."

A prospectus circulated in late 1951 detailed the premises for the festival. The document outlined the first fifty years of the century as one of intense "ideological conflict" and simultaneous "intense creative activity."[158] It continued:

> Powerful states have arisen whose governments have attempted and are attempting to stifle the free effort of artists and to transform them into obedient instruments of the state, serving the political ends and ideologies of its leaders. They have declared invalid, corrupt, and decadent nearly all the highest artistic achievements of the last fifty years.

Rather than engage in an "ideological polemic" about the validity of "Free culture," the Congress for Cultural Freedom intended to let the "products" of this culture "speak for themselves." Nicolas Nabokov, the prime mover behind the operation, contended that "no ideological polemic about the validity and meaning of our culture can equal the products of this culture itself."[159]

Cultural production is certainly a difficult process to analyze and it is unclear to what extent one can speak of the pieces in "masterpieces of the twentieth century" as products of "Free culture." Some of the artists presented were, or had been, critical of their cultural milieu. One piece presented, Edvard Munch's *The Scream,* is hardly a ringing endorsement of Western Civilization. Nevertheless, the organizers of the conference decided that it would be better to err on the side of inclusiveness. By casting the net as wide as possible, the Congress for Cultural Freedom maximized the co-optation. The organizers recognized that turning the most important art of the twentieth century into anti-Communist totems was a long-term project. The dominant position of the United States in global communications and media was certainly an advantage. The prospectus for the festival explained that mass audiences necessarily followed mass media. The global implications of this for the projection of American power were significant: "Vast geographical areas which formerly were in cultural isolation have been drawn into active participation in the cultural life of the Western world."

Ideologically, "masterpieces of the twentieth century" operated along two axes. The first was to identify the United States as the protector of the Western Canon, including the works consecrated that May in Paris; the second axis identified "Freedom" with the ability and leverage to globally market and distribute this Canon as a means of ending the cultural "isolation" of the periphery.[160] To fulfill these objectives the festival sought out partisan conflict. Nabokov claimed that the festival would avoid overt propaganda.[161] However, the four public debates provided a context of partisan conflict for the art showings: "Isolation and Communication"; "Revolt and Communion"; "The Spirit of Painting in the Twentieth Century"; "Diversity and Universality." There were also anti-Communist events such as a church service for victims of "totalitarian oppression" and performances of works by Prokofiev and Shostakovich, which were forbidden in the Soviet Union.[162]

May 1952 was also a period of intense activity by the Communist party. It had been mobilizing for action against the new premier, the conservative Antoine Pinay. The arrival of the new military leader of NATO, the American General Matthew Ridgway, provided a crystallizing event for a mass demonstration against the Pinay government and French involvement with the United States. "Masterpieces of the twentieth century" thus occurred in a politically supercharged environment. Two weeks prior to Ridgway's arrival Communists destroyed an American labor exhibit touring the provinces. The discontent reached a crescendo on 28 May. As the *Academia Nazionale di Santa Cecilia* performed in the *Théâtre des Champs-Elysées* and Raymond Aron and Parisian intellectuals debated "Diversity and Universality" some twenty thousand Parisians rioted in protest of Ridgway's presence in Paris. Dozens of protesters and police were hurt, and one protester died.[163]

It was not surprising, therefore, that the festival did not hit its intended target. Indeed, it provoked a certain amount of cultural chauvinism from French intellectuals. Barrett and *The New York Times* were quite naïve to herald the festival as a demonstration of American culture. There was very little American content at all. The presence of the Boston Symphony Orchestra and the New York Ballet underlined the American tone of the exhibit, but most French commentators quickly pointed out that the director of the Boston Symphony, Charles Münch, was French, as were many of the dancers in the Ballet.[164] Jean-Paul Sartre's *Les Temps modernes* encouraged its readers to visit the Art exhibit of the festival because most of the pieces were by French artists.[165] "The exhibit shows paintings," explained the editors, "that one no longer sees, or cannot see, because they belong to private, principally American, collections." The neutralist periodical *L'Observateur* thought the atmosphere of the "super-festival" was "a bit too showy," but it commended the organizers for bringing Stravinsky back to Paris to direct *Oedipus Rex.*[166] As for *L'Humanité*, the Communist paper attacked the festival as an attempt to "ideologically occupy" the country.[167] According to the editors, the festival was an effort to "enlist" French intellectuals in a fascist "cultural army." They also noted the ostentatious nature of the festival and questioned who could be footing the bill.

The Swiss journalist Herbert Leuthy provided what was arguably the most insightful analysis of the festival. Writing in *Commentary*, Leuthy described the presentation of the festival and French reaction in detail. Although he acknowledged that the festival as an attack on Stalinism was a "noble and generous" idea, Leuthy quickly pointed out that great works of art were not easily converted to ideological warriors.[168] One problem Leuthy identified was the speciousness of claiming that the works of artists somehow argued for or against the conditions under which they were produced. It was misplaced for the organizers to celebrate the work and life of Bartok, who died in poverty, as an endorsement of Western Civilization. According to Leuthy, rather than "Freedom" the societies under which such geniuses as Bartok, Van Gogh, or Berg strove supplied the "vital minimum of freedom" called "indifference." Such a society, concluded Leuthy, should hardly congratulate itself on its generosity.[169]

The festival closed without incident at the end of May. Nicolas Nabokov, the primary organizer, acknowledged in a letter to Sidney Hook that the festival had not received the desired acceptance by the French press.[170] Arthur Koestler described it as "an effete gathering."[171] Nevertheless, most commentators accepted that the festival had established a presence in some elite circles. *Elle* magazine even devoted an issue to the fashion of celebrities at various festival events. Although the press was generally negative, the high-priced

tickets sold well.[172] Yet the festival did generate some positive feedback. For example, *L'Observateur* argued that if many of the works
were American-owned French pieces it was because the United States
was more accepting of innovation. These pieces had found their way
to the United States only after being rejected by the status quo in
France. Nevertheless, the conditions of their prodigal return caused
no small amount of confusion. As Leuthy concluded: "Far too many
people wondered whether their approval—or disapproval—would be
entered to the account of Arnold Schoenberg or General Ridgway."[173]

From Psychological Warfare to Waffle Irons

"Masterpieces of the twentieth century" was indicative of a new high
culture emphasis in the American public diplomacy effort. In 1953
museums in the United States sent eighty works of abstract expressionism for an exhibit at the *Musée d'Art Moderne*. Jackson Pollock
was the featured artist. *Le Monde* commended the works for their
"sense of humanity" but also commented on their "excess of energy."
"All these tendencies," the paper stated, "prepare in a very particular way the art of tomorrow: we cannot ignore that fact, even if art
in our country follows a different path."[174]

The exhibitions in France illustrate the evolution of U.S. public
diplomacy. During the Marshall Plan American public diplomacy
moved away from overt ideological confrontation, and the naïve assumption that increased knowledge of the U.S. was sufficient to make
the French population amiable to American foreign policy. In the absence of assistance from the French government, American information specialists learned how to reach their French targets the hard
way. They often missed their mark, and the damage done to French
public opinion was significant. The use of the car-mounted loudspeaker, for example, to promote the traveling agricultural exhibit
did more harm than good. American pamphlets also inadvertently
reinforced Communist criticisms of the Marshall Plan. American exhibits, pamphlets, and other material that stressed the benefit of the
Marshall Plan did not square with the reality of life for the average
worker or farmer. As long as such individuals failed to see themselves as beneficiaries of the Marshall Plan they were impervious to
the American programs.

At times the American programs amounted to little more than
meddling. The results of overt programs such as the traveling agricultural exhibit and "the true face" vis-à-vis their stated objectives
were unclear at best. A 1950 report by Mission France to the Secre-

tary of State admitted that knowledge of the Marshall Plan did not affect the average French person's opinion of it; well-informed individuals were just as likely to be hostile to it as the uninformed.[175] Much of the American material succeeded in reinforcing French stereotypes about the United States, or, as with the agricultural exhibit, further strengthening the symbolic link between the United States and modernity. Yet, the indirect efforts of the American Embassy yielded only marginally better results.

As problematic as discussions about public opinion are, the responses to the traveling agricultural exhibit bear a striking resemblance to the attitudes of the French villagers Laurence Wylie studied during 1950 to 1951. The conclusion of Mission France and Vergil Reed that the French rural population had the highest "undecided" rate about the value of the Marshall Plan is similar to Wylie's observation that "most of the people agree that both the Russians and Americans seem spoiling for a fight, and France is nothing but a pawn in the struggle between these two giants."[176] The remarks of one French farmer regarding a political poster are also revealing. "All that," the farmer told Wylie, "is propaganda, and propaganda does not interest me. All sides have thrown it at us since 1939—we don't pay attention to it anymore."[177] The pessimism and cynicism described by Wylie resemble the comments reported by Bauche. Because the plan had negligible effects on the lives of the visitors to the exhibit, many concluded that the French government was misusing Marshall Plan funds. Furthermore, as Bauche reported, even many non-Communists thought the Marshall Plan was a means for the U.S. to dump its surpluses.

The display at the Marseille fair in 1952 provides one last example of the transformation in U.S. public diplomacy. Where previously American officials had provided explanations of counterpart funds and refutations of Communist charges, they now displayed Hamilton-Beach mixers; an Oasis hair dryer; an electric broiler, knife sharpener, and waffle iron; a garbage disposal; cosmetics; plastic nursing bottles; and raincoats.[178] Where previously French visitors had taken offence at the anti-Communist content of American exhibits, this time the resentment of French crowds centered on the unwillingness of the exhibit's staff to sell the display items. In other words, the labor-saving consumer goods on display evoked a curiosity and fascination different than that demanded by headlines about Korea, U.S. funding for the war in Indochina, or the European Defense Community. This exhibit illustrated the ambivalence of some French visitors toward the fruits of American mass culture. As Susan Caruthers points out, "Ordinary people may have ambiguous responses to

'Americanization,' even as they may simultaneously enjoy American products."[179] By 1952 American public diplomats had learned to exploit this ambivalence.

The French visitors to U.S. exhibits saw a vision of modernity that was explicitly American. Indeed, the argument of these exhibits was that it was necessary to adopt American values and methods in order to modernize at all. The political message was also explicit and global: the Cold War was a battle between Freedom—the American way of life—and the Soviet Union, and the French farmer or worker who adopted American methods, who produced more for the good of *his* country was aiding the side of Freedom. The politicized content of the exhibit may help explain why the "undecided" rate of the French rural population was so high. French farmers may have been willing to accept the value of hybrid corn from the United States, but they were less enthusiastic about the presence of American troops, for example.

Scholars have considered how representations of America act as metonyms for modernity.[180] Others have examined French representations of modernity that avoided the American model.[181] Shanny Peer argues that representations of rural life as dynamic and adaptive during the late Third Republic marked an attempt to create a French path to modernization, one that avoided the contradiction between tradition and American modernity.[182] The traveling agricultural exhibit and "the true face of the United States" contributed to the contested nature of representing modernity and modernization in twentieth century France. Yet the involvement of the United States was direct. The exhibits were an unprecedented attempt to place a specifically American face on modernization. That they occurred as a condition of an economic aid package for French reconstruction only strengthened the claims of American universality.

Notes

1. Robert H. Haddow, *Pavilions of Plenty: Exhibiting American Culture Abroad in the 1950s* (Washington, D.C.: Smithsonian Institution Press, 1997), 2.
2. Projet d'exposition rurale itinérante du Plan Marshall en France, September 1948, NARA, RG. 469, entry 1193, box 44.
3. The French staff used two terms when discussing the rural population: *paysan,* literally "peasant" and *fermier,* which translates more generally as "farmer." Generally, *paysan* was used most often by the staff members in their reports. Projet d'exposition rurale itinérante du Plan Marshall en France.

4. Projet d'exposition rurale itinérante du Plan Marshall en France.
5. Letter from David K. Bruce, head of Mission France, to Pierre Pflimlin, 15 December 1949, NARA, RG. 469, entry 1193, box 52.
6. Ibid.
7. *L'aide Américaine à la France,* 1 Mai 1949.
8. Letter from David K. Bruce to Pierre Pflimlin, 15 December 1949.
9. Letter from Pierre Pflimlin to David K. Bruce, 23 December 1949, NARA, RG. 469, entry 1193, box 52.
10. Itinerary of agricultural exhibit, NARA, RG. 469, entry 1193, box 52.
11. *La Croix,* 1 June 1949.
12. Traveling Agricultural Exhibit, memo John L. Brown, chief information officer Mission France, to David K. Bruce, 5 March 1949.
13. Rapport de M.J. Bauche sur les modifications qu'il semblerait judicieux d'apporter à l'organisation de l'exposition agricole itinérante du Plan Marshall pour la deuxième partie de son voyage à travers la France, 16 August 1949, NARA, RG. 469, entry 1193, box 52.
14. *La France agricole,* pamphlet, NARA, RG. 469, entry 1193, box 54.
15. Letter from John L. Brown to David K. Bruce, 5 March 1949.
16. *Parisien Libéré,* 7 June 1949.
17. *L'Aube,* 8 June 1949.
18. Rapport de M. Jacques Bauche à M. John L. Brown, 7 June 1949, NARA, RG. 469, entry 1193, box 52.
19. Rapport de M. Jacques Bauche à M. John L. Brown, 20 June 1949, NARA, RG. 469, entry 1193, box 52.
20. *L'Epoque,* 15 June 1949.
21. *L'Aube,* 15 June 1949; *Le Populaire,* 17 June 1949.
22. Exposition Agricole, Itinéraire 1949-50, NARA, RG. 469, 1193, box 52.
23. June Activities Report, 1 July 1949, NARA, RG. 469, entry 1193, box 48.
24. Exposition Agricole, Itinéraire 1949-50.
25. Rapport de M. Jacques Bauche, 1 July 1949, NARA, RG. 469, entry 1193, box 48.
26. Agricultural Tour Film Showings, NARA, 13 June 1949, NARA, RG. 469, entry 1193, box 48.
27. Impressions, critiques, et suggestions, Letter from G. Laupretre to John L. Brown, 20 June 1949, NARA, RG. 469, entry 1193, box 44.
28. Letter from Strauss Sagan to John L. Brown, 22 June 1949, NARA, RG. 469, entry 1193, box 44.
29. Rapport de Jacques Bauche, 11 July 1949, NARA, RG. 469, entry 1193, box 48.
30. Letter from Helen Kirkpatrick SGCI, F60 *ter* 393.
31. Ibid.
32. Ministère des Affaires Etrangères, relations culturelles 1945-1947, 1.
33. Rapport de Jacques Bauche, 15 July 1949, NARA, RG. 469, entry 1193, box 48.
34. Rapport de Jacques Bauche, 20 July 1949, NARA, RG. 469, entry 1193, box 48.
35. Rapport de Jacques Bauche, 6 August 1949, NARA, RG. 469, entry 1193, box 48.
36. Letter from Bauche to Brown, 16 August 1949, NARA, RG. 469, entry 1193, box 52.
37. Suggestions for Improvement of Traveling Agricultural Exhibit, Mission France Information Division, 19 August 1949, NARA, RG. 469, entry 1193, box 52.
38. Rapport de Jacques Bauche, 30 August 1949, NARA, RG. 469, entry 1193, box 48.
39. Exposition Agricole, Itineraire, 1949-1950.
40. *L'Informateur Rouennais,* 26 August 1949.
41. *Ouest-France,* 27 August 1949.
42. *Paris-Normandie,* 26 August 1949.
43. Rapport de Jacques Bauche, 26 August 1949, NARA, RG. 469, entry 1193, box 48.

44. Rapport de Jacques Bauche, 11 September 1949, NARA, RG. 469, entry 1193, box 48.
45. Rapport de Jacques Bauche, 15 September 1949, NARA, RG. 469, entry 1193, box 48.
46. Ibid.
47. Rapport de Jacques Bauche, 20 October 1949; 23 October 1949; 27 October 1949; NARA, RG. 469, entry 1193, box 48.
48. Further notes on the Propaganda Battle in France, NARA, RG. 469, entry 1193, box 49.
49. Rapport de Jacques Bauche, 20 October 1949.
50. Ibid.
51. Rapport de Jacques Bauche, 27 October 1949, NARA, RG. 469, entry 1193, box 48.
52. Ibid.
53. Rapport de Jacques Bauche, 30 October 1949; 9 November 1949; 14 November 1949; NARA, RG. 469, entry 1193, box 48.
54. Rapport de Jacques Bauche, 4 November 1949, NARA, RG. 469, entry 1193, box 48.
55. Compte-rendu de M.J. Bauche à Miss H. Kirkpatrick, 21 December 1949, NARA, RG. 469, entry 1193, box 52.
56. Ibid.
57. Reims, the largest stop of the exhibit, had the lowest reported turnout: merely six hundred.
58. Compte-rendu de M.J. Bauche à Miss H. Kirkpatrick, 21 December 1949; Rapport de M. Lauprêtre, 12 October 1949.
59. Ibid.
60. Letter from Helen Kirkpatrick to Robert Huse, Information Director, ECA Washington, 8 December 1949, NARA, RG. 469, entry 1193, box 48.
61. Compte-rendu de M.J. Bauche à Miss H. Kirkpatrick, 21 December 1949.
62. Etudes et suggestions sur l'exposition agricole itenérante du Plan Marshall faites par M. Bauche, 3 January 1950, NARA, RG. 469, entry 1193, box 52.
63. Rapport de Jacques Bauche, 13 January 1950, NARA, RG. 469, entry 1193, box 48.
64. Rapports de Jacques Bauche, 23 January, 26 January, 1 February, 5 February, 12 February 12, 1950, NARA, RG. 469, entry 1193, box 48.
65. ECA Special Mission to France monthly report, January 1950; ECA Special Mission to France monthly report, February, 1950; NARA, RG. 469, entry 1048, box 8.
66. Rapport de Jacques Bauche, 2 March 1950, NARA, RG. 469, entry 1193, box 52.
67. Comments by A.E.; letter from Ann H. Eskin to H. Kirkpatrick, 12 March 1950, NARA, RG. 469, entry 1193, box 52.
68. Letter from Ann H. Eskin to H. Kirkpatrick, 12 March 1950.
69. Rapport de Jacques Bauche, 19 March 1950, NARA, RG. 469, entry 1193, box 52.
70. Ibid.
71. Rapport de Jacques Bauche, 22 March 1950, NARA, RG. 469, entry 1193, box 52.
72. Rapport de Georges Laupretre, 3 May 1950, NARA, RG. 469, entry 1193, box 52.
73. Rapport de Jeanne Blanc, 29 March 1950, NARA, RG. 469, entry 1193, box 52.
74. Mission France May monthly report, NARA, RG. 469, entry 1193, box 49.
75. Rapport de Jeanne Blanc, 29 March 1950.
76. Rapport de Jeanne Blanc, 2 April 1950.
77. Rapports de Jacques Bauche, 14 April, 18 April, 29 April 1950, NARA, RG. 469, entry 1193, box 52.
78. Circular of A. Eskin, Information Division, Mission France; Rapport de Jeanne Blanc, 2 April 1950, NARA, RG. 469, entry 1193, box 52.
79. Ibid.

80. The PCF pamphlets were not specific about which war the Marshall Plan was responsible for. The pamphlets seemed to argue that it contributed to war in general because the ultimate aim of the United States was to launch a war against the Soviet Union. Mission France May monthly report, 1950, NARA, RG. 469, entry 1048, box 8.

81. Pamphlet by Combattants de la Paix et de la Liberté, NARA, RG. 469, entry 1193, box 52.

82. Handbill signed "PCF, section de Toul," NARA, RG. 469, entry 1193, box 52.

83. *Le Patriot,* 13 May 1950.

84. Communist Attacks on ECA Agricultural Exhibit, 8 June 1950, NARA, RG. 469, entry 1193, box 52.

85. Ibid.

86. PCF pamphlet "Paysan de France, le-sais-tu?" This was a copy of a limited circulation American pamphlet, NARA, RG. 469, entry 1193, box 52.

87. Rapport de Georges Laupretre, 14 May 1950.

88. Mission France June monthly report 1950; Rapport général sur l'activité de l'-Exposition Agricole itinérante du Plan Marshall, 25 May 1950; NARA, RG. 469, entry 1193, box 52.

89. Mission France June monthly report 1952; letter to Ann Eskin from Elmer Dorsay, 24 January 1952; NARA, RG. 84, entry 2462, box 34.

90. ECA France Information Division, Exhibits Program 1951, NARA, RG. 94, entry 2462, box 34.

91. Rapport général sur l'activité de l'Exposition Agricole itinérante du Plan Marshall, 25 May 1950.

92. Ibid.

93. 1950 Report of the Information Division, ECA Mission to France, NARA, RG. 469, entry 1193, box 45.

94. Fourth Quarterly Report, 1950, of Information Division, ECA Mission to France, 2 January 1951, NARA, RG. 469, entry 1193, box 51.

95. ECA-France Information Division Exhibits Program 1951, RG. 84, entry 2462, box 34.

96. ECA Mission Speciale en France, exposition "Le vrai visage des Etats-Unis," SGCI, F60 *ter* 394.

97. ECA France Information Division, Exhibits Program 1951, NARA, RG. 94, entry 2462, box 34.

98. Manifestation à Vierzon contre l'exposition "Le vrai visage des Etats-Unis," SGCI, F60 *ter* 394.

99. "A report covering the findings and recommendations of Vergil D. Reed under a contract between E.C.A. and J. Walter Thompson Company," 2 September 1950, NARA, RG. 469, entry 1193, box 51.

100. Exhibit for French fairs, Mission France, 2 March 1950, NARA, RG. 469, entry 1193, box 45.

101. Fairs-General, 1950-1960, 9 March 1950, NARA, RG. 469, entry 1193, box 45.

102. Exhibit for French fairs, Mission France, 2 March 1950.

103. Ibid.

104. Ibid.

105. 1950 Report of the Information Division, ECA Mission to France.

106. Rapport de M. Bauche sur le stand du Plan Marshall à la Foire de Strasbourg, 19 September 1950, NARA, RG. 469, entry 1193, box 46.

107. Rapport de M. Bauche sur le stand du Plan Marshall à la Foire-exposition de Metz, 11 October 1950, NARA, RG. 469, entry 1193, box 46.

108. Translation of address by Monsier Weydert, NARA, RG. 469, entry 1193, box 46.

109. Rapport de M. Bauche sur le stand du Plan Marshall à la Foire-exposition de Metz.
110. Report from Oran Fair, 30 October 1950, NARA, RG. 469, entry 1193, box 46.
111. Ibid.
112. Letter from Helen Kirkpatrick to Everett Cook, 24 November 1950, NARA, RG. 469, entry 1193, box 45.
113. Letter from Martin to Kirkpatrick, 1 August 1950, NARA, RG. 469, entry 1193, box 46.
114. Letter from Martin to Kirkpatrick, 3 June 1950, NARA, RG. 469, entry 1193, box 46.
115. Ibid.
116. *Le Provençal,* 29 September 1950.
117. Rapport de Madame Blanc sur la foire de Marseille, 19 September 1950, NARA, RG. 469, entry 1193, box 46.
118. *Le Provençal,* 27 September 1950.
119. Ibid.
120. Rapport de Madame Blanc sur la foire de Marseille.
121. Ibid.
122. 1950 Report of the Information Division, ECA Mission to France, NARA, RG. 469, entry 1193, box 45.
123. Interview with Julian Stein, Mission France Information Division, 20 October 1997.
124. Central decimal files of the State Department, 511.512/7-2650.
125. Semi-annual evaluation report for period ending May 31st, 1951, Exhibits-Photo Section, NARA, central decimal files of the State Department, 511.51/10-1350 to 511.51/12-2951.
126. Semi-annual evaluation report for period ending May 31st, 1951.
127. Exhibition of 68 Contemporary American Prints at the Cultural Relations Section, 11 December 1951, NARA, central decimal files of the State Department, 511.512/12-1151.
128. Telegram from David K. Bruce to Secretary of State, 12 December 1951, NARA, central decimal files of the State Department, 511.512/12-1251.
129. Undated translation in Exhibition of 68 Contemporary American Prints at the Cultural Relations Section.
130. Ibid.
131. Ibid.
132. Exhibition of 68 Contemporary American Prints at the Cultural Relations Section.
133. Telegram from David K. Bruce to Secretary of State, 12 December 1951.
134. Guilbaut, 3–5; 148–153; 203.
135. Frank Lloyd Wright exhibition at the *Ecole Nationale des Beaux-Arts,* NARA, central decimal files of the State Department, 511.512/5-2652.
136. Ibid.
137. Ibid.
138. *Les Lettres françaises,* 10 April 1952.
139. *Le Monde,* 3 April 1952.
140. *Le Figaro littéraire,* 12 April 1952.
141. *Carrefour,* 30 April 1952.
142. *Le Monde,* 3 April 1952.
143. *Le Figaro littéraire,* 12 April 1952.
144. *Les Lettres françaises,* 10 April 1952.
145. *Le Figaro littéraire,* 12 April 1952.
146. *Les Lettres françaises,* 10 April 1952.
147. Frank Lloyd Wright exhibition at the *Ecole Nationale des Beaux-Arts.*

148. Memo from State Department to Paris Embassy, central decimal Files of the State Department, 511.512/5-2652.
149. Pierre Grémion, *Intelligence de l'anticommunisme: Le Congrès pour la liberté de la culture à Paris, 1950-1975* (Paris: Fayard, 1995), 80.
150. Peter Coleman, *The Liberal Conspiracy: The Congress for Cultural Freedom and the Struggle for the Mind of Postwar Europe* (New York: Free Press, 1989), 55.
151. Frances Stoner Saunders, *The Cultural Cold War* (New York: the Free Press, 1999).
152. Coleman, *The Liberal Conspiracy*, 46–50.
153. Memo to Howland Sargeant, Assistant Secretary of State for Public Affairs, from John Devine, 7 December 1951, NARA, RG. 59, lot 61D53, box 67.
154. Letter from Edward Barrett to Ralph Reed, 17 October 1951, NARA, RG. 59, lot 61D53, box 67.
155. Ibid.
156. A copy of the editorial was circulated in the State Department; Memo to Howland Sargeant, Assistant Secretary of State for Public Affairs, from John Devine, 7 December 1951; Memo to Mr. Edwards to Shepard Jones, 4 December 1951, NARA, RG. 59, lot 61D53, box 67.
157. One official, John Devine, told Sargeant that the editorial was unjust, but that "trying to correct it would probably create more difficulties." Memo to Howland Sargeant, Assistant Secretary of State for Public Affairs, from John Devine, 7 December 1951.
158. Masterpieces of our century, 1 October 1951, NARA, RG. 59, lot 61D53, box 67.
159. Quoted in Frances Stoner Saunders, *The Cultural Cold War*, 114.
160. Locations of other conferences by the Congress for Cultural Freedom included Bombay, Rangoon, Mexico City, Rhodes, Tokyo, Vietnam, Cairo, Khartoum, Dakar, Manila, Montevideo, Kuala Lumpur, and Nairobi; see Coleman, 253–257.
161. Saunders, *The Cultural Cold War*, 116.
162. Coleman, *The Liberal Conspiracy*, 56.
163. USIS semi-annual evaluation report for period 1 December 1951–31 May 1952, NARA, RG. 84, entry 2462, box 8; see also Kuisel, *Seducing the French*, 48–50.
164. *Le Monde*, 29 April 1952; *La Revue Musicale*, no. 212, April 1952.
165. *Les Temps modernes*, no. 81, July 1952.
166. "En marge de *L'Œuvre du XXe siècle*," *L'Observateur*, no. 103, 30 April 1952.
167. *L'Humanité*, 26 April 1952.
168. "Selling Paris on Western Culture," *Commentary*, July 1952: 70–75.
169. Ibid.
170. Coleman, *The Liberal Conspiracy*, 56.
171. Quoted in Coleman, *The Liberal Conspiracy*, 57.
172. Koestler told Hook: "We would also have had a finer press reaction, but then again the action we had undertaken was aimed at this area, and I still believe that it was the only kind of action we could have undertaken here in Paris which would have established the Congress in the minds of the European intellectuals as a positive, and not only a political, organization." Quoted in Coleman, *The Liberal Conspiracy*, 56.
173. "Selling Paris on Western Culture," 75.
174. *Le Monde*, 25 April 1953.
175. Telegraph: TOECA 196 from ECA France to Secretary of State, Summary of Public Opinion, 20 February 1950, NARA, RG. 469, entry 1029, box 17.
176. Laurence Wylie, *Village in the Vaucluse*, second edition (Cambridge: Harvard University Press, 1964), 34.
177. Wylie, *Village in the Vaucluse*, 215.

178. Marseille exhibit, Memo from Tate to Robert Sivard, Acting Chief, Information Division, MSA Mission France, 11 October 1952, NARA, RG. 469, entry 1193, box 45.

179. Susan Caruthers, "Not Like the U.S.? Europeans and the Spread of American Culture," *International Affairs* 74, no. 4 (October 1998), 891.

180. Jean-Philippe Mathy, *French Resistance: the French-American Culture Wars* (St. Paul: University of Minnesota Press, 2000); Philippe Roger, *L'Ennemi américain: Généalogie de l'antiaméricanisme français* (Paris: Seuil, 2002).

181. Gabrielle Hecht, *The Radiance of France: Nuclear Power and National Identity after World War II* (Cambridge: M.I.T. Press, 1998).

182. Shanny Peer, *France on Display: Peasants, Provincials, and Folklore in the 1937 Paris World's Fair* (Albany: S.U.N.Y. Press, 1998), 2–3; 19–20.

Chapter 3

THE MARSHALL PLAN AND TRANSATLANTIC TOURISM[1]

Anxieties multiply into a growing feeling of helplessness for the new passenger when he or she deplanes at an intermediate station. This loss of orientation is compounded if the strange passenger finds himself or herself in a foreign country. "I can't read the signs in the foreign language!" ... "How long will we be here!" ... "Might I miss the plane when it leaves!" ... "Where are the rest rooms?" ... "Should I try to eat here on the ground, or do they feed us after we take off again?" ... "Is my money good here?" These are just a few typical frantic questions which race through the head of a passenger devoid of orientation at a strange airport in a strange country.

Howard G. Kurtz, "The Common Man—Up in the Air"
IATA Bulletin 1953[2]

In 1949 French officials at the Chicago consulate issued an urgent memo to Henri Bonnet, the French ambassador, about the consequences of new French and American programs aimed at promoting transatlantic tourism. Americans, the consul warned, "think that France, and particularly Paris, is becoming the playground of America."[3] Paris, the consul continued, was perceived as an essentially tourist space, a place "where the citizens of the United States can free themselves of all constraints." Concluding his letter, the consul wondered how the American public would ever be able to understand the "difficulties of life faced by the mass of the French population."

This chapter examines the promotion of American tourism to France during the Marshall Plan, 1948 to 1952. It addresses two sets of questions. The first relates to policy issues. How did French and American officials and tourism promoters develop and implement policy, and what goals did the program hope to achieve? What was their assessment of the program at the conclusion of the Marshall Plan?

A second set of questions concerns the relationship between the tourism program and the Americanization of France. To what extent did promoting American tourism contribute to the Americanization of France? Did the French tourism industry resist or desire Americanization? The Marshall Plan programs to promote tourism provide an opportunity to further elucidate the relationship between Americanization and globalization. Tourism marketing is an example of global consumerism. The anthropologist Jon Abbink refers to tourism as an "avant-garde" of globalization because it illustrates the impact of a global and globalizing consumer identity.[4] Furthermore, transatlantic air travel is arguably the paradigmatic example of time/space compression for globalization theorists.[5] The question of cultural homogenization is another important issue in the debate about the consequences of globalization. Tourism entails commodification, often seen as a homogenizing force, but exposure to distinctness and concepts of authenticity are central appeals of tourism. French and American planners were aware of this tension, I argue, and attempted to balance homogenization and distinctness. Mainstream French leaders have embraced key economic aspects of globalization while resisting the very cultural changes these economic transformations entail.[6] My analysis of American tourism in France provides a historical case study of how French leaders responded and adapted to globalization with an American face, that of a tourist.

Rebuilding Tourism in Postwar France

Public officials on both sides of the Atlantic promoted the development of international tourism in response to the tough challenges of economic recovery in France after the Second World War. A 1944 study by the Brookings Institution illustrated the importance with which policy makers and planners viewed tourism. "The surplus of our national production not absorbed at home must be sold to others," the report explained, "But other countries' currencies ... have a limited value in, say, Kankakee, Illinois. Only as dollars are supplied in one way or another to the rest of the world can American goods find foreign markets."[7] Three years later counterpart funds would provide one source of dollars, but for the moment the Brookings Institution concluded that tourism was an ideal means:

As the world's great creditor nation we have a tremendous stake in making it possible for American residents in ever-increasing number to travel abroad; for the dollar credits they transfer help to protect our investments, sell our export surplus, and put a solid economic foundation under peace.[8]

Economic imperatives thus compelled the Economic Cooperation Administration and the French government (specifically the Commissariat général du plan) to develop programs to increase the number of American tourists in France, especially the *nouvelle clientèle*— middle-income Americans. After the Second World War, tourism figured consistently as the largest dollar-earning industry in France until it was surpassed by military aid during the rearmament years of the Korean War. In addition, American tourists spent more in France than any other group of international tourists. Indeed, tourism seemed a faultless way to close the so-called "dollar gap" between the United States and France: not through aid, but by the physical importation of dollars into France in the pockets of tourists.

U.S. planners' enthusiasm for the potential of tourism was equaled only by their preoccupation with the dollar gap. As the comments of this U.S. commerce department official demonstrated, tourism was perceived as an almost magical solution to economic woes:

> The exploitation of the travel resources of a country lead to an increase in these resources rather than depletion as in the case of coal, oil, and other extractive industries. The more travel service is used, the larger it grows. Once seen and enjoyed, the people, scenery, art and culture remained unimpaired to be appreciated again and again.[9]

These remarks conceal the Faustian nature of tourism. The development of transatlantic tourism had economic, cultural, and environmental consequences. The Marshall Plan made the attraction of American tourists and the dollars they brought the central goal of French tourism. This had consequences not only for the character of the French tourism industry, but also the perception of France abroad.

The tourism program had cultural as well as economic goals. American policy makers stressed the cultural impact of tourism. "A measure, and one which is often overlooked," argued Senator J. William Fulbright in 1950, "for breaking down the barriers of ignorant prejudice between ourselves and our allies is tourism."[10] For French officials, tourism offered an "efficacious instrument" for ensuring international prestige. The head of the French Commissariat général au Tourisme, Henry Ingrand, lamented the "almost vertical" decline of France as a tourist destination. In 1928 France had received more tourists than any other country in Europe. In 1938 it was fifth behind Austria, Switzerland, Germany, and Italy.[11] Nevertheless, officials in

the French and American tourism industry argued that cultural barriers needed to be overcome for tourism to be successful. The French
tourism industry needed to learn about American tourists. It was the
task of both American and French planners to prepare the French
public for the influx of American tourists.

Several essential conditions made it possible for Americans to
travel in France with "the Tourist's Gaze."[12] ECA and French tourism
officials created tourism infrastructures that facilitated American
visits.[13] Three delegations of French hotel and restaurant owners
were brought to the United States in an effort to educate the French
about the habits of American tourists and the characteristics of
American hotels. No less important, officials and entrepreneurs created the Parisian *Salon du Tourisme,* first held in 1950, as a way of
fostering transatlantic tourism. The Salon hosted a large display by
the ECA detailing the benefits of American tourism to France as well
as the likes and dislikes of American tourists. These efforts demonstrated that the process of preparing the locals (or at least the tourism
professionals) to receive the tourist was essential for the creation of
transatlantic tourism.

French and American planners sought to shape the tourist experience itself. Tourism had long been associated with the cultural
capital and social prestige that visitors were assumed to acquire as
a result of their vacation in France. Yet, most of the new middle-class
consumers of the French travel adventure were unfamiliar with the
country's history, culture, and language. American and French officials worked to ensure that American tourists would not feel like
fishes out of water. They sought to domesticate the exotic, and in so
doing they made French vacations a part of American consumer culture. To the extent that they succeeded, they may have undermined
one of their principal goals: making tourism a vehicle for enhancing
Franco-American understanding. In turn, the structure required to
receive and profit from American tourists influenced the development of the French tourism industry. Through pamphlets, press releases, visitor centers, and advertising campaigns Americans were
told what to say and not to say to the French, where to go and stay,
what to see, and how to recognize "communist lies."[14] This is not to
say that the tourist's experience was somehow less authentic than
everyday life. Responding to this traditional elite criticism of tourism, John Urry and Scott Lasch point out: "What is consumed in
tourism are visual signs and sometimes simulacrum; and this is what
is consumed when we are supposedly not acting as tourists at all."[15]

The drive by French and American officials to attract large numbers of middle-class American tourists was predicated on appeals to

consumer values.[16] France had long been the destination of the American elite. In their publications and publicity, French and American tourism officials exploited the popular image of France as the travel destination of the elite, and as the world capital of high fashion and art. The American perception of Paris as the playground of the rich and expatriates dates from at least the interwar period. A French publication noted in 1918 that "family vanity" was the main reason for a French tour by Americans. [17] The transposition of this meaning to the culture of mass consumption was a characteristic of postwar tourism. American and French planners portrayed French vacations as an opportunity to increase one's cultural capital, allowing the middle-class person to be an upper-class tourist. Analyzing tourism in 1958, Hans Magnus Enzensberger noted, "The last stage of the tourist endeavor is the return, which turns the tourists themselves into the attraction."[18] Another important element of French vacations as consumer goods was their portrayal as special periods of recreation, what Ellen Furlough describes as "the time in parentheses."[19] Middle-class American tourists were consumer-pilgrims seeking not blessings but the bestowal of social and cultural capital. The implications for transatlantic tourism were significant.

The French dimensions of the program as a component of the Monnet Plan began in 1948. World War II had destroyed the tourism industry. Enemy and allied bombardment had destroyed twenty-five thousand hotel rooms, gutted sixty thousand, and moderately damaged eight hundred thousand.[20] In addition, allied and German occupation forces had ruined over a half-million rooms. France possessed only two passenger ships and one, *La Liberté*, was in dry dock (it would later be repaired with ERP funds). Half of the trucks in France had been destroyed. The Commissariat au Tourisme estimated that France had lost half of its tourist capacity and the half that remained was of inferior quality.[21] A 1946 memo from the Minister of Foreign Affairs cautioned tourism officials about promoting international tourism until facilities could be reconstructed.[22] These conditions were even more alarming given the historic economic importance of tourism: 1.2 million people in France depended on it for their livelihood.[23] In 1929, the high point of French tourism between the wars, the receipts from 2.2 million tourists accounted for 20 percent of French exports.[24] On the eve of the Second World War tourist receipts still accounted for 10 percent of total exports.[25]

In 1948 a report by the French authority on tourism, the Commissariat général au Tourisme, presented the French plan for reconstruction. It called for a substantial investment program. By 1952 it hoped to attract more than three million tourists bringing the equivalent of $450 million annually.[26] This figure represented a sine qua non for equilibrium in the balance of payments.[27] The Marshall Plan's financial contribution to this program was significant. In 1949 the counterpart expenditure for the tourism industry amounted to 326 million francs.[28] In addition, the Monnet Plan made available 1.2 billion francs in loans and 750 million francs for hotel modernization.[29] Still, this figure was only one-fifth of the amount originally planned for that year.[30]

Expenditures increased for the fiscal year of 1950. Previously the ECA had reserved twenty billion francs for use in high priority areas. On 22 August 1950, the Minister of Finance, Maurice Petsche, requested the release of one billion francs for the tourism program.[31] This was in addition to a previously agreed upon release of two billion francs in counterpart funds for loans to private industry. The total 1950 counterpart contribution to Monnet Plan tourism development projects amounted to over two million dollars. In addition, the U.S. approved the use of over five million dollars of counterpart funds in the form of private loans to the tourism industry. American officials claimed to have financed over 85 percent of all 1950 tourism development projects in France.[32] American funds contributed to the construction of airports at Aix-les-Bains and Biarritz, facilities improvements at ski resorts in the Alps and seaside resorts, hotels in Paris, and the purchase of overnight wagon-lits for trains.[33] Counterpart funds were also used to aid casinos at Le Havre and Cannes (according to Barry Bingham, head of the French Mission, casinos were "social centers" where "civic activities" occurred in addition to gambling).[34] The Korean War and rearmament, as we will see, limited tourism development funding and the 1951 tourism budget remained at approximately the 1950 level.[35]

Financial instability was an immediate constraint on tourism profits at the start of the program in 1948. The strength of the underground economy was telling. Tourists could obtain a better exchange rate for their currency on the underground economy than through official channels. A study of the underground economy concluded that it absorbed 57 percent of the tourist receipts for 1948.[36] In that year the underground exchange rate was 440 francs to the dollar, compared to the official rate of 305. High prices and inflation ensured that American tourists would avoid official transactions wherever possible. In many cases the hotel clerk was the tourist's easiest connection to the underground economy. Tourists were also awarded gasoline coupons due to rationing, regardless of whether or not they possessed a vehicle. Tourists often sold these coupons on the underground economy. Moreover, Americans in Paris and the Riviera became vic-

despite destruction of fr tourist industry in WWII, tourists increased early 1950s

tims of overpricing. As one official explained, "Resentment centers on alleged high prices charged Americans over those charged tourists of other nationality, plain gouging, short changing, and ubiquitous requests for tips."[37] The French ambassador in the U.S., Henri Bonnet, warned the foreign minister, Robert Schuman, that high prices in Paris would turn tourists away from France. Bonnet suggested that Ingrand take immediate actions to address the problem.[38]

In 1949 the French authorities tried to mitigate some of these circumstances by granting French hotels the right to exchange francs and dollars at the official free rate; each hotel would receive 16 percent of the dollars exchanged in this way for publicity abroad and the import of equipment.[39] The French Commissariat général au tourisme implemented the "prix fixe" scheme in November 1949, to curb abuse. Dinner prices were fixed at 300, 500, 750, or 1000 francs.[40] Despite these efforts, the underground economy and high prices remained chronic weaknesses for the tourism industry.

American tourists complained about customs as well, and officials tried to make these less burdensome for Americans. In June 1949, Paul Hoffman's special assistant, Mrs. H.H. Woods, conducted a fact-finding trip across Western Europe. Woods concluded that border crossings were characterized by "prolonged, repetitious, and apparently empty procedures."[41] The *New York Herald Tribune* made similar charges about customs at Orly airport. The Commissariat au Tourisme responded energetically. Ingrand issued a directive ordering French customs officials to treat Americans in an "esprit liberal."[42]

Nevertheless, individual complaints by American tourists to the State Department or the ECA were exceptional. Despite frequent complaints about the prices, American tourists were satisfied with their vacations. In 1951 the ECA conducted an exit poll of more than two thousand American tourists leaving France. It concluded that only 5 percent of the tourists had been dissatisfied with their visit and that 25 percent had found their expectations exceeded.[43] As Hans Enzensberger points out, complaining about a vacation upon returning is a "confession of defeat," and amounts to a "social failure."[44]

The immediate postwar years saw a rapid return in the number of tourists. Five hundred thousand visited France in 1946, but close to a million (mostly from Britain) came in 1947.[45] Despite this increase tourist receipts continued to lag well behind prewar figures. This was due not only to lower numbers, but also to reduced spending. In 1938 the average American tourist spent $553 in France; in 1949 the average was as low as $208.[46] Worse still, the number of American tourists in France actually declined from 160,000 in 1947 to 120,000 in 1948.[47] The drop in American tourism was all the more alarming because tourism was the most important single export to the United States. In 1949 American tourism receipts comprised almost half of all French exports to the U.S.[48]

It was no surprise, therefore, that the promotion of American tourism was a priority for both the ERP and the Monnet Plan. Tourism was an industry where French and American officials agreed on both goals and methods. Not only was tourism's importance accepted, there was little disagreement between French and American officials over the measures to promote it. Section 117(b) of the Economic Co-operation Act called for the promotion of American tourism in all ECA countries. The U.S. went so far as threatening to reduce aid to countries that did not promote transatlantic tourism.[49]

French and American officials identified two necessary steps in order to reach their economic goals: stabilizing prices in France and increasing the length of the tourist season. The Commissaire général au Tourisme, Henri Ingrand, pointed out that as the primary export industry, tourism was especially vulnerable to inflation. He warned that inflation would negate the effects of any devaluation of the franc. To increase the tourist season the Plan recommended off-season rate reductions in hotels and transport.

The question of publicity figured prominently in the French Plan. The target goal of three million tourists in 1952 represented a 50 percent increase over the best year of prewar French tourism. This would require a substantial outlay for publicity. Ingrand explained: "We can't imagine a manufacturer who had decided on such a sales program would try to achieve it without recourse to massive publicity."[50] He warned that a publicity campaign might not bring immediate results. It was the task of a publicity campaign to bring Americans tourists to France who would otherwise travel to different European countries or even Mexico and Canada.

Thus by 1949 both the French and Americans had begun to address formally the tourism question. Other measures soon followed. A European Commission of Tourism was created in the OEEC and both the Department of Commerce in Washington and the ECA created tourism or travel development offices. In August Barry Bingham, the head of Mission France, hosted the first meeting of the Tourist Advisory Committee. Continuing the close relationship between American business and the ECA, the committee was composed of officials from Pan-American Airlines, Trans-World Airlines, American Express, United States Lines, and the European edition of the *New York Herald Tribune*.[51]

The French press reaction to transatlantic tourism promotion was ambivalent. French newspapers followed tourism initiatives as they developed in 1949. According to *France Soir* the presence of Americans threatened to break the National Bank. This paper headlined: "With American tourists dollars flood France."[52] According to the author, so many dollars were coming into France that the Bank of France was running out of francs to exchange them: "The demand of American tourists alone already attains $100,000 to $150,000 per day. At 330 francs to the dollar, one can see the franc payment that amounts to at the end of a few months for the treasury." *France Soir* warned that the ceiling set for advances to the Treasury from the Bank of France would have to be adjusted so that tourist dollars did not break it, leaving French exporters unable to collect dollars.

In March *Combat* reported some of the details of the Monnet Plan for tourism.[53] Three million tourists were expected for 1952. Modernization was to occur throughout France. "In particular," explained the article, "several very pretty regions, ignored by visitors and even the French, of the Basse-Alpes and Massif Central will be developed."[54] *Le Parisien Libéré,* sounding an optimistic note, stated that for every hundred dollars spent in France by an American, hotel and transportation each received twenty-five dollars. The remaining was shared between purchases and "distractions."[55] According to *Le Parisien Libéré* tourist dollars were "invisible imports" because the country that received them did not have to give hard merchandise in return. For *Le Parisien Libéré* France's cultural and natural resources were inexhaustible: "The country which welcomes tourists sells them, above all, services and scenery, in other words, invisible merchandise which cannot be exhausted."[56]

The French Meet Monsieur and Madame Amérique

Hotel modernization and renovation proceeded apace. Demand in Paris was heavy due to the concentration of Americans, but by late 1950 France could boast more hotel rooms than any other country in Europe: 452,472.[57] As the French hotel industry modernized, the ERP sought to convince owners to modernize in specific ways that would attract Americans. They needed little convincing. The three groups of hotel and restaurant owners brought to the United States under the Marshall Plan's Technical Assistance Program stayed for six weeks. The Technical Assistance visits did not always meet the expectations of either the Americans or the French, but the hotel industry visits were an unqualified success.[58] Their reports provide insight into French perceptions of American life. The leader of one group observed, "The American clientele, especially the new clien-

tele, has its method of living and eating which differs markedly from
our own. Should we apply their method or seek a compromise?"[59] In
seeking the best means to attract American tourists, hotel and restaurant owners tried to distill the essence of American culture that
represented the least common denominator for service in France.
Although they did this self-consciously in an attempt to preserve what
was most French, the desire to attract Americans compelled some
deviation from tradition.

The first hotel and restaurant group left France in January 1950.
The purpose of the visits was to "assure the development of Europe
for the American clientele."[60] The report noted that thirty million
Americans were of European origin and that if 3 percent of these individuals could be brought to Europe, the balance of payments would
be positive. In order to do this, the authors concluded that the sanitary equipment of French hotels was most in need of modernization: "Meticulous cleanliness and the state of sanitary conditions are
the points on which an establishment are judged. At the present time,
all our efforts must be concentrated on the amelioration and modernization of our sanitary conditions, particularly the toilet."[61] Contrary to traditions in the French hotel industry, hotels in the United
States treated bathrooms as items of utility, not luxury. One French
observer described the standard American hotel bathroom in this
way: "Of reduced dimension, it nevertheless contains the required
equipment for a demanding clientele whose dominant preoccupa-
tions are hygiene and cleanliness."[62] The visitors were surprised to
find hotel rooms in the United States that lacked windows, nevertheless, had bathrooms.[63] The same group returned to France with blue-
prints of American bathrooms ("note the absence of a bidet").

The visitors under Lucien Serre provided the most detailed report of their visit. Serre, the director of hotels in Biarritz, Cannes,
and Paris, was accompanied by Pierre Lafon, owner of *La Coupole*
restaurant in Paris, and Jacques Gauthier, another hotel manager
from Paris. During their visit to the United States the three identified
three forms of American hotels: transient hotels, traditional or resort hotels, and the novel "motel." Motels made an indelible impression on the three. They marveled at the inexpensive construction of
motels and their layout: "construction at a price more than a third
less than ordinary hotels, and a less onerous upkeep through the
elimination of elevators and useless areas."[64] Motels were generally
less expensive than hotels and seemed to offer equivalent comfort,
that is a lavatory in every room. Nevertheless motels were a function
of the automobile industry in the United States, Serre concluded, and
thus they could not easily be adapted to France. In addition, Serre

noted that Americans possessed unique relationships with their automobiles: "One can say that Americans virtually live in their cars and love to have them in the course of their travels."[65] He suggested that if Americans could more easily transport their automobiles across the Atlantic they would be more likely to visit. Motels could then be constructed to respond to this market.

If motels proved impractical for France, Serre was nevertheless able to make recommendations for the French hotel industry based on American hotels. The expansion of motels had caused hotels to add new services to attract visitors. Many hotels, for example, now offered to park guests' cars in nearby garages. More intriguing was the development of "conventions," which Serre described as the equivalent of French "congrès professionnels." He was astounded to learn that many New York hotels could stay in business with only the profit earned by conventions. Yet conventions also were problematic for the French hotel industry because space in French hotels was scant, and few possessed meeting rooms. Nevertheless, he hoped that France could attract small to medium-sized convention groups for off-season package deals.[66]

The contrasts between French and American hotel operations provided the most useful bases for French adaptation. Serre was impressed with the standardization of front-office operations in American hotels. It provided uniformity in the presentation of bills and the methods for dealing with guests. Standardization also allowed for employees to be easier to both train and replace. American hotels divided the functions of the concierge among mail clerks, telephone desks, and information desks. Yet Serre concluded this was impractical in France due to the inability of most Americans to speak French. A concierge could coordinate these services for the American tourist and in this way the "old system" was preferable.[67]

Serre's group identified twenty-two details in American hotels that should be adopted by French hotels. These adaptations would preserve the character of French hotels while at the same time Americanizing them enough to provide the conveniences that Americans seemed to take for granted. Serre wrote,

> We realize we cannot become identical in appearance and customs with American hotels. Moreover, we feel that the foreign traveler to European hotels expects something different and new, and that European hotels would lose some of their atmosphere should they try to copy completely the American hotel practices.[68]

Serre's proposals showed two sides of Americanization: on the one hand, changing French ways to become more like Americans—which he tried to minimize—and on the other hand, adapting American innovations, as was the case with the "gift shop." Serre concluded that the middle-income status of American tourists had forced hotels to use "every possible portion of their premises to earn revenue." "The 'gift shop,'" noted Serre, "is quite developed in American hotels and brings in a substantial return."[69]

The spending habits of American consumers highlighted the revenue potential of gift shops. American tourists in Europe spent more in retail stores (31 percent of their vacation expenditure) than they did on transportation or lodging (13 percent and 23 percent respectively).[70] Serre suggested small shops be created in French hotels on the ground floor as long as they did not detract from the appearance of the entrance hall. The middle-income guest also determined the content of the gift shop. Because Americans spent more in shops than other tourists, their needs determined the items to be carried, making it essential that French shops sell English-language maps that informed Americans of the principal sites in the area. According to Serre, "a large and persuasive publicity campaign will be necessary to get these people conscious of the attractions that Europe has to offer."[71] If a region possessed a specialty craft, such items should also be sold in the gift shop. In addition, each hotel was to "contain an abundance of leaflets" explaining the significant facts of a given area, including a list of monuments and churches to visit.

Serre offered several other observations about American practices and hotels. He noted that for the majority of Americans wine lists were a "puzzle." Hotel menus needed to suggest the appropriate wine for each meal. Americans also liked to be served ice water before a meal; meals should be presented in a "prix fixe" scheme that would include the cost of tea or coffee and could offer different meals for the same price. Americans preferred to drink their tea or coffee (served "rather light") during their meal. Few Americans liked to eat breakfast in their rooms. Instead, small tables should be provided in a room for this purpose, or failing that, in the regular dining room. Hotel rooms should be heated between 20 and 22°C. At the same time, the windows in a room should be easily opened because most Americans preferred to sleep with them open. Electric lights should be placed at the head of every bed and hot water should be available twenty-four hours a day. If possible a small bar of soap should be placed on every sink and an English-language newspaper should be provided free every day.

Serre's report was well received by Mission France. They decided to use it as the basis for the American display at the first *Salon du Tourisme* held at the Porte de Versailles.[72] Antoine Pinay, then minister of public works, transport, and tourism, inaugurated the twenty-day event on 3 November 1950.[73] The Salon contained over 150 exhibits from various countries, airlines, shipping lines, and equipment manufacturers. Mission France's exhibit, strategically placed just inside the main entrance, highlighted the results of the Technical Assistance (TA) visits, as well as the contribution of the Marshall Plan to hotel reconstruction. Over 60,000 people visited the American stand. Particularly striking was the representation of American tourists. "Monsieur et Madame Amérique" provided the theme of the exhibit: what they looked like, who they were, why they came to France, and other information.

M. et Mme. Amérique were life-sized illustrations on vertically standing wooden panels. Against the backdrop of a U.S. flag lined with skyscrapers the white couple followed arrows to France. They were clearly well-to-do. Mme. Amérique was clad in a shimmering dress, earrings, and pearls. She wore a hat with a feather as long as her body arcing back over M. Amerique. The latter was clad in checkered suit, polka-dot shirt, and a black tie. Two suitcases dangled from ropes around his right shoulder and he carried a larger suitcase in hand. Both were bespectacled. Both showed gum and teeth through a wide smile. As for children, it may have been difficult to discern, but

Figure 3.1

A visitor to the Salon du Tourisme (NARA, RG. 469, entry 1193, box 47)

a five-pointed star with legs did appear to be alongside Mme. Amérique. The value of American tourism was clearly evident in the several
panels that showed M. and Mme. spending money in various shops.
In addition, the widely distributed pamphlet *Le Touriste et Vous* emphasized the high per-capita spending of American tourists.

Who were M. and Mme. Amérique? They represented "typical
Americans," and the American family was a common feature of other
U.S. exhibits.[74] According to one panel, 24.6 percent of American tourists were housewives and 22.6 percent were businessmen. Professors
and students made up 13.5 percent and the liberal professions another
10 percent. "Employees and workers" constituted 9 percent, which
was just more than the number of journalists, writers, and artists at
7.5 percent. The remaining portions were divided between farmers,
civil servants, military personnel, and "various." According to another
panel, all came to enjoy—in this order—the inhabitants of France,
its scenery, architecture, museums, theaters, concerts, and cabarets.
The next panel, only appropriately it seems, pictured a Frenchman
holding up his palm and the caption: "Can more Americans come?"
Quoting Serre's report, the panel explained: "At the moment only .28
percent of the American families who can come to Europe do so."

Five panels summarized the TA visits. All twenty-two of Serre's
suggestions were presented. One picture showed a confused American tourist staring at a wine list. Attached to the American's head
was a funnel through which a French waiter was suggesting a wine.
Following a list of amenities for hotel rooms another illustration
showed a room with a dozen lamps.

The ECA exhibit also contained a number of panels that portrayed
the benefits of tourism to Franco-American understanding. Because
of their trip American tourists were exposed to *la grandeur de la civ-
iliasation française.* They had met and spoken with French people,
had eaten French cuisine and drunk French wine. Returning to the
United States, the tourist communicated these "unforgettable experiences" to neighbors and friends and "thanks to that a better understanding is established between free peoples."

The panels were the creation of a French artist, André François.
It is not surprising, therefore, that they reflected common French assumptions about Americans. What was notable, however, was the
uncritical acceptance of the display by both the exhibits officer and
the head of the visual information unit of Mission France.[75] The head
of the visual information unit had criticized the display as "rather
flat." The exhibit was then broken up with plants and railings. An
eight-foot-high pair of clasped hands was also added to symbolize
Franco-American understanding.

Monsieur and Madame Amérique were representations of "typical" American tourists based on a French perception, but one tacitly accepted by U.S. officials. The reliance on François and Serre illustrated Mission France's reliance on French artists and publicists to reach the French population. As we saw, by 1950 even the most sympathetic French commentators had criticized virtually all of the information material generated by Mission France. As was the case with the material for the *Salon du Tourisme,* Mission France's solution to these criticisms was to increasingly turn to the French for guidance and material. The ironic result was that although the material was less offensive to a French audience (in some cases it was not) it also reflected a French perception of Americans and the United States that may not have been congenial to the U.S. policy it ostensibly promoted.

The attendant at the display reported that the display received an average of three thousand visitors per day.[76] This figure, if accurate, suggests that the fair attracted the general public in addition to industry representatives. According to the report, the French visitors resented the wide smiles of Madame and Monsieur Amérique: "Some French people thought they were being laughed at."[77] The best spin he could put on the affair was: "Visitors were always interested, never indifferent, which was the objective to be attained."[78]

Tourism Takes Off

The largest single factor for the increase in transatlantic tourism was the creation, in 1952, of tourist-class airfares. The economic importance of tourism was clearly demonstrated in the ECA's early and sustained commitment to a tourist-class fare for transatlantic flight. Tourist-class airfares crystallized several factors of concern to the ECA. The creation of medium income air travel was an essential condition for the increase in the total number of American tourists visiting Europe. Air travel also provided a means to increase off-season tourism. Finally, an increase in air travel would benefit American commercial and industrial interests.

The Civil Aeronautics Board (CAB) regularized tourist fares within the United States in 1948. The first route operated at night between New York and Chicago. Discussion for transatlantic tourist fares occurred at the Bermuda meeting of the International Air Transport Association (IATA) in 1948.[79] The issue was not resolved and it was tabled until the 1949 IATA meeting in Nice, France. Paul Hoffman took a personal interest in promoting tourist airfares. Another major proponent was Juan Trippe, the president of Pan-American Airlines.[80]

Thomas K. Finletter, chief of the ECA mission to the United Kingdom, opposed the fare. He argued that the bulk of the U.K. air fleet would be rendered obsolete if tourist fares were implemented.[81] It was first class only by virtue of it being the only air transport available (during this period, airplanes were not divided into coach and first class areas). Tourist fares implemented on these planes would have negated any reason to purchase a first class ticket. Averell Harriman, acting as mediator, suggested that British opposition could be overcome if Hoffman made a personal appeal to the Chancellor of the Exchequer, Sir Stafford Cripps. According to Harriman, Hoffman could argue that the loss to the air transport industry of Britain would be made up for with increased dollar revenues as a result of the greater number of tourists that the tourist fares were sure to bring.[82]

The debate intensified when the chairman of the CAB, Joseph J. O'Connell, weighed in negatively. The CAB, not the ECA, was the U.S. representative at IATA meetings. O'Connell argued that there was no indication that tourist service could be performed at a cost lower than regular service.[83] Aircraft that could effect a reduced operating cost such as the Lockheed Constellation and Boeing Stratocruiser were not yet in widespread service. Finally, O'Connell stated that the physical characteristics of transatlantic flight precluded class distinctions. The CAB had allowed tourist fares on domestic flights only after conditions had been established that clearly distinguished coach from first class. Initially, domestic tourist rates could only be applied to off-peak flights with planes (usually a DC-4) configured for high-density seating.[84] There was no such thing as off-peak hours for a fourteen-hour transatlantic flight. Another factor was the subsidy provided to U.S. carriers in the form of mail transport fees. According to O'Connell, the tourist fares would result in a decrease in profits. The CAB would have to increase its mail subsidy as a consequence:

> While it is recognized that tourist services would create traffic that would not otherwise move, and that such traffic to Europe would further the ECA program, we feel that the possible detrimental effect on the sound development of our air carriers, and the increased cost to the government which would result, argue against the institution of 'tourist' fares at this time.[85]

Another official told Hoffman that only Pan-American was in the position to reduce fares without cutting profits, "due largely to a fortunate and far-sighted equipment procurement policy."[86] Public records that showed airline profits did not reveal the extent to which the mail subsidy sustained transatlantic carriers.[87]

In another letter to Hoffman, O'Connell was more explicit about the negative effect of granting air travel to the middle and working classes. He told Hoffman that he doubted tourist-class passengers to Europe would benefit European recovery because they would spend less.[88] In addition, the transatlantic shipping companies relied on middle-class passengers. The tourist fare would detract from the shipping profits of European lines, further impeding economic recovery. Finally, O'Connell stated that tourist-class passengers were more prone to the vagaries of the economy. First-class travel was consistent and easy to predict. O'Connell suggested that a more prudent measure would be to decrease off-season fares.

O'Connell's decision effectively killed the measure at the Nice conference.[89] In addition to the CAB, Air France, British European Airways (B.E.A.), and virtually every other European carrier opposed tourist fares.[90] ECA officials were not pleased. For them, the possibility of increasing the airline subsidy was less important than the benefits increased tourism would bring to European economies:

> Of course, there will always be reasons why there should not be low cost transportation, but the several billion dollars spent yearly on Marshall aid would not prove as large a dollar earner as a few millions invested in subsidizing low-cost transportation. It is about time that a firm stand is taken in Washington ... even though we have to fight a CAB decision.[91]

Congress was also beginning to take an interest in tourist fares. In August, Senator Owen Brewster from Maine called for a one hundred and fifty dollar round-trip airfare to Europe.[92] John D. Rockefeller told Hoffman that lower cost travel would encourage young Americans to travel abroad.[93] In March 1950, Senator Claude Pepper and Representative Michael Mansfield wrote Harriman letters critical of the ECA's tourism promotion program. "By far the largest source of dollars abroad in the last generation," wrote Mansfield, "has been the American tourist dollar. It is also the most painless and the cleanest dollar from the standpoint of the U.S. because it does not adversely affect home industry."[94] The same month Senator Fulbright entered his statement in favor of tourism promotion into the congressional record. By April the ECA had convinced Congress that it was doing everything in its power to promote tourism; the fault lay with the CAB.[95] These efforts culminated in the 24 April 1950 Senate Resolution targeted at the CAB:

> In view of the contribution of the travel of U.S. residents to the creation of vitally needed dollar exchange in Europe and the inability of many Americans to visit Europe due to lack of adequate transatlantic passenger capacity at rates within the reach of the middle-income market the Civil Aeronautics Board is directed to explore every available means of providing additional and lower cost transatlantic air passengers ser-

vice including the maximum utilization of existing capacity under special low-fare arrangement, charter, and group contracts. If the CAB
finds its authority inadequate to facilitate and encourage such low cost
air transportation, it shall recommend the necessary legislation for the
consideration of congress.[96]

The CAB moved slowly, but it could no longer resist such pressure. In March 1951 the CAB attacked companies that specialized in
charter flights, nonscheduled airlines such as Flying Tigers, Trans-
ocean, Seabord, and Western.[97] Henceforth, only authorized carriers
could operate charter flights. Charter companies could operate only
where regular carriers were either unable or unwilling to provide service. The CAB further encouraged airlines to provide low fares for
individual passengers. Wilkinson told Theodore Pozzy that the decision would "tremendously influence" the IATA to establish tourist
rates at its next meeting.[98] Pozzy concluded that the CAB decision
was "probably one of the biggest steps in the development of travel
to Europe."[99] Free of charter flight competition, the major carriers
could organize low fares and charter flights through the IATA.

The IATA met throughout 1951 and 1952 to discuss the implementation of tourist class fares. B.E.A. and Air France now favored
their implementation. Like Pan-American, they possessed extensive
routes (mainly to colonial possessions) and, like other long-distance
carriers, they faced competition from nonscheduled carriers.[100] With
American backing, the IATA agreed to implement tourist fares for
transatlantic flights in 1952 and tourist fares for intra-European travel
in 1953.[101] The IATA set the price for London–New York flights at
$486 round-trip and $270 one-way, approximately a third less than
first class.[102] In contrast, budget passage on a steamship cost about
$300 round-trip in June 1952.[103]

The arrival of new aircraft into service was crucial for the implementation of tourist fares. Both Lockheed and Boeing converted
heavy bombers to civil aviation after the war. It was a win-win situation for both companies. The military budget financed the development of the B-29 (upon which the Stratocruiser was based) and the
Lockheed L-049 Constellation. The latter did not enter service until
the end of the war; the former was produced in large numbers beginning in 1944. Both possessed pressurized cabins, which aided their
conversion to cargo and passenger craft after the war. With the end
of the war, American airplane manufacturers sought new orders to
replace military subsidies. France had originally sought to develop
its aircraft industry after the war, but the ECA refused export of Pratt
and Whitney engines for use in the French Bréguet and SO-30P.[104] As
a result Air France relied on U.S. planes for transatlantic flights.

O'Connell had originally thought that the Boeing B-377 Strato-cruiser would reduce costs, but Boeing had miscalculated. The two-floor Stratocruiser was initially designed as a luxury aircraft from top to bottom. It contained a cocktail lounge, a "ladies' lounge," and sleeper compartments. The Constellation changed that. Entering widespread European service in 1951, it was easily configured to either tourist or first class service and it possessed an operating cost significantly lower than did the Stratocruiser.[105] Air France and KLM ordered large numbers of the Constellation. B.E.A. achieved similar results with the Vickers Viking and Elizabethan.[106]

The first arrivals of tourist class passengers on an international flight landed in London and Paris on 2 May 1952. Trans-World Airlines, Pan-American, and Air France began the flights simultaneously. At Orly, the occasion received extensive publicity from the Municipal Council of Paris, the Commissariat Général du Tourisme, and the American Embassy.[107] The latter was particularly concerned with "briefing" the new arrivals about hotels and restaurants that "were in keeping with a coach air ticket."[108] Plans were later added for the mass distribution of pamphlets to the American tourists and the creation of a tourist information center at Orly. "Representative couples" were selected from the incoming flights and given publicized tours of Paris.[109] The Commissariat Général au Tourisme organized a reception for the first arrivals. The theme was *"À Paris pour 10 dollars par jour."*[110] Other activities included a display of modern airplanes at Orly and a poster exhibit at the Aéro-Club of Paris.

The effects of the tourist fare were dramatic. In 1951 two hundred and eighty thousand Americans had visited France. Three hundred and sixty thousand Americans visited in 1952.[111] Of those, nearly one-third traveled by air.[112] Two-thirds of all air passengers in 1952 traveled tourist class, and 1953 saw a 25 percent increase in air traffic from the United States to France.[113] Tourist fare traffic increased by 70 percent in 1953. Americans were more common in France than Germans, Italians, or Spaniards.[114] Only the British, with four hundred and eighty thousand tourists in 1952, were more numerous. However, the data show why Americans were the most important group for the French tourism industry: Americans outspent the British by over a million dollars.[115] Spending by air and ship passengers was not disaggregated. However, according to the IATA, during the five years following the start of tourist class fares, these passengers had spent an amount equal to one-fifth of the Marshall Plan.[116]

The increase in American tourists in France was also the result of increased French publicity in the United States and an increase in tourist services in France. The OEEC sponsored a $350,000 joint publicity program in the United States to promote tourism during 1951. France was the largest contributor to the fund.[117] The results were not meager. From 22 April to 15 June 1951, one hundred thousand dollars were spent in the United States promoting the 2000th birthday of Paris. Administratively, the program was streamlined in June 1952, with the creation of the Conseil Superieur du tourisme. Composed of thirty individuals drawn from the French tourist industry, it reported directly to André Morice, minister of public works, transport, and tourism.[118]

The Commissariat général au Tourisme also increased its subsidy to the Comité de tourisme de Paris et du département de la Seine. The Comité established three welcome centers in Paris during 1950, at the Gare Saint-Lazare, at l'Aérogare des Invalides, and on the Champs Elysées.[119] Young women in uniform—"hostesses of Paris"—staffed these offices. Other "hostesses of Paris" could be found on trains from Le Havre to Paris and on the passenger ship *Liberté* providing public relations information and distributing the pamphlet *Connaissance de Paris.* Throughout the holy year of 1950 the Comité coordinated its efforts with the Comité Catholique des Amitiés françaises à l'étranger. It claimed to have welcomed over forty thousand pilgrims from the Western Hemisphere as they made their way to Rome.[120] The Comité also organized the reception of the U.S. radio star Bobby Benson when he came to France to adopt a child.

The 1951 celebrations and publicity surrounding the 2000th birthday of Paris illustrate the characteristics of transatlantic tourism promotion. Publicity in the United States was concentrated in Boston, Chicago, New York, and San Francisco. Jules Romains, the prominent writer and president of the organizing committee, came to the United States to promote the event. The Boston Symphony, conducted by Frenchman Charles Munch, held a concert in celebration.[121] The Boston department store Jordan Marsh featured French merchandise in elaborate window displays. Windows lined with posters of the Eiffel Tower and Notre Dame displayed Christian Dior dresses and Chanel perfume.

Articles, most likely coordinated with Mission France, began appearing in late 1950.[122] In November the *New York Herald Tribune* published a special supplement called "Paris Plans a Party!"[123] "A party to end all parties will celebrate the city's 2000th birthday next year," declared the author, William Attwood,

> Most Parisians don't know it yet, but their city's going to start a 12 month birthday party next January—its first in 2000 years. That's roughly how old Paris is supposed to be. No one knows for sure … the main thing is having a good party.

The author described a series of meetings he held with two members of the organizing committee in Paris. "We want to reflect Paris's role as the capital of Western Civilization," one member told Attwood, "We want to strike a note that will attract Americans." Between meetings Attwood related his walk to Notre Dame where he found "Americans swarming all over the ancient island from stem to stern." Heartened by this site and a group of GIs in the Bois de Boulogne wooing French women, Attwood assured one of the organizers, who feared Americans would not come, "I wouldn't worry about the Americans. As far as they're concerned, the party has already started and they are having a swell time at it."

Attwood's article was also intended to serve a didactic purpose. He told of meeting a flustered American tourist arguing with a Parisian taxi driver: "'What's a matter with this guy?' he complained, 'He won't take good American money.' I suggested to him what might be the reaction of a New York cabby to a proffered 500 franc note. He began to grin and relax." Attwood befriended the tourist, "Fresh from the states and still smarting from a 3,000 franc dinner tab at one of the gilded tourist traps near the Champs-Elysées." He brought the American to a restaurant on a side street where they ate for less than a dollar and the proprietress explained the secret of her *sauce béarnaise.*

In addition to the didactic element—indicative of the influence of the ECA travel development officials—Attwood presented himself as something other than a tourist; he was what Chris Endy identifies as an expert traveler.[124] In addition to Attwood's advice to the American about the taxi and dinner, he also went to a café in St. Germain-des-Prés where French intellectuals debated and played chess. Attwood smugly explained that Americans could learn more about Paris in these cafés than in any by Notre Dame.

The *San Francisco Chronicle* published a travel supplement on the 2000th Birthday Party of Paris in April 1951. Like other publicity, the paper emphasized the cultural betterment entailed by a French vacation and the strength of the dollar: "Revel in the beauty of the country, in the cultural and artistic things that set France apart from the world. See the great museums, hear the finest concerts, study the architecture ... and remember this: your dollar goes far in France."[125] "Beauty Comes First when One's in Paris," headlined a two-page spread on perfume ("France's pedigreed industry") and fashion. As for entertainment, one article recommended smoky spots on the Rue Pigalle where "the ladies discard their G-strings before the dance, and champagne is just another reminder that one should have left his wife at home."

Four pages detailed the epicurean pleasures of Paris. "France has placed food in a special niche with love-making and wine-making as one of the honorable adornments of civilization." This article reminded readers that because most restaurants post their menus on windows they would have only themselves to blame if they erred on price. A facing page contained French recipes such as filet of sole *chambord* and deer stew *à la française*.

An important element of the tourism promotion program was contact between the press and agencies, both private and public, which promoted tourism.[126] The European Travel Commission, an American industry group that met in New York, worked with the ECA on a number of projects. Several guides illustrated the general trends outlined by the ERP tourism promotion officials. The 1951 *Fielding's Travel Guide to Europe,* for example, promoted travel away from Paris, an important goal of both French and American tourism officials. The guide recommended a trip to Montfort-l'Amaury, "an unspoiled, lovely little French village ... only an hour from the teeming Champs-Elysées."[127] Another guide explained, "The fact is that, from a tourist standpoint, France is suffering from too much Paris."[128] Other guides also recommended excursion away from Paris.[129] Nevertheless, like most tourists, the majority of guides concentrated on Paris.[130]

In addition to publicity, Marshall Plan officials also worked with the European Travel Commission to address a broad range of transatlantic tourism issues. The price complaints of American tourists were a major concern. The committee members agreed that many Americans visiting the Riviera and Paris complained about high prices. Harry Hill, the American Express representative, suggested distributing an article to the major American newspapers that would emphasize the strength of the dollar compared to the franc. Hill pointed out that although prices were high, American tourists were still getting a better deal than the average French person was. Another pressing concern was the concentration of Americans in Paris and the Riviera. According to Hill, tourists, both French and American, had to wait in line, sometimes for thirty-six hours, to book reservations on sleeper-cars. Bingham suggested a campaign to divert Americans to "out of the way" areas of France after counterpart funds had been used to increase sanitary conditions in these areas. According to the representative of the *New York Herald Tribune,* this "siphoning" would have immense benefits: "It would lessen the traffic load on Paris and the Riviera, would increase the tourist attractions in France, and would make the American visitor happier in that lower prices are usually available in such out of the way areas." In addition, new sources of competition would cause price reductions in Paris and the Mediterranean.[131] Addressing the goal of increasing off-season travel, Bingham suggested that counterpart funds be used to develop French alpine ski areas. This was already a priority under the Monnet Plan. Hill pointed out that "the French people themselves generally fill up the available space."

Committee members seemed hopeful that American tourists could be diverted away from France and the Riviera. Hill reminded those present that 1950 was a Holy Year and that thousands of pilgrims would be coming through France on their way to Rome. He suggested that the ERP develop points of interest in France for groups of American pilgrims, including a large group led by New York Cardinal Spellman. Hill admitted that he was having trouble finding accommodations for Cardinal Spellman's group in Lourdes (again, more French) but that France had other shrines that could be developed. In 1950 Ingrand's office released an English language illustrated pamphlet on cathedrals; another one on chateaux quickly followed.[132]

The boom in American tourism in France, however, did not fulfill every expectation French officials had for this critical sector of the economy. On 27 January 1953, the minister of public works, transport, and tourism, André Morice, briefed American officials. Morice stated that the number of foreign tourists to France during 1952 was virtually the same as in 1951: 3.2 million.[133] Tourist visits from Great Britain had decreased, but visitors from the United States increased. The minister pointed out that although official receipts for tourism had declined across the board, dollar receipts were the only currency to decline in face of an increase in tourists. They had dropped from $47 million in 1951 to $36 million in 1952. Morice identified several causes for the decline. One was the persistence of the underground economy for converting dollars. Another was consumer resistance to high prices in France. As we saw, French officials in the U.S. warned of this problem as early as 1949. Three years later high prices continued to be the most common complaint of American tourists returning from France. The French consul in Chicago reported that as a result of the high prices in Paris many tourists preferred to spend the majority of their time in Italy or Austria, passing through Paris for a few days en route.[134] Finally, Morice stated that a larger percentage of travelers were from "lower income classes" and this had caused per-capita spending to decline.[135] This suggested that indeed the nature of transatlantic tourism was changing during these years. It was not the case that these middle-class tourists were merely an addition to France's traditional, elite American tourists (in which case per-capita spending would have dropped but gross receipts would have

increased). Rather, the entire bloc of American tourists was spending less, traveling more on the off-season, and staying for a shorter
duration.[136]

France's economy had also become closely tied to the performance of its tourism market in general and American tourists in particular. It was an important component of the French economy and
the dollars brought by Americans were both a boon and a problem.
The drop in the value of the capital franc during the height of the
1953 tourist season illustrated the delicate relationship between the
French economy and American tourist dollars.

As *France Soir* had pointed out in 1949, part of the problem was
the availability of francs for dollar exchanges. The French had adopted
a stopgap solution involving U.S. film companies. These companies
sought guarantees for the convertibility of profits to dollars. The Informational Media Guarantee Program provided some assurance,
but this required approval by the State Department for individual
projects. A more general agreement was reached with the French government. According to this agreement, franc earnings from U.S. films
were used to exchange tourist dollars.[137] Profits were "unblocked" at
the beginning of each tourist season for conversion.

This system showed its faults during the 1953 tourist season. The
French government had increased the amount of unblocked movie
profits in anticipation of an increase in tourists. In August large strikes
led by Force ouvrière occurred in the public sector.[138] The strikes reduced tourist arrivals and the unblocked movie profits glutted the
franc market.[139] The exchange rate went from 352 francs to the dollar before the strikes to a high of 385 in late August, and because prices
remained stable tourism profits declined.[140] Profits from tourism
dropped as a result of both the weak franc and cancellations due to
the strikes.

France achieved its 1952 goal of three million tourists but it did
not achieve the projected earnings.[141] Why? Morice was correct in
identifying the underground economy and high prices (coupled with
inflation). Other factors inflated the number of American tourists in
France without the commensurate profit. One was the role of Paris
as a geographic hub for European travel. Tourists staying for one
night in Paris en route to another city were included in the French
tourism figures, but their spending in Paris was negligible. Another
source of American tourists was the American army in Germany. GIs
on a two-day leave from Germany lowered the figure for per-capita
spending while increasing the number of American tourists.[142]

The rearmament program following the outbreak of the Korean
War also had a significant effect on the tourism investment program,

which, in turn, affected profits. In 1950 the head of the French Mission, Henry Parkman, told the ECA that it would be impossible to increase the level of expenditure on tourism due to the need for rearmament following the start of the Korean War.[143] However, if the tourism program could not be increased, both French and American officials agreed it should not be decreased. This, nevertheless, amounted to a budget cut because the French plan called for increased spending on a yearly basis to achieve its goals.[144] Officials were still attracted to the unparalleled dollar earning potential of tourism. A top State Department official, Ralph I. Straus, issued a statement to the ECA Missions in late 1950 outlining the effects of the rearmament program.[145] Straus stated that because rearmament made "general exhortations to export difficult," each country should develop one or two key export industries.

According to Straus, tourism should be given priority because it was "the most important invisible earner of dollars for the participating countries."[146] Henceforth, rearmament would be given top consideration, but tourism was an example of a dollar earning industry that would not interfere with defense efforts. Or rather, tourism was a source of dollars in addition to rearmament: "It may be possible to have both our cake and eat it too and both rearmament and dollar earnings in certain cases may be profitably continued side by side." "Thus," continued Straus, "we do not see a fundamental inconsistency between continued efforts to increase dollar earnings from tourism and collective effort toward Western defense."[147] In practice, however, it remained difficult to sustain the tourism investment program at the level originally intended. In 1948 Ingrand had seen tourism as the sine qua non for closing the trade deficit with the United States, but by 1953 France had become dependent on U.S. military aid in Indochina to balance its trade deficit.[148] The ECA and the Commissariat général au tourisme compensated for decreased building and modernization credits by increasing tourist promotion programs. The tourist class airfare was one by-product of this effort. Another was the effort to increase off-season traffic.

Nevertheless, the number of tourists in 1952, 3.2 million, was impressive. Tourist class airfares and off-season deals accounted for some of the gains. Another factor was the French government's role in promoting intra-European tourism in OEEC countries. From 1951 onward the French government became increasingly concerned with tourism while the ECA contracted its tourist promotion programs.[149]

The tropes created by French and American tourism publicity were durable. A 1959 study for the European Travel Commission showed the extent to which American tourists understood France as a unique blend of elite culture and hedonism.[150] The report further revealed that many American tourists perceived a distinct French hostility toward Americans. The study interviewed one hundred and six "upper-middle class" people from Detroit, Boston, and Atlanta. Half of the individuals had been to Europe in the past two years ("travelers"), the other half had not ("non-travelers"). The two groups' perceptions of France converged.

In order to test the hypothesis that European hostility to Americans was a deterrent to travel, the interviewers presented a picture of an American husband and wife in front of the Eiffel tower. A caption above the head of the woman read, "I can't wait to get home." People were asked why the woman wanted to return home. "That looks like Paris to me," responded one non-traveler, "There's a lot of women in Paris and she wants to get her husband away." Another one explained, "The people in Paris are not very cordial to Americans." Virtually all of the "travelers" responded that the French disliked Americans. Some characteristic responses were:

> "She's in Paris. Practically nobody in Paris hide their contempt for and dislike of Americans."
> "In Paris people are very unfriendly toward Americans and she wants to get away from Paris because of that."
> "She is in Paris. The Frenchmen over there."

"In conclusion," explained the report, "it would seem that there is a tendency for Americans to feel that they are not regarded entirely favorably by Europeans."[151]

Yet the report concluded that the status of a French vacation offset the deterrence of perceived European hostility. The report explained, "Another frequently mentioned reason for wanting to go home was the desire to tell people at home about the trip." Here, too, the opinions of travelers and non-travelers converged. The ideal advertisement, the report suggested, was one that combined culture and pleasure:

> Just to illustrate this point, the picture in a travel advertisement might show man and wife studying a monument or other cultural artifact while a kiosk in the background displays a poster of can-can girls, presumably advertising a local revue.... One such cartoon might show the wife studying her guidebook as she walks down the street while her husband is momentarily distracted by a shapely leg.

As this and other advertisements indicated, gender was an important element of tourism as a consumer enterprise. Advertisements celebrated French fashion and perfume as opportunities for the middle-

France
=
Culture + Sex

class housewife to become sophisticated and glamorous. Conversely, popular literature and tourism publicity sexualized Parisian women in an appeal to American men.

As these examples show, in their efforts to publicize tourism, French and American tourism officials and promoters presented a version of Frenchness that was both conservative and titillating. Tourism publicity represented France as the land of vineyards and peasants, the Louvre, Notre Dame, and the Eiffel Tower. In addition to this message, the publicity also revealed that France (particularly Paris) offered opportunities for gratification unavailable anyplace else. Cabarets and the Rue Pigalle promised men, with or without a wife, sexual adventure.

By 1952 American tourism in France was not only an example of a specific consumer identity, it was also geographically concentrated in Paris and the Riviera. During 1952, American tourists in France occupied 90 percent of the beds in four-star hotels, and 87 percent of the beds in three-star hotels. In the same year, the only demographic group more numerous than Americans in Paris was Parisians.[152] On the Cote d'Azur, only the British (58,103) were more numerous than the Americans (53,106). The American tourist flow to Biarritz and Bordeaux increased from 1950 to 1952 as a result of publicity in the American press, but the numbers remained smaller than Belgians, Spanish, and British visitors.[153]

The concentration of Americans in Paris and the Riviera helped to reinforce French stereotypes about Americans. Paris was the favored leave destination for American soldiers stationed throughout Europe. Lapses of discipline by American soldiers in Paris were covered in *L'Humanité* and such incidents were a concern for French and American diplomats.[154] Contrary to the assertion by a U.S. official that tourism's "contribution to mutual social and cultural appreciation among all nations are similarly immeasurable in terms of money," the evidence suggests that American tourists in France did little to disabuse the French public of common stereotypes.[155] Americans had been associated with materialism for over a century. The new American tourists concentrated in Paris did little to change this. Nevertheless, increasing international understanding was often presented as a bonus to the economic benefits of tourism. In early 1950 the ECA sponsored a poster program offering $2000 in prizes for posters with the theme: "Understanding through travel is the passport to peace."

Tourists were good for bringing dollars to France but they were not equally effective as proselytizers for the American way of life. As one ECA official explained:

students better than ~~previous~~ tourists

We have found, surprisingly, that a single individual brought to this country and indoctrinated somewhat with our methods and manner of living, on his return to his country is of much greater value as an emissary
of good will and the interchange of friendly relations, than two dozen
or two-hundred American tourists who, for a brief period, visit the country in question.[156]

yes!

This statement reflected a growing belief in the State Department of
the importance of educational exchanges and visits by industry and
government elites. American tourists were less effective than such
visits for a number of reasons, one being that the State Department
had only a limited influence on what tourists said, or what might be
said to them. In theory, every American going abroad received the
State Department pamphlet, "Tips for Your Trip." Its purpose was to
prevent the more embarrassing behaviors of American tourists. The
reaction of one woman, "I'm from the country giving yours so much
money," to a French customs official was common enough.[157] "Tips
for Your Trip" cautioned: "Don't forget that you're a guest in Europe—
politeness and respect for European customs and habits are always
the best policy."[158] Another fear of the State Department was that
Americans going abroad would be exposed to criticism of the United
States. Printed in bold letters on the pamphlet was a reminder of the
Marshall Plan's significance: "It is a vital arm of U.S. foreign policy directed toward postwar recovery in Europe and the establishment of
a new pattern of world trade."

The efforts by the French press to counter stereotypes of Americans as wanton consumers provide an indication of their strength.
According to *Le Figaro,* the Organization for European Economic Cooperation expected a half-million American tourists in 1952.[159] The
paper warned that the French must not imagine American tourists "rolling in dollars." Citing Theodore Pozzy, *Le Figaro* wrote: "The 'deluxe'
American tourist has disappeared. It's now the average American who is
going to come to France."[160] *La Croix* criticized the Marshall Plan and
the French government for financing high-priced resorts: "The era of
billionaires is past and the hotel industry must face up to new conditions."[161] The paper argued that downward flow of bourgeois tourists
who could no longer afford the accommodations and expenses of luxury vacations was meeting the increase in tourism among individuals
of modest income, even from the United States. The paper happily reported that even Americans had adopted cost-saving habits. According to *La Croix:* "Nobody wants to be 'taken for an American' any more."
Ostentation was no longer in line with the new conditions of tourism.

Even if the common view of Americans had not been based on long-
standing perceptions of Americans as shallow and materialistic, the

[handwritten margin note: Marshall Plan reinforced Fr belief w rich Americans]

Marshall Plan program, which emphasized tourists as purveyors of dollars, would have created the image. The *Salon du Tourisme* was a case in point. By emphasizing the economic contribution of tourists, the Marshall Plan reaffirmed French assumptions about the affluence and materialism of Americans. However, if tourism tended to reinforce stereotypes about Americans, the same cannot be said for French views of American consumer goods tourists brought with them. During this period Marshall Plan exhibits that displayed such consumer goods as mixers, hair dryers, electric broilers, waffle irons, and garbage disposals were well-received by French audiences. Nevertheless, tourism planners represented American tourists in simple terms to the French and presented France simplified to attractions and pleasure to Americans. This simplification of understanding corresponded to the needs and conditions of postwar tourism and was characteristic of both American and French officials. Furthermore, the Cold War rhetoric— "free"—underlying much of the discussion of tourism showed that "international understanding" contained a partisan political message.

The Marshall Plan's impact on the French tourism industry was significant and formative. The economic imperative strengthened the ties between the French and American economies; new regulations governing international air travel were adopted; Marshall Plan reconstruction funds helped rebuild and modernize French hotels; the concentration of Americans in Paris occasioned the creation of sites and activities that were conducive to tourist leisure; advertising for internationalism tourism targeted the American market. In 1955, a report from the Commissariat general au plan explained that American tourism to France accounted for 93 percent of French exports to the U.S. "With little risk," the report concluded, "we can envisage that American tourism to France will constitute 50% of the market in the years to come."[162] Ingrand suggested that modernization continue to focus on increasing the number of hotels for international tourists possessing modest resources, "such as those that will take the recently created transatlantic tourist class flights."[163]

Did Marshall Plan tourism development contribute to the Americanization of France? Indeed it did. Although the cultural and social changes the tourism program promoted in France were minor, the Americanization of France for American tourists did occur through this program. The success of the program was contingent on the extent to which a French vacation could be a part of a middle-class American consumer enterprise. Elite tourism no longer provided the numbers or the dollars that postwar France needed. Yet, it was exactly the elite status entailed by a trip to France that made French tourism appealing to middle and upper-middle class American consumers.[164]

The Marshall Plan created the conditions for the postwar success of the tourism industry in France, either directly, as was the case with the creation of tourist class airfares, or indirectly through underwriting the Monnet Plan. After the Marshall Plan the apparatus and initiative for the development of the tourism industry lay within the French government. French tourism has flourished. In 2001, 76.5 million tourists visited France, more than any other country in the world and over 10 percent of all international tourism.[165] Spain and the United States placed a distant second and third with 49.5 and 44.5 million, respectively. In 2002 American tourists spent € 5,785,000 in France, more than any other group and about 17 percent of France's total receipts from international tourism.[166]

In 1948 the Commissariat général au Tourisme referred to tourism as the "highest French industry."[167] It represented the "healthiest and most authentic" source of French influence and prestige abroad. International tourism had become an element of the State's cultural policy. The French government thus instrumentally embraced a key aspect of globalization, and selectively Americanized it in an attempt to maximize the economic benefit. To take this analysis to its conclusion, from 1948 to 1952 the French tourism industry Americanized in order to increase the reach of French culture. Given French apprehensions about globalization and the impact of American mass culture, the results of this strategy at times appear paradoxical. Recently Planet Hollywood outlets have failed throughout the world, but the Champs-Elysées location is alive and well, as evidenced by the thousands of people who were on hand to cheer Sylvester Stallone during a recent visit.[168] Ten years after the French government won the competition for the new European location of a Disney resort the park is one of the most popular tourist destinations in Europe … an "insolent success" in the words of Agence France Presse.[169] To the extent that France sees tourism as both essential for the *rayonnement* of its culture and a key industry, it will have to manage the commodifying logic tourism brings with it.

Notes

1. Portions of this chapter previously appeared as "Creating a Tourist's Paradise: the Marshall Plan and France, 1948 to 1952," *French Politics, Society, and Culture* 21, no. 1 (2003): 35–54.

2. Howard G. Kurtz, "The Common Man—Up in the Air," IATA bulletin (mid-year, 1953), 9–10.
3. J.J. Viala to Bonnet, 19 September 1949, Ministère des Affaires Etrangères, Paris, Relations culturelles 1945-59/echanges culturelles 1948-55/126.
4. John Abbink, "Tourism and its discontents: Suri-tourist encounters in southern Ethiopia," *Social Anthropology* 8, 1 (2000), 1–2.
5. John Tomlinson, *Globalization and Culture* (Chicago: University of Chicago Press, 1999), 4.
6. Philip H. Gordon and Sophie Meunier, *The French Challenge: Adapting to Globalization*, 62–64, 114–117.
7. *Civil Aviation and Peace* (Washington: the Brookings Institution, 1944), 64–65.
8. Ibid., 94.
9. Contribution of Travel Development to Closing the Dollar Gap, prepared by the Travel Branch of the Office of International Trade, Department of Commerce, 15 August 1950, NARA, RG. 469, entry 928, box 2.
10. U.S. Congressional Record, Promotion of tourism can supply Europe, Wednesday, 26 April (legislative day of Wednesday 29 March), 1950.
11. Étude sur le tourisme en France de 1946 à 1948, Annex I, Part de la France dans le tourisme international en Europe, NARA, RG. 469, entry 928, box 2.
12. John Urry, *The Tourist's Gaze* (London: Sage, 1990); Annabel Black, "Negotiating the Tourist Gaze," in *Coping With Tourists: European Reactions to Mass Tourism*, ed. Jeremy Boissevain (New York: Berghahn Books, 1996), 116–118.
13. For a discussion of tourism infrastructures and national identity in an earlier period, see Rudy Koshar, "'What ought to be seen': Tourists' Guidebooks and National Identities in Modern Germany and Europe," *Journal of Contemporary History* 33, 3, (1998): 323–340.
14. Letter from Robert R. Mullen, E.C.A. office of information, to Roscoe Drummond, Mission France: information division, 7 May 1951, NARA, RG. 469, entry 302, box 18.
15. John Urry and Scott Lasch, *Economies of Sign and Space* (London: Sage, 1994), 272.
16. Ellen Furlough, "Making Mass Vacations: Tourism and Consumer Culture in France, 1930s to 1970s," *Comparative Studies in Society and History* vol. 40 no. 2 (April 1998), 274.
17. Pierre Chabert, *Le tourisme Américain et ses enseignements pour la France* (Paris: Librarie Hachette et Cie, 1918), 78.
18. Hans Magnus Enzensberger, "A Theory of Tourism," trans. Gerd Gemünden and Kenn Johnson, *New German Critique* 68 (Spring-Summer 1996), 134. First published as Hans Magnus Enzensberger, "Vergebliche Brandung der Ferne: Eine Theorie des Tourismus," *Merkur* (August 1958): 701–720.
19. Ellen Furlough, "Making Mass Vacations: Tourism and Consumer Culture in France, 1930s to 1970s," 276.
20. Plant Conditions of French Tourism, in Report on Information Activities August through November 1948. NARA, RG. 469, entry 1193, box 3.
21. Ibid.; The Commissariat Général au Tourisme was created by the Monnet Plan and the commissioner's post was initially held by Henri Dussauze-Ingrand.
22. Archives du Ministère des Affaires Etrangères, relations culturelles, 1945-1947, Oeuvres diverses, 1.
23. Plant Conditions of French Tourism.
24. Ibid.
25. Ibid.
26. Étude sur le tourisme en France de 1946 à 1948, action entreprise—résultats—perspectives d'avenir, NARA, RG. 469, entry 969, box 3.

27. Étude sur le tourisme en France de 1946 à 1948.
28. 1949 counterpart expenditures on tourism, memo from ECA/F to ECA administrator, 24 March 1950. NARA, RG. 469, entry 333, box 10. In many cases the counterpart expenditures were "hidden" under the general category of "Reconstruction," Short Summary of the ECA Program in France: April 1948–December 1950, NARA, RG. 469, entry 1193, box 44.
29. Ibid.
30. Report on the French Tourist Industry, November 1950. NARA, RG. 469, entry 969, box 3.
31. Memo from Henry Parkman to ECA/W, 2 October 1950. NARA, RG. 469, entry 333, box 10. See also Irwin Wall, *The United States and the Making of Postwar France, 1945-54* (Cambridge: Cambridge UP, 1991), 182.
32. Travel Development Section, E.C.A. France, NARA, RG. 469, entry 969, box 3.
33. Letter to E.C.A. Washington from E.C.A. France, 2 October 1950, NARA, RG. 469, entry 333, box 10; Memo from Henry Parkman to ECA/W, 2 October 1950, NARA, RG. 469, entry 333, box 10.
34. From Paris to ECA Administrator, 15 May 1950, NARA, RG. 469, entry 353, box 10.
35. To ECA/W from ECA/F, 2 November 1950, NARA RG. 469, entry 969, box 3; Report on the French Tourist Industry.
36. Black Marketing by Tourists, Appendix A in Report on Information Activities.
37. Memo from American Consulate Algiers to Dept. of State, 6 September 1949, NARA, RG 469, entry 969, box 3.
38. Telegram from Bonnet to Robert Schuman, 7 Juillet 1949, Ministère des Affaires Etrangères, Paris, série B/Relations culturelles/Échanges culturelles/126.
39. Memo from American Embassy in Paris to Dept. of State, 12 April 1948, NARA, RG. 469, entry 969, box 3.
40. Minutes of the European Travel Commission, 22 November 1949, NARA, RG. 469, entry 928, box 3.
41. Letter from Theodore Pozzy to Ingrand, 8 June 1949, NARA, RG. 469, entry 969, box 3.
42. Letter fron Ingrand to Pozzy, 13 June 1949, NARA, RG. 469, entry 969, box 3.
43. Report on Tourism, NARA, RG. 469, entry 928, box 2, Julian Street, Jr., conducted the poll. Julian Street, Jr., interview by Linda and Eric Christenson, 16 August 1993, Norfolk CT, VHS recording, Christenson Associates.
44. Hans Magnus Enzensberger, "A Theory of Tourism," 135.
45. French Tourist Trends, Dispatch no. 1665 from American Embassy to Department of State, NARA, central decimal files of the State Department, 851.181/12-2953.
46. French Tourism, in Report on Information Activities. Factoring out the underground economy's 57 percent leaves an average of $484, still lower than prewar spending.
47. French Tourist Trends.
48. "Le tourisme international en Europe," *Études et conjoncture* No. 4, 1950, juillet-août, published by the Ministère de finance et des affaires économique.
49. Whelan, 337.
50. Étude sur le tourisme en France de 1946 à 1948.
51. Telegram TOECA A-163, NARA, RG. 469, entry 969, box 3.
52. *France Soir,* 25 June 1949.
53. *Combat,* 29 March 1949.
54. Ibid.
55. *Le Parisien Libéré,* 11 June 1949.
56. Ibid.
57. "Le tourisme international en Europe."

58. See Richard F. Kuisel, *Seducing the French: the Dilemma of Americanization*, chapter 3, "Missionaries of the Marshall Plan"; Richard F. Kuisel, "The Marshall Plan in Action: Politics, Labor, Industry and the program of Technical Assistance," in *Le Plan Marshall et le relèvement économique de l'Europe*, eds. René Girault and Maurice Lévy-Leboyer (Paris: Comité pour l'histoire économique et financier de la France, 1993).

59. Voyage d'études aux Etats-Unis organisé sous les auspice de l'ECA, Rapport, NARA, RG. 469, entry 969, box 3.

60. Groupe de travail n. 5 du comité du tourisme pour l'Étude de l'assistance technique dans le domaine du tourisme, NARA, RG. 469, entry 969, box 8.

61. Voyage d'études aux Etats-Unis organisé sous les auspice de l'ECA, Rapport.

62. Ibid.

63. Ibid.

64. Ibid.

65. Ibid.

66. Ibid.

67. Ibid.

68. Ibid.

69. Ibid.

70. "Le tourisme international en Europe," *Études et conjoncture.*

71. Voyage d'études aux Etats-Unis organisé sous les auspice de l'ECA, Rapport.

72. Memo from William H. Wise, travel development officer, to Helen Kirkpatrick, October 23, 1950, NARA, RG. 469, entry 1193, box 47.

73. Marshall Plan Aid to French Tourism at Paris Exposition, NARA, RG. 469, entry 1193, box 47.

74. Laura A. Belmonte, "A Family Affair? Gender, the U.S. Information Agency, and Cold War Ideology, 1945-1960," in *Culture and International History,* Jessica C.E. Gienow-Hecht and Frank Schumacher, eds. (New York: Berghahn Books, 2003), 79.

75. Memo to Robert Sivard from Peter G. Harnden, 23 October 1950, NARA, RG. 469, entry 1193, box 47.

76. Report on Salon du Tourisme, NARA, RG 469, entry 1193, box 47.

77. Ibid.

78. Ibid.

79. Stephen Wheatcroft, *The Economics of European Air Transport* (Manchester: Manchester University Press, 1956), 136.

80. Support for the tourist fares came from airlines that possessed the largest network of routes, such as Pan-Am.

81. Letter from W. Averill Harriman to Paul G. Hoffman, 5 April 1949, NARA, RG. 469, entry 970, box 1.

82. Ibid.

83. Letter from Joseph J. O'Connell to Juan Trippe, 27 April 1949, NARA RG. 469, entry 970, box 1.

84. Wheatcroft, 136.

85. Letter from Joseph J. O'Connell to Juan Trippe.

86. Personal Memo to Hoffman from Russell S. McKlure, 24 August 1949, NARA, RG. 469, entry 928, box 7.

87. Ibid.

88. Letter from Joseph J. O'Connell to Paul G. Hoffman, 27 April 1949, NARA, RG. 469, entry 970, box 1.

89. The CAB had no control of international fares and rates as such, but it did have the power to approve or disapprove any agreement between U.S. carriers and

foreign airlines. Since all IATA decisions had to be unanimous this gave it an effective veto. See Wheatcroft, 221–226.

90. Outgoing telegram, American Embassy Paris to Secretary of State, 3 May 1949; Memo from Pozzy to Wilkinson, 17 May 1949, NARA, RG. 469, entry 928, box 7.
91. Letter to Wilkinson from Pozzy, 24 August 1949, NARA, RG. 469, entry 928, box 7.
92. *New York Herald Tribune International Edition,* 19 August 1949.
93. Letter from Averill D. Harriman to John D. Rockefeller, 9 February 1950.
94. Letter from Senator Claude Pepper to Harriman, 15 March 1950; Letter from Representative Mansfield to Hoffman, 14 March 1950. Representative Mansfield was not entirely accurate, of course, because American tourism abroad had a negative effect on a major industry: domestic tourism. NARA, RG. 469, entry 928, box 29.
95. Letter from Harriman to Senator Claude Pepper, 28 March 1950, NARA, RG. 469, entry 928, box 29; Letter from Kirkpatrick to Senator J. William Fulbright, 12 May 1950, NARA, RG. 469, entry 968, box 4.
96. A copy of the resolution is contained in NARA, RG. 469, entry 928, box 7.
97. Letter from Pozzy to Wilkinson, 23 March 1951; Civil Aeronautics Board press release, 22 March 1951. Both in NARA, RG. 469, entry 970, box 2.
98. Wilkinson also brushed aside the Charter companies' complaints: "Documentation shows abuse by these groups of the exemptions previously accorded them and practices contrary to the public interests servicing the traveler." Letter from Pozzy to Wilkinson, 23 March 1951.
99. Pozzy to Wilkinson, 3 April 1951, NARA, RG. 469, entry 970, box 2.
100. Wheatcroft, 138.
101. Ibid., 139.
102. *Tourist 5: Five Years of Transatlantic Airline Tourist Service* (Montreal: IATA, 1957), 2.
103. *The New York Times,* 1 June 1952.
104. Gérard Bossuat, *La France, l'aide américaine et la construction européene 1944–54* 1: 367–369.
105. Ronald Miller and David Sawers, *The Technical Development of Modern Aviation* (New York: Praeger Publishers, 1970), 291–295.
106. Wheatcroft, 173–176.
107. Telegram from American Embassy Paris to Department of State, 18 February 1952, NARA, RG. 469, entry 969, box 3.
108. Telegram from American Embassy Paris to Department of State, 18 February 1952.
109. From Paris to State Department. NARA General Records of the State Department, 851.181/3-752.
110. *Le Monde,* 2 May 1952.
111. French Tourist Trends, 851.181/12-2953.
112. Tourist Traffic to France by Air, 851.181/1-1454.
113. *Tourist 5,* 3; Tourist Traffic to France by Air, 851.181/1-1454.
114. Tourism Developments, France, 851.181/1-2853.
115. Ibid.
116. *Tourist 5,* 6.
117. Joint Publicity Program for 1951, European Travel Committee, NARA, RG. 469, entry 928, box 3.
118. Tourism, France (Conseil Superieur du Tourisme), 851.181/12-552.
119. Compte-rendu annuel d'activité, Comité de Tourisme de Paris et du departement de la Seine, NARA, RG. 469, entry 969, box 3.
120. Compte-rendu annuel d'activité.

121. From Bonnet to Schuman, 21 Decembre 1950, Ministère des Affaires Etrangères, Paris, Quai d'Orsay, série B/1944-52/États-Unis/fête du bi-millinaire de Paris, 280.

122. I have been unable to find direct links between specific articles and agency decisions. However, it is likely given the close ties between Mission France and press agencies, as evidenced by the planning participation of William H. Wise of the *New York Herald Tribune.* Furthermore, the funds allotted by the OEEC for the promotion of the event were spent by the European Travel Commission in New York. The ETC had direct contact with both Mission France and the Commerce Department, "Minutes of the European Travel Commission," 22 November 1949, NARA, RG. 469, entry 928, box 3.

123. *New York Herald Tribune,* 17 November 1950.

124. Christopher Endy, "Travel and World Power," *Diplomatic History* 22, no. 4 (Fall 1998), 569.

125. *San Francisco Chronicle,* 29 April 1951.

126. Theodore Pozzy, chief of the Travel Development Section of the ECA's Office of the Special Representative, worked closely with the European Travel Commission office in New York and the J.M. Mathes advertising agency. He disseminated press releases regarding changes in price structure, customs procedures, and special events. Minutes of the European Travel Commission, 22 November 1949, NARA, RG. 469, entry 928, box 3.

127. Temple Fielding, *Fielding's Travel Guide to Europe* (New York: William Sloane, 1951), 338.

128. Richard Joseph, *Richard Joseph's Guide to Europe and the Mediterranean* (New York: Doubleday, 1956), 145.

129. Frederick E. Tyarks and Normand D. Ford, *Europe on a Shoestring* (New York: Harian, 1956); Stuart Murray, *A Traveler's Guide to France: the Country, the People and the Language* (New York: Sheridan House, 1948); Harold Newman, *Newman's European Travel Guide* (Baltimore: I & M Ottenheimer, 1955).

130. See, for example, L. Russell Muirhead, *Short Guide to Paris* (Chicago: Rand McNally, 1952); Clara E. Laughlin, *So You're Going to Paris!* (New York: Houghton & Mifflin, 1948); Horace Sutton, *Footloose in France* (New York: Rinehart, 1948); Eric Whelpton, *Paris To-day* (New York: Macmillan, 1950).

131. TOECA A-163.

132. *Travel in Europe: A Selective Reading List* (Washington, D.C.: Library of Congress—European Affairs Division, 1950), 28ff.

133. Tourism Developments, France, 851.181/1-2853.

134. Telegram from François Briere, consul general de France à Chicago to Henri Bonnet, 29 September 1952, Ministère des Affaires Etrangères, Paris, série B, Amérique 1952-1963, Etats-Unis, 327. Industry professionals felt that Spain and Italy could make significant gains in the tourism market at France's expense. See "Le tourisme étranger en France en 1952," *Études et conjoncture* No. 9 Septembre 1953.

135. Tourism Developments, France, 851.181/1-2853.

136. Sixty percent of American tourists to France during 1952 traveled during the off-season. Le tourisme étranger en France en 1952.

137. Recent developments in Paris Capital Franc Market and Outlook for the Future, Central decimal files of the State Department 851.131/8-2553.

138. Wall, 270.

139. Recent developments in Paris Capital Franc Market and Outlook for the Future, 851.131/8-2553.

140. Ibid.

141. French Tourist Developments, Central decimal files of the State Department 851.181/ 2-1054.
142. "Le tourisme etranger en France en 1952."
143. To ECA/W from ECA/F, 20 September 1950, NARA, RG. 469, entry 969, box 3.
144. Étude sur le tourisme en France de 1946 à 1948, action entreprise—résultats—perspectives d'avenir.
145. Statement by Ralph I. Straus to Mission Heads, NARA, RG. 469, entry 968, box 4.
146. Ibid.
147. Ibid.
148. Wall, 251.
149. The Travel Development Section of Mission France was absorbed by other departments in April 1951. Airgram from ECA/France to ECA/Washington, 20 April 1951, NARA, RG. 469, entry 969, box 3.
150. "Motivations Related to Pleasure Travel in Europe, a Pilot Study for: European Travel Commission, Holiday Magazine, Time Magazine," prepared by the Opinion Research Corporation, August 1959 (Princeton: Opinion Research Corporation, 1959).
151. Ibid., 33.
152. "Le tourisme dans les regions de France," British and Belgian tourists often surpassed Americans in number, but it was the Americans who flocked to Paris. *Études et conjoncture* no. 9 Septembre 1953.
153. "Le tourisme étranger et le relevement de la France," *Cahiers francais d'information,* No. 171, 15 January 1951.
154. See, for example, *L'Humanité* 23 Mai 1951; Factors Adversely Affecting the Acceptance of U.S. Troops in Europe, NARA, RG. 469, entry 302, box 10.
155. Contribution of Travel Development to Closing the Dollar Gap.
156. Minutes of Travel Advisory Committee, Department of Commerce, Office of International Trade, 5 October 1950, NARA, RG. 469, entry 928, box 7.
157. Memo to Theodore Pozzy, NARA, RG 469, entry 928, box 6.
158. Tips for Your Trip, NARA, RG. 469, entry 928, box 6.
159. *Le Figaro,* 7 June 1949.
160. Ibid.
161. *La Croix,* 4 June 1949.
162. Commissariat général au plan, commission de modernization du tourisme—rapport général, AN, AJ 80, box 67.
163. Memorandum concernant le 2eme plan de modernization et d'equipement du tourisme, AN, AJ 80, box 67.
164. As Chris Endy points out, as early as 1909 the question was not "Can I afford to travel?" but "Can I afford to stay at home?" Endy, "Travel and World Power," p. 570.
165. Bilan de l'année touristique 2001, Secrétariat d'État au Tourisme, www.tourisme.gouv.fr. Retrieved 3 June 2002.
166. Dépenses des touristes étrangers en France, Secrétariat d'État au Tourisme, www.tourisme.gouv.fr. Retrieved 28 July 2003.
167. Étude sur le tourisme en France de 1946 à 1948, NARA, RG 469, entry 969, box 3.
168. *Le Figaro,* 9 Septembre 2002.
169. Agence France Press, 10 Avril 2002.

Chapter 4

THE LABOR INFORMATION PROGRAM: "AN INFORMATION PANZER FORCE"

I never have been more convinced of anything than I am that communist imperialism would long since have overrun Western Europe had we not stepped in to the picture with our offer of succor in the crucial hour. It is not just that millions of innocent people ... would have starved to death or died for want of shelter and clothing ... but the fate from which we have thus far saved Western Europe is one I consider infinitely worse than death, a fate from which for many hapless victims thereof death would be a welcome relief.[1]

Harry Martin, Director, Labor Information, 1949

In 1950 Kenneth Douty, the chief labor officer of the French Mission of the ERP, presented his assessment of the Marshall Plan's impact on the lives of French workers. His findings were stark. "We have furnished neither the moral nor the material antidote," he wrote, "that has gained worker acceptance. Until tangible results underscore our moral position, we can count only on the mistakes of the Communists to help us in the battle for the allegiance of French workers."[2] Douty worried that the U.S. emphasized productivity over wages. He pointed out that the Marshall Plan had not increased the standard of living or the wages of French workers in light of productivity gains that were, ostensibly, a by-product of the Marshall Plan. In 1950 productivity was one-fifth higher than it had been in 1938. Wages, on the other hand, were fully a third lower than the 1938 level.[3] In Douty's words, "The results can be seen in the opulent Paris store windows and in the clothes and physique of the workers who pass by them." He cautioned that consumption, not production, was soon to be France's major economic concern.

Notes for this section begin on page 184.

[handwritten margin note: Marshall Plan effort Fr to convert to workers way of life to combat communism]

Douty was also concerned about the "moral position" that the lack of concrete results threatened to wipe away. A central goal of the Marshall Plan was establishing the moral authority of the United States in Western Europe. The U.S. based its claim to moral authority on anticommunism within Western Europe and opposition to the Soviet Union beyond. Ultimately, however, many U.S. officials believed that the most powerful source of moral authority was the American way of life. For American public diplomacy, exposure to the American way of life was the best way to win support for the policies of the U.S. "Freedom" and consumption were inextricably linked elements of the American way of life. French workers were shown American workers who owned houses, cars, and appliances. All these, they were told, could belong to them if they emulated American practices. Yet for French workers this was a fantasy. Douty explained: "The pie-in-the-sky we've been offering workers has not helped them economically or us politically."[4]

This chapter examines the attempts of Mission France and the Labor Information Division (part of the Office of the Special Representative in Europe, OSR) to win the support of French workers for the Marshall Plan and demonstrate that the United States was an economic and social model to be emulated. The program to reach French labor was extensive. Although some of the material was technical and specific, the majority of its output was intended for general consumption. The program included films, exhibits, and printed material. Another aspect of the program was the Technical Assistance program which sponsored transatlantic visits of union and industry officials. Finally, Labor Information worked to undermine the Confederation générale du travail, the strongest French trade union.

The staff behind Labor Information was a cadre of Congress of Industrial Organization (CIO) members led by Harry Martin, the president of the American Newspaper Guild. They viewed themselves as being on the front lines of the propaganda battle in Europe. In theory, the standing of the members as CIO cardholders imparted credibility to their efforts. They spoke to French workers as union brothers, not American bureaucrats. The majority of the staff were newspapermen, although some had backgrounds in broadcasting. A number of them had worked in the domestic operations of the Office of War Information during the Second World War. They worked closely with the respective labor officers of the country Missions of the ERP.

American leaders perceived the support of labor, both foreign and domestic, as crucial to the success of the Marshall Plan.[5] The support of labor was important for two reasons. It provided domestic support for the program, but most importantly, at least from a foreign policy perspective, the intervention of U.S. labor in Marshall Plan countries provided a counterpoint to Soviet influence in Western European trade unions.[6] Indeed, the Marshall Plan was the central issue in the schism of the World Federation of Trade Unions and the creation of the pro-U.S. International Confederation of Free Trade Unions (ICFTU) in 1949.[7] Both James Carey, secretary-treasurer of the CIO and George Meany, secretary-treasurer of the American Federation of Labor (AFL) served on the Harriman Committee, which determined the scope of the Marshall Plan offer to Europe. After the beginning of the aid program, both union officials served on the Public Advisory Board that oversaw its implementation. For the AFL, the Marshall Plan represented an opportunity to extend its fight (already well advanced with the arrival in Europe of Irving Brown in 1945) against communism.[8] The CIO's support was more ambivalent. It couched its initial support in terms of political nonalignment.[9]

Nevertheless, by 1949 the CIO's involvement with the Marshall Plan had led to a tightening of relations with the Truman administration and a purge of its left-wing members.[10] U.S. Secretary of State Dean Acheson met with AFL and CIO leaders after the November 1949 London meeting that created the ICFTU. Labor leaders described the new organization as "completely non-Socialist in character," and they further agreed that the growth of communism should be fought "in every way possible."[11] In early 1950 the CIO issued a foreign policy statement. It pledged to increase its ties with labor organizations in Europe, Latin America, and Asia. The statement also reiterated the organization's opposition "to all forms of totalitarianism, Fascist, Communist, and Falangist."[12] "We know," explained the CIO, "that there can be no democracy in any nation without the existence of an alert and effective trade union movement."[13]

The Weaknesses of the Labor Information Program

The involvement of U.S. labor in France suffered from a number of fundamental weaknesses. On the other hand, the program possessed an extensive budget and a dedicated staff. As an element of U.S. foreign policy Labor Information possessed access to French workers unprecedented in the history of international labor relations. Thus the impact of the program cannot be measured solely in whether or not it succeeded in achieving some or all of its policy objectives. One problem was that it was charged with selling a product, the ERP, that it did not make. It was soon apparent that labor was deemed vital in support, useful for publicity, but unnecessary for policy-making. And yet, ironically, the efforts of Labor Information were some of the most visible components of the Marshall Plan. The Labor Information program attempted to sell the French on the Marshall Plan by presenting it as a solution to France's economic problems and a purveyor of individual prosperity. This exceeded even the most ideal outcome of the Marshall Plan. There was, in fact, a disjuncture between presentation and policy, further exacerbated by the impressive resources and autonomy of Labor Information. Anti-inflationary policies remained at the center of ERP/MSA aid. Thus while ECA officials pushed for—indeed demanded—deflationary policies and strict budgetary controls, the staff of Labor Information sponsored speakers who called for higher wages; while some American officials called for closer cooperation between employers and non-Communist labor, others called for non-Communist labor to "prove" itself through militant action.

Anthony Carew suggests that the lackluster performance of the ECA Labor Advisers in Washington, D.C., Clinton S. Golden of the CIO and Bert Jewell of the AFL, was one reason for the disjuncture between economic and labor policy.[14] However, as Federico Romero argues, the reasons for Labor Information's failures were more complex, and related to the very nature of European labor relations:

> The Labor Division and the Labor Information Division were given the task of assuring that the workers and the "free" unions were integrated in the plan ... but the most serious problem was to persuade business and conservative politicians to cooperate with non-Communist unions and to meet the most basic claims of the workers half-way.[15]

The domestic context in France was uncongenial for Labor Information operations. The difficulties arose because the commencement of the Marshall Plan was met in France and Italy with the return to power of bourgeois political parties. One of the consequences of this political realignment, what Romero terms "anti-Communist stabilization," was that industry and government were not eager to grant concessions to labor unions of any political stripe.[16] In practice, therefore, the desire of the Marshall Plan administration and of West European governments for anti-Communist stabilization was incompatible with Labor Information's goal of promoting the interests of the working class. This created early tensions between non-Communist trade unions, Marshall Plan officials, and the French government. During the Marshall Plan, Labor Information was unable to convince French workers that it had their interests at heart.

Labor relations were of central concern to the U.S. in France from the outset of the Marshall Plan. The creation of the Marshall Plan had occasioned a schism in France's largest trade union, the Confédéra-

tion générale du travail (CGT).[17] The labor situation rapidly deterio-
rated. The CGT, following the general line of the Soviet Union, had
denounced the Marshall Plan as a tool of American imperialism. In
December 1947 the non-Communists united around Léon Jouhaux to
form the Confédération générale du travail—Force ouvrière (FO).
Then, during a wave of miners' strikes in October 1948, the CGT declared it would not cooperate with the ECA. This left the U.S. with
the support of only the minor Confédération française des travailleurs
chrétiens (CFTC), Confédération général des cadres (CGC), and FO.
Relative to the CGT, all were weak, but especially in terms of blue-
collar representation. In 1948 a top secret CIA memo declared that
the situation in France was critical. The memo argued that "everything should be done by way of giving support to anti-Communist
elements of French labor."[18] FO was sustained by the infusion of dollars from the CIA and the AFL.[19] Despite this aid, FO had trouble expanding its working-class base.

Virulent anticommunism further weakened U.S. efforts. U.S. planners often forgot that not all CGT members carried membership cards
in the French Communist Party. The often-held assumption that CGT
entailed PCF was a formidable obstacle to understanding the nature
of trade unionism in France. Given the antagonism of the French
patronat, other unions could offer little programmatically or organi-
zationally to compete with the benefits of belonging to the most
powerful union in France. The common recourse of FO and the CFTC
to criticize CGT strikes as "political" even when they contained demands for collective bargaining and wage increases illustrated the
problems faced by these unions in gaining worker support.[20]

Preventing the convergence of Communist and non-Communist
unions on labor issues was a problem for Labor Information. Ironically,
even the largest sector of non-Communist union members, French
civil servants, was critical of the Marshall Plan. The secretary general of the Syndicate général de l'éducation nationale, Paul Vignaux,
warned in 1949 that civil servants would soon lose confidence in the
government because of its failure to grant wage increases. According to Vignaux, "The opposition of the government and the employer
to the wage earner's demands is generally motivated by the need to
keep a balanced budget, which is required, it should be added, by
the United States government, the distributor of Marshall Plan aid."[21]
Vignaux urged an immediate reclassification for civil servants and
expanded efforts to establish collective bargaining agreements, without which non-Communist trade unions would have little authority,
either with workers or the government. He further called on the ECA
to make its criticism of the French wage/price structure more ex-

plicit.[22] U.S. aid was intended to strengthen non-Communist unions, but it risked having the opposite effect. Any explicit connection between non-Communist unions and the U.S. government invariably brought the charge that the former were mere "stooges."[23] FO was particularly vulnerable to this charge. To the frustration of American officials, the same argument was not as effective against the CGT vis-à-vis the Soviet Union.[24]

Ultimately, the labor staff of the Marshall Plan was unable to resolve the fundamental policy contradictions. By 1952 American labor officials in France were explicitly critical of the effects of the Marshall Plan on European labor. They had also become critical about their own role in promoting it.[25] The chronology reveals not only disaffection with the program by the staff of Labor Information but also a gradual recognition of the hubris underlying the premise that "informational media" could effect substantial changes in the French economy and labor relations.

A final paradox of the involvement of U.S. Labor in France was that it reinforced French stereotypes and assumptions about the materialism and "utilitarianism" of American culture. The Labor Information program was not limited to workers. Millions of French citizens visited its exhibits, read its pamphlets, and saw its films. For these citizens productivity, rationalization, and consumerism animated the United States.

Productivity: the Key to Plenty

If anti-Communist stabilization was the political imperative of the Marshall Plan, productivity was its economic leitmotif. As Richard F. Kuisel explains, American economic planners viewed industrial productivity as a panacea.[26] For the economists of the ERP, productivity promised to increase the wages of workers, fight inflation, reduce the French trade deficit with the U.S., and insure that rearmament efforts did not result in a drop in workers' living standards.[27] In sum, the effects of increasing industrial productivity were socially as well as economically beneficial.

Why did productivity develop as a priority for ECA labor officials and what role did Labor Information hope to play in increasing it? Despite some tentative efforts with the beginning of the Monnet Plan in 1946, a dedicated program to increase French industrial productivity did not begin until 1948.[28] Structurally, the Marshall Plan increased productivity because it expedited reconstruction and the import of heavy equipment from the United States. However, the Marshall Plan also caused a renewed interest in the "politics of productivity" as it applied to Western Europe.[29] U.S. planners sought to apply the lessons of the New Deal to postwar European economies. That is, they sought to create a consensus for economic growth based on rising productivity, rising wages, and decreased class conflict while fighting restrictive industrial practices at the same time.

The consensus model proved to be difficult to adopt in France. The ECA drive for productivity faced outright opposition from the CGT. The non-Communist unions and the Conseil national du patronat français (CNPF) were unenthusiastic supporters initially, but the former would soon become explicitly critical of the drive to increase productivity. One FO official told American officials that productivity should be used to increase wages, not profits.[30] The same official stated that any productivity program must include a full employment policy, including retraining for technological unemployment.

The resistance of the French *patronat* proved to be more frustrating to American officials because they had the most to gain from increased productivity. Yet French employers proved surprisingly unwilling to adopt American productivity methods. Charles Edmundson, an official with the Industry Division of the OSR, related this encounter with a "wealthy industrialist who holds the reins in an important national industry":

> On a man to man basis, this industrialist talked frankly. Yes, he made more money than he needed to make. Yes, he might very well increase output, lower prices, boost sales and make still more money. But why rock the boat? Labor was restless and intractable, and the present setup gave him a club over the unions. His price umbrella enabled a bevy of marginal producers to remain in the field. These smaller companies could barely afford to keep their plants open and their workmen knew it. So they got by with paying low wages and set a pattern to justify low wages for the prosperous company. Why disturb a comfortable setup?[31]

This industrialist, like others, did not distinguish between Communist and non-Communist unions. Another high-ranking official related the story of an American technical expert who had discovered a way to double the output of a French mine in Morocco. The mine's owner, however, was not interested in increasing the output of the mine. "Why should I do that?" asked the owner, "I've got all the money I want. My wife has what she wants, my children are in the best schools. If my mistress wants pearls, I buy her pearls. I like partridge for lunch, but I can't have two partridges, I only have one stomach."[32] In Europe, it appeared, it was possible to be sated. Such attitudes were far from the consumer culture promoted by U.S. public diplomacy.

U.S. planners were certainly not optimistic about the prospects for a productivity drive given the opposition of the CGT on the one hand and the conservatism of the *patronat* on the other. Toward the end of 1950 the director of ECA Information in Washington, D.C., told officials, "There is universal agreement, so far as I know, that productivity drives, per se, are useless in France today."[33] He stated that a major task of any productivity program would be to "bring the French owners to their senses." As we will see, Labor Information played an important role in the productivity drive precisely because the ECA had identified the *mentalité* of French employers as one of the main obstacles.

The onset of the Korean War caused U.S. planners to renew their efforts to increase productivity. Only this, they argued, could ensure that the living standard of workers remained stable in the face of a general rearmament program that would invariably siphon funds from social programs. A further impetus for a renewed productivity effort was the failure of the Marshall Plan to grant workers benefits commensurate to those enjoyed by industry. A report from ECA headquarters in Washington declared that France was "both the most important and the weakest link" in Western Europe.[34] The report explained:

> A considerable part of French labor is living close to, or below, a minimum subsistence standard of living.... Some increase in the real standard of living for lower income groups is a sine qua non of any effective policy to combat Communism in its trade union stronghold in France.[35]

Increasing wages was deemed essential, but the report warned that growing military expenditures had increased inflationary pressures. A general wage increase risked touching off an inflationary wage-price spiral.[36] Instead, increases in French wages needed to be selective and directly related to heightened productivity.[37]

The formal call for a productivity information program came from the ECA in early 1951.[38] The program was understood to be an intensification of current efforts, and the administration placed the emphasis on expanding the audience of the program: "It is important to cover the *widest possible geographical area* and to *reach all classes* of the population since productivity must be the concern of *all*—labor, top management and the 'intellectuals.'"[39] In line with an expanded audience, the content of the program was to downplay technical information about productivity. The country missions were instructed to "emphasize the relationship between increased productivity and an improved standard of living for everybody."[40]

The information staff responded enthusiastically to the renewed call. The head of the Information Division of the OSR declared that "informational techniques can contribute directly to the solution of specific and priority economic objectives."[41] This was because "psychological problems" were a major impediment to achieving U.S. objectives.[42] France was the most important target for "information-propaganda." The ECA's chief information officer told other officials that Labor Information could achieve increased productivity by generating enthusiasm among workers and creating "a supporting atmosphere of demand on the part of the general public."[43]

Labor Information's own proposal demonstrated equal optimism in the efficacy of "information activity" to increase productivity. It hoped to be successful by generating public demand for productivity.[44] Such public interest might also create initiatives independent of the ECA program. Propaganda could also serve as "preventive medicine," influencing public attitudes and decreasing opposition to difficult decisions about wages and business practices. Finally, the United States would benefit because of the "continuous public association of our country with this 'good' idea."[45] There was, however, an important caveat in the Labor Information program: to be effective, the U.S. propaganda would have to taper off and be replaced by indigenous efforts.[46]

Some in Labor Information recognized that the ECA and Labor Information had set out upon a dangerous road. One official warned:

> It would be a major mistake for those of us in the information field to try to sell the completely false idea that we hold the key to a real productivity drive and that our role is more important than it actually is.... Imagine for a moment, if you will, the manner in which a gigantic propaganda drive could backfire—ideologically and otherwise—if we really turned on the heat, shouted to the housetops about the glories of productivity—and THEN NOTHING WORTHWILE RESULTED.[47]

On the Road with Labor Information

Nothing like Labor Information had ever been tried, and the staff learned by doing. The staff of Labor Information, although primarily union members, were unfamiliar with the political culture of French labor.[48] As one member of the staff later recalled, "We tried to apply American media methods. They were not only surprising to Europeans, but probably were often ineffectual. We were feeling our way all the time."[49]

The centerpiece of the Labor Information program was a traveling labor exhibit entitled *D'homme à homme* ("from man to man"). Most importantly, from the perspective of Labor Information, the exhibit displayed the active role of both American and non-Communist

French labor in the ERP. The exhibit also displayed sponsorship from FO, the CFTC, and the OEEC. It consisted of twenty panels that could be mounted on the three to four trucks used to transport them, or set up in an exhibit hall. The panels showed how productivity increased the standard of living of American workers. Several panels juxtaposed the number of labor hours required to purchase sundry objects (bread, shoes, a bicycle, an automobile) in the U.S. with the number required in France, Great Britain, and the Soviet Union.[50] Other panels depicted the amount of Marshall Plan aid France received and the mechanism behind the Marshall Plan. The exhibit did not possess its own traveling cinema, but when possible the exhibit made contact with a local United States Information Service (USIS) office that could supply a movie projector. The exhibit also carried a large supply of pamphlets and publications, including the Labor Information publication *Bulletin syndical* and the Mission France periodical *Rapports France—Etats-Unis*. Labor Information was unable to provide an American staff for the exhibit, so French nationals were hired instead. This provoked some of the first criticisms of the exhibit: the French expected to talk to Americans at an American exhibit.[51]

The exhibit began its tour of France in late 1950. The first showings were problematic. An early swing through northern coal mining regions was scrapped because it risked creating a counterpropaganda triumph for the CGT.[52] The exhibit boldly displayed a panel: "Wage gains are won by strong unions." An official quickly pointed out that the CGT was the strongest union in the mines and thus the ECA was giving credit to the CGT for wage gains. Another panel stated that through his hard work, the French miner had "freed Europe from dependence on U.S. coal." The official objected that this implied that the U.S. was taking advantage of France's weaknesses.[53]

The exhibit arrived in Grenoble in mid-October 1950.[54] The chief of the exhibit, J.R. Schmitt, attempted to contact the local representative of FO, but he ignored the presence of the exhibit. The representative of the CFTC responded in a similar manner. However, one group that did react enthusiastically to the exhibit was the employer's association, the local branch of the CNPF. Schmitt contacted the USIS office to arrange the cinema, and he also placed notices in two local newspapers. The exhibit opened the following day to a small audience. Fifty people attended a film showing of newsreels and about two hundred people, primarily pensioners, employers, and merchants, visited the exhibit proper.[55] The results for the next day were similar, and only twenty-five people attended the official ceremony and *vin d'honneur* in the evening.[56]

The exhibit's chief concluded that the exhibit "did not obtain the success it merited."[57] He cited several factors. First, the exhibit did not occur in conjunction with any local event. Another reason was the apathy of the non-Communist union officials. In the future, Schmitt reported, their participation would have to be secured well in advance of the exhibit's arrival. The report was rather circumspect about the low turnout of workers. According to Schmitt, it was because workers preferred to relax on the weekend and attending an exhibit devoted to labor would remind them too much of work.[58] But Schmitt made no explicit connection between the strength of the CGT, the support of the CNPF, and the absence of workers. Yet it was precisely in such towns as Grenoble where the PCF was strong that FO and the CFTC had to be most cautious about supporting the Marshall Plan. More than half of the organized workforce in the department of Issère belonged to the CGT and between 40 and 50 percent of the population voted for the PCF.[59] Finally, the exhibit was held in a hall used regularly by the CGT for meetings. Some workers saw this as a provocation.

The debacle in Grenoble provided valuable lessons and the next showing in Marseille was a well-managed affair. Schmitt contacted the local FO representative well in advance. The latter arranged an emplacement at a "neutral location, not associated with any political party or union."[60] Furthermore, posters were placed around the city and press releases were given to sympathetic newspapers before the exhibit's arrival. The USIS consul in Marseille also provided assistance by arranging an interview of Schmitt on French radio.

Over three thousand people visited the exhibit during its two-day presentation. According to Schmitt, "A festival attitude prevailed," and workers "could not hide their pride and joy" at being associated with the Marshall Plan.[61] More than three hundred people participated in the official opening of the exhibit, including the departmental secretaries of the CFTC and FO. The prefect of the department gave a speech exhorting the workers to increase their productivity. He also called upon owners to show more understanding of France's economic difficulties. Schmitt concluded the exhibit was a success: both the prefect and the unions were eager for its return.

What can be made of the "success" of the exhibit in Marseille? The numbers, about eighteen hundred people per day, are not extraordinary given Marseille's population, over a half-million at the time. However, this showing must also be measured against the strong support in Marseille for the CGT and the PCF. Yet unlike Grenoble, the non-Communist unions had achieved a small but loyal following.

Only a few months prior to the arrival of the exhibit, Marseille was the site of violent confrontations between the Seamens' and Dockers' International (a member of the World Federation of Trade Unions) and thugs hired by Irving Brown under the "Mediterranean Port Committee."[62] During the "Battle for the Docks" Brown's goons weakened the influence of the CGT on the dockers through violence and intimidation. The hired muscle temporarily gave FO some breathing room in Marseille, but the ploy eventually backfired: by 1952 the FO organization among the dockers was dissolved.[63] The exhibit arrived in Marseille at a time when the workforce was polarized, with the non-Communist unions clearly in the minority. The arrival of the exhibit provided an opportunity not to increase support for FO, but rather to consolidate and reassure the support it already possessed. Like other instances of American cultural interventions, the labor exhibit preached to the converted.

In 1951 the exhibit visited thirty-four cities, beginning the year in Dax and finishing in Dieppe eleven months later. Like the previous year, the exhibit achieved mixed results. In St. Etienne FO officials refused to assist with the exhibit because of the presence of the *patronat*. They claimed that associating themselves with the exhibit would damage their credibility among local workers.[64] The mayor of Castres refused to let the exhibit in to the town.[65] In Sète the crowd was hostile. A bundle of five thousand copies of *Bulletin syndical* was tossed off a dock.[66] As the exhibit approached Tarbes the mayor and an entourage of officials drove out to meet it. They begged Schmitt not to enter the city and they further implored him not use their names if he contacted any of the regional newspapers about publicity for the exhibit.[67]

Positive experiences for the exhibit included Périguex, where the exhibit reportedly attracted six thousand visitors in its three-day presentation.[69] The Secretary-General of FO, Robert Bothereau, reported that the exhibit was a great success in Tulle.[70] Almost three thousand people visited it in two days. At Carcassone (population thirty-eight thousand), some six thousand people attended the exhibit.[71] The head of Labor Information reported, "The exhibit is exciting comment, causing controversy, and making the French worker think" (positive thoughts? He did not speculate).[72]

One of the most important tasks of the labor exhibit was to disseminate printed material. Labor Information produced pamphlets and one serial publication, *Bulletin syndical*. They were meant to serve three purposes. First, *Bulletin syndical* and various pamphlets were intended to increase understanding of the Marshall Plan: its mechanism, the noble purposes behind it, and the benefits that accrued to

Table 4.1 Exhibits Program 1951: D'homme à homme[68]

January	Dax Mont de Marsan Agen Villeneuve Angoulême
February	Lognes Niort Chatellerault Poitiers Guéret
March	Tulle Brive Perpignan Narbonne
April	Sète Carcassone Decazeville Carmaux Mazamet
May	Tarbes Limoges Grenoble
June	
July	La Rochelle
August	Douarnenez Nantes Concarneau Brest
September	Morlaix Saint-Nazaire Saint-Malo Cherbourg Caen
October	Rouen Evreux Dieppe

France as a result of it. A second purpose was to promote productivity via two strategies. The first was to publish specific, technical information and articles. A second strategy was to generate enthusiasm for productivity by demonstrating its benefits, as illustrated, for example, by the ability of American workers to own an automobile and a refrigerator. *Bulletin syndical* printed stories of French Technical

Assistance visits to the United States, the enthusiasm of American labor for productivity, and statements by French labor leaders and officials in support of productivity. The *Bulletin* also carried articles that were explicitly anti-Communist. One article "exposed" Communist tactics in worker elections.[73] Finally, the printed material of Labor Information, especially *Bulletin syndical,* bolstered non-Communist labor by providing the financially strapped unions with a publication for their use.

At its peak, *Bulletin syndical* boasted seventy-five thousand subscribers.[74] In 1951, the *Bulletin* made the transition from a monthly to a weekly periodical. However, like other ECA publications, this figure needs qualification. The periodical was free, and it is not clear that all the "subscribers" wanted it. In fact, it is difficult to determine the number of individual subscribers because the majority of subscriptions appear to have come from bulk orders. The FO secretary in the Nord, for example, received five thousand copies each month for distribution to sections in the department.[75]

Nevertheless, *Bulletin syndical* did possess an impressive distribution. Labor Information targeted the so-called "three fortresses" of communism, loose groupings of thirty-three departments where the PCF had received more than 30 percent of the vote in 1951.[76] In Paris, one copy of *Bulletin syndical* existed for every 330 people. In the Nord, the ratio was even greater, 1:160. Overall, the ratio for the thirty-three departments of the "fortresses" was 1:450. However impressive these figures were, they represented sheer weight of numbers, not what workers actually thought of the publication.

André Drom, a French national working for Labor Information, advised that the *Bulletin* was "unworthy of a conscientious worker."[77] The problem, according to Drom, was that the average worker was bombarded with publications from close to a dozen sources. *Bulletin syndical* failed to attract workers because the articles were "desultory." In addition, the composition was "far from satisfactory" and misprints were common. It was not rare to see the "remarkable blunders" of the *Bulletin* pasted on the walls of French newspaper editing rooms.[78]

Jacques Masson-Forestier, another French national on the ECA payroll, recommended that the ECA label be removed from the *Bulletin syndical* because that in itself stopped workers from reading it.[79] This suggestion was rejected, but in 1951 the *Bulletin* added the FO label when its printing moved to an FO shop.[80] Another factor that may have cooled workers' enthusiasm for the *Bulletin syndical* was the wholehearted support accorded to it by the French *patronat.* The director of Labor Information stated that employers were eager to distribute it to workers because they knew "that the *Bulletin syndical* is waging battle against the Communist labor publications."[81] Masson-Forestier concluded that the *Bulletin* used the subjunctive tense too often: "The use of [it] is extremely good in French, when it is used in a classical text, but when used in a labor text made for labor people it sounds absolutely ridiculous, and in some cases a provocation."[82] The staff dismissed this last criticism as uncalled for and "entirely exaggerated." "It is an implied insult to labor people," stated one American, "to say that they do not understand, or resent good grammar."[83]

More critical than grammar questions was the denunciation, albeit privately, of *Bulletin syndical* by the CFTC. The move to the FO print shop had caused resentment in the CFTC. Both trade unions regarded the *Bulletin* as a useful, if flawed, publication.[84] It was free, but equally important, Mission France ensured it achieved a wide distribution. However, at the policy level the clear preference of the United States was for FO. This preference was manifest in the content of *Bulletin syndical* even before the move to the FO print shop. The secretary-general of the CFTC complained to Labor Information in 1951. He said that he had read the latest issues with "genuine stupefaction."[85] He wanted to know why the *Bulletin* was merely a "propaganda organ" for FO and furthermore, should he consider it as opposed to the principles of Christian syndicalism.

In 1952 an effort was made to determine the number of individual subscribers to *Bulletin syndical.*[86] The staff inserted a postage-paid questionnaire in three consecutive issues asking for editorial feedback. The total print run for the period was 233,000. The office received only 254 responses, barely a tenth of 1 percent. A few months later Labor Information sent letters to 3,006 individual subscribers. The readers were simply asked: "Do you still want to receive *Bulletin syndical*?" Two hundred and seventy three individuals responded, but only 227 responded positively.[87] In early 1953 *Bulletin syndical* ceased publication. The last issue explained: "During the past year the regular information services of the free trade union movement have increased to the extent that we now feel no useful purpose would be served by the continuation of the *Bulletin syndical.*"[88]

This brief history of *Bulletin syndical* demonstrates that it encountered many of the same problems that all such endeavors met in France. On the one hand, the American staff was unfamiliar with the political culture of French syndicalism. On the other, the rank and file of French labor, Communist and otherwise, were quite critical of the Marshall Plan and productivity. To those who did read *Bulletin syndical,* FO militants, officials, and employers, it provided useful information about trade unionism in the United States and Marshall Plan projects in France. Any broader expectations were wholly unrealistic.

Bulletin syndical was but one publication distributed by Labor Information. There were several others. The most common form was the pamphlet. Labor Information distributed general pamphlets such as *A B C's du Plan Marshall,* as well as ones that specifically targeted French labor. Two such pamphlets were *Joe Smith, travailleur améri-cain* ("Joe Smith, American worker") and *L'Homme au cigare entre les dents* ("The man with the cigar between his teeth").

"Joe Smith" was a forty-eight page pamphlet that sought to in-form French workers about the lives of American workers.[89] The pamphlet explained that American workers enjoyed material abun-dance because of strong unions and high productivity. Numerous photographs showed American workers in pristine factories, or re-turning from work in an automobile to a house with a garden. The pamphlet also sought to counter a common French stereotype about the United States: that its wealth, and consequently the high stan-dard of living enjoyed by Joe Smith, was the result of fortuitous nat-ural resources. According to the pamphlet, this was not the case; rather it was the "constant growth of productivity" which lowered costs and raised the standard of living. The other reason for Joe Smith's comfort was the influence of American unions on national politics, suggesting that better cooperation between French unions and government would yield similar results.

"The man with the cigar" used a different approach. Two French writers for the satirical *Canard Enchaîné* wrote and designed the pamphlet, which was evidently intended as a satire. The pamphlet depicted American children smoking cigars in imitation of an Amer-ican industrialist. The industrialist, the man with the cigar between his teeth, worked hard to ensure the success of the Marshall Plan, without which France would be reduced to horse-buggies for trans-portation.[90] Other drawings provided basic information about the Marshall Plan.

Mission France was enthusiastic about the pamphlet when it ap-peared in 1950.[91] It increased the original print run of one and a half million by one hundred thousand.[92] This was a misjudgment. The French reaction was so negative that the pamphlet was pulled from circulation a year later. Referring specifically to *Joe Smith, travailleur américain* and *L'Homme,* one French staff member of Labor Informa-tion stated: "The infantile nature of such propaganda makes it impos-sible for us even to criticize it. The techniques used for the realization of these pamphlets are matched only by those used by German pro-paganda during the last war."[93] FO officials thought the pamphlet was good only for children; they were not disposed to distribute it in large numbers.[94] Mission France made vain efforts to recover the pamphlets already distributed.[95]

In 1951 the renewed productivity drive featured several other efforts at labor promotion. Labor Information tried to take advantage of the Voice of America (VOA). The proposed radio program stated: "The information policy of the ECA is now committed to a more aggressive information program in Europe, i.e., what can be called 'political warfare.'"[96] Productivity did not subsume all other material on VOA, but its presence increased dramatically. VOA featured at least one major productivity story each week.[97] American officials made declarations in support of productivity, and the issue was regularly included in USIS press releases. Some official statements emphasized how workers benefited from increased productivity.[98] A statement by William Joyce, the assistant director of the ECA, was typical. In September 1951 he traveled to Paris to meet with the OEEC to discuss productivity. According to Joyce, increased productivity needed to impart higher wages, greater profits, and lower prices.[99] The previous March Barry Bingham, the head of the French Mission, had told a meeting of the French Regional Press Association that the wage/price structure in France was inequitable to workers.[100] Such statements provided much needed high-level public support for French labor. The director of Labor Information, Harry Martin, welcomed such comments:

> For the sake of ECA's place in history ... we ought to be shouting from the house tops in Europe that we do know about the worker's plight, we do feel that something should be done about it, and we do try to persuade the powers-that-be as to their responsibilities in this field. That, it seems to me, is the very least that we can do.[101]

Another expression of the renewed productivity drive was the Train of Europe. This exhibit was not, however, the creation of Labor Information but rather the ECA Information Division in Washington and the Office of the Special Representative.[102] As such it touched on themes like European unification often neglected by Mission France. The train consisted of seven cars, each devoted to a theme of the Marshall Plan.[103] Every participating country was represented to some extent, usually by displaying the amount of aid it received from the U.S. The last car of the train addressed productivity exclusively. After its inauguration in Paris the train traveled to every Marshall Plan country save Ireland. During its two-week stay in Paris the train had just over two hundred thousand visitors.[104] This impressive attendance was the result of good weather as well as location: the train was located on the esplanade in front of Les Invalides.

Shortly after its inauguration, an official from Labor Information visited the train. He was horrified by what he saw. Reporting to his chief, he declared: "This bloody thing is a fiasco!"[105] The official catalogued a list of errors: the mere presentation of the dollar amount of aid did not indicate the nature of the Marshall Plan's benefits to France; throughout the rolling exhibit trade union material was scarce and the car devoted to productivity contained no trade union content at all. This last car was the most disturbing for the official. It displayed a series of cartoon panels telling the story of productivity. "There was one really fantastic touch," reported the official, "One panel showed a worker knocking himself out for dear old productivity, while the next one, captioned 'Everybody benefits from productivity,' showed a wealthy family, complete with servant, eating a lush meal." Likewise, the remaining panels showed the "benefits flowing to the upper middle class from increased productivity." The official concluded: "If the commies had designed this particular sequence they couldn't have done a better job."

A commentator for the newspaper *Ouest-Matin* visited the train just before it crossed into Germany. "I have been to see the famous exhibit train," he declared,

> The noisy American type propaganda which had heralded its passage for several days in advance entitled me to believe that I would meet a crowd of farmers and 'consumers' who had come there to obtain valuable advice. Instead I only met a few scattered visitors. Poor American leaders ... in order to persuade us of their kindness, they send us an exhibit train full of nice pictures accompanied by figures, and the result: nobody is interested. What a want of gratitude![106]

The reporter entered the car devoted to agriculture and was happy to find a French wine exhibitor offering a Pinot from Charentes: "An excellent wine, such was the unanimous opinion." But the visitors left the car when the exhibitor asked them to purchase a dozen bottles ("You are sure to need a few bottles for Christmas") for slightly more than four thousand francs. "Alas," concluded the reporter, "the lovely Pinot from Charentes will not appear on the tables of the workers." The train left France, never to return.[107]

A few blocks away from the inauguration of the Train of Europe, the French Mission had a productivity exhibit at the annual Paris automobile show on the Champs Elysées. The show featured the latest models from French, European, and American automobile manufacturers.[108] The Mission estimated that one hundred thousand people visited the productivity exhibit on their way in to the automobile show.[109] A specialist critiqued the exhibit at the behest of American officials. According to the specialist, the exhibit lacked the aesthetic appeal that was important to a French audience. She explained,

> Having started off already on the wrong foot by creating an atmosphere which for a Frenchman is somewhat bizarre [the exhibit was primarily yellow], the exhibit proceeds to the fatal mistake of failing to state the one thing which is of real interest to the average person: what this increased productivity has meant to them personally.[110]

She commended the Americans for avoiding the claim that the increased productivity meant that automobiles had become more accessible to the majority of the French populace.[111] However, it was important to show that the average person received some benefit from the decrease in production costs. She suggested that the Americans argue that increased productivity in the automobile industry made a wider variety of produce available and less expensive as a result of cheaper truck and bus transports.

The American propaganda effort received a boost from the film *Productivity, Key to Plenty.* The film made its debut in February 1951 at the Normandy Theater on the Champs Elysées.[112] Over two thousand people crowded the eighteen hundred seat Normandy to watch four films: *Productivity, Key to Plenty; Ideas at Work; High Induction Frequency Heating; The Fork Lift Truck.* The films were presented under the auspices of the French Machine Tool Association. *Productivity* was the main feature.

The film was a veritable siren song of consumerism. Dubbed in French (the film was shown throughout Europe in various dubbed versions), the film had two primary components. The first was an ostentatious display of middle-class America: automobiles, kitchen appliances, houses with picket fences, and wide paved streets. The narrator intoned, "In such a street we would be happy to be able to own a small house, or even rent one ... a bungalow with a garden where week-ends would be calm and peaceful, where we could relax and rest after work."[113] Into this image of bourgeois tranquility came a gleaming automobile. It pulled into a paved driveway, in front of a garage: "What is so extraordinary about having an automobile?" asked the narrator, "Yet, except when it is actually an instrument of work, it still remains a luxury for us." The camera switched to the interior of the house, a well-lit kitchen with shiny appliances reflecting the light, formica countertops, and a garbage disposal, refrigerator, and electric blender. "What housewife has not dreamed of a kitchen like this one?" asked the narrator. Just then, at the very moment when some of the audience may have been breaking free of the spell, others with eyes still wide with wonder, came the second component, a gentle reassurance:

> We must not deceive ourselves. One can remain attached to moral val-
> ues which give a precise meaning to existence without neglecting the
> material factors which contribute to the good things in life. The social
> conditions of life can be improved without impairing these moral values.

Quite simply, luxury need not entail either guilt or Americanization. It was possible to have all these things and remain French. And yet some change was inevitable to achieve such bounty: "Goods and material riches within the reach of every individual—this is not something which happens by itself." Indeed, it happened, the audience was in-formed, only in "free societies" where workers and unions endorsed productivity. *Productivity, Key to Plenty* continued to play to full houses on the Champs-Elysées and elsewhere. While the film illus-trated the French fascination with American consumerism, it also demonstrated that such propaganda was far more acceptable to a general audience than it was to labor. Yet, in depicting America's "good life" as a middle-class utopia of kitchen appliances, American prop-aganda reinforced French assumptions about American materialism.

The experience of Labor Information with other film projects was altogether different than that with *Key to Plenty.* Any attempt to reach workers with American films was an uphill battle. The CGT had estab-lished a *ciné-club* in every factory it could. These clubs showed com-munist films such as *Give us This Day* whose creator, Edward Dmytryk, had been persecuted by the House Un-American Activities Commit-tee. Far more popular, however, were self-critical American films such as *Citizen Kane* and *Grapes of Wrath.*[114] According to the staff of Labor Information these films had "done much to establish the myth of cap-italist, lynch-happy, race-mad America in the French mind."[115] The ECA considered organizing its own anti-Communist *ciné-clubs,* but for the moment the presence of U.S. propaganda films was limited to six projectors shared by FO and the CFTC.[116] The U.S. supplemented these meager resources with film showings by the USIS. Even when the material resources were available, there existed a shortage of acceptable films.[117] Yet if CGT members were unreachable by such propaganda—most simply walked out on ECA sponsored films—the non-Communist unions were also critical of American films.

In 1950 the American embassy in Paris rejected a suggestion from the ECA Washington office that "Walt Disney type films" be created to educate the French about the "Negro question," the construction of skyscrapers, Thanksgiving, U.S. labor unions, Johnny Appleseed, Paul Bunyan, Daniel Boone, and other "Indian and cowboy heroes." However popular Walt Disney films were in France, the embassy pointed out, cartoons about such issues as race relations and labor unions might create the appearance of talking down to the French.[118]

Several Marshall Plan documentaries dubbed in French existed, but Labor Information found these to be unsuitable because in most instances they did not demonstrate any benefit for labor as a result of Marshall aid.[119] Some were of manifestly poor quality. The ECA canceled a contract with Tadie-Cinema after the latter produced a documentary on the ERP-restored French liner *La Liberté*. According to American officials, the film suffered from droning music, bad camera shots, and poor editing.[120]

The film *With These Hands* produced by the International Ladies Garment Workers Union was an hit among U.S. labor unions, but its adaptation to France proved problematic. The film celebrated the formation of the ILGWU and presented a moving story about the struggle of immigrant labor to organize. Checking the influence of Communists was a key theme. An initial screening to French unionists was disappointing. The anti-Communist sequences, in particular, struck the French as "a typical Hitler approach" to propaganda.[121]

In early 1952 Labor Information completed a film specifically for a French audience. It was called *Jour de Peine* and told the story of a strike at a large factory.[122] The film portrayed the organization of an FO section in a factory and a one-day strike. The aim was to show that the FO was as militant as the CGT. An initial screening of the film to FO officials did not go well. They protested that the film made no reference to the key problem of the union: its coexistence with the CGT.[123] One union official from Renault complained that the reasons for the strike were not clearly given and thus the film unintentionally emphasized the CGT doctrine of striking for any reason or none at all. Others rejected the ending of the film, which showed the resolution of the strike, because no mention was made of the general assembly of workers. That is, the strike resolved itself rather than being resolved by a vote of the workers to return to work. The leader of FO told the Americans that the film needed to be altered to take into account these criticisms as quickly as possible because there were no other acceptable films available.[124] Another FO leader stated that it would be better "to wait months than use it in its present form."

Labor Information encountered similar problems with a film devoted to the fledgling foundry program. The foundry program consisted of nine plants selected by the National Productivity Committee (Comité national de la productivité) for productivity incentives.[125] For Labor Information, these plants represented "object lessons" through which productivity could effectively be "sold" to ERP countries.[126] A film about the program was finished in 1952. Like other Labor Information film projects, this one never made it past the screening audience.[127] FO officials were disappointed to see that the film neglected to show workers as "equal partners" with the patrons at the pilot plants. They objected to the paternal implications of numerous scenes that showed the plant manager handing out prizes to productive workers.[128] Labor Information began to correct these mistakes, but the project was cancelled when FO pulled out of the program and it collapsed.[129]

One of the ironies of the productivity drive was that French productivity increased throughout these years (and well beyond) despite the negative reception of the U.S. programs that sought to promote it. Gains in productivity were not dependent on changes in French labor relations.[130] Yet productivity was one area in which the French government was willing to cooperate with the ECA on publicity. Both the Comité national de la productivité (CNP) and the Association française pour l'accroisement de la productivité conducted publicity in favor of the productivity drive. Elgozy coordinated a series of broadcasts on French radio.[131] In addition, the CNP produced a traveling exhibit that showed how handtools increased productivity.[132]

However, official French enthusiasm for American labor publicity was also tempered. American forays into French colonial possessions provoked a number of high-level exchanges between French and American officials. Ken Douty visited Tunis in March 1950. The purpose of the visit was to discuss the Marshall Plan with unions there and to assess its impact on their standard of living. Local French officials expressed surprise at the visit because the Marshall Plan was an economic policy, but Douty assured them that its "social goals" were just as important.[133] After spending some time in Tunis, Douty expressed several concerns to his hosts. Most importantly, he thought that the standard of living for workers was quite poor. He was also disappointed that French unions (he met with the CFTC and FO) in Tunis were unaware of the Marshall Plan's role in aiding French recovery. Douty also spent a lot of time speaking with CFTC and FO leaders about the strength of communism in Tunisia. The French administrator complained to Robert Schuman that "foreign agents" could conduct "purely political missions" under the guise of the ECA.[134]

An ECA photographer caused a scandal on a visit to Algeria when she repeatedly and "violently" criticized French colonial policies.[135] French foreign affairs officials concluded that American policies toward the colonies suffered from an "internal contradiction."[136] It promised economic growth without freedom. Communist propaganda, on the other hand, promised colonial subjects their freedom in addition to improved standards of living. The French could not refuse U.S. visits to the colonies—Article VIII ensured access—but they were able to reduce the breadth and depth of these visits, and they also rejected U.S. requests for further cooperation in this area.

The Role of Technical Assistance Visits

As Richard F. Kuisel demonstrates, the Technical Assistance visits were an important component of the Marshall Plan in general and the productivity drive in particular.[137] By 1953, almost three thousand French citizens had visited the United States as part of the program.[138] However, traffic was not only one way from France to the U.S. Several teams of American labor leaders visited France. Labor Information attempted to exploit both of these kinds of visits for their propaganda value.

Despite the technical knowledge gained from these visits, they also reinforced French stereotypes of America and American stereotypes of France. The visits of Americans to France, in particular, revealed the limits of understanding embodied in the Manichean world-view of American anti-Communists. One of the earliest transatlantic technical assistance visits to France occurred during the summer of 1950. J. William Belanger, president of the Massachusetts CIO industrial council, Harold Gibbons, secretary-treasurer of Local 688 (St. Louis) of the International Brotherhood of Teamsters, and Carmen Lucia, vice president of the South Eastern Region of the United Hatters International Union spent six weeks touring France.[139] The team visited Paris, Lille, Tourcoing, Roubaix, Lyon, St. Malo, St. Etienne, and Marseille.

Toward the end of their visit the three visited an FO labor education program in St. Malo and met with union representatives from England and France.[140] Gibbons delivered a terse speech detailing what, in the eyes of the three, was wrong with French labor. According to Gibbons, French labor was too idealistic and philosophical. FO was simply not militant enough. Gibbons stated that French workers refused to take militancy seriously. The French workers objected that Gibbons did not understand the reactionary nature of French employers. Gibbons took strong exception to this. He told the audience he was "impatient" with the French for saying that everything in France was "complicated and complex." He told the workers they were "cheating themselves" by not going after higher wages through militant action. Finally, Gibbons told the assembled workers that French labor refused to recognize their weaknesses: low membership and a reluctance to pay union dues.[141] After Gibbons finished his harangue a French unionist told him that the French situation was "too deep" for an American labor leader to come up with solutions in five weeks.[142]

There was an abundance of militancy in French labor, clearly, but Gibbons did not speak with any members of the CGT.[143] To the assembled FO unionists, talk of militancy coming from an American may have provoked confusion and frustration. It was, after all, American officials who had worked hard from 1947 to 1949 to prevent FO members from striking with the CGT on such common issues as wage increases. It was also Americans who had urged FO workers to adopt the "idealistic" approach of seeking concessions from the *patronat* as an alternative to militant action. Most surprising, however, may have been the fact that Gibbons based his call for militancy on the failure of the Marshall Plan to provide benefits to French workers.[144]

The trip of another labor specialist, Harry Turtledove, revealed both French misconceptions of the Marshall Plan and the paradoxes of Labor Information propaganda. Turtledove spent three weeks in Marseille with FO and management. He did not spend any time with the CFTC because their strength was "negligible."[145] As for the CGT, Turtledove reported: "I carefully avoided them and was more circumspect in my contacts than I usually am."[146] He claimed this was necessary because Marseille Communists claimed there were several U.S. spies in the area and he was fearful that his presence would "prove" these allegations.

Turtledove was taken aback by the lack of knowledge most workers and managers possessed about the Marshall Plan. "A general proposition," he reported, "is that the average worker seems to have few thoughts about the Marshall Plan and fewer accurate ideas."[147] Managers invariably told him his questions about the use of counterpart funds could be better answered in Paris. He visited one shipyard that, according to Mission France, received four million dollars in counterpart. The assistant chief, however, professed no knowledge of the counterpart funds. Turtledove was incredulous:

> When the assistant chief of a four thousand man shipyard doesn't know whether or not they have received four million dollars from the Marshall Plan in a single year, I do not consider it a particularly remarkable fact that most of his workers don't know it either.[148]

Turtledove's analysis of the labor situation in Marseille was prescient. He stated that FO was not gaining members at the rate at which the CGT was losing them. Nevertheless, the decline of the CGT in membership was, he stated, not necessarily indicative of a decline in influence. The CGT made some unpopular political moves, but when it came to wage demands it could always count on support from union members and nonmembers alike. According to Turtledove, the CGT could count on the support of nonmembers for strikes protesting wages "regardless of what [nonmembers] may think of the CGT."[149] "Free labor" was powerless. It did not have the resources to back a strike, nor did it want to risk a strike for fear of co-optation by the CGT. It was, pointed out Turtledove, caught between "the Commies who want strikes and trouble; the patrons, who want the eighteenth-century to go on forever; and the government, who seem to want nothing so much as their own self-perpetuation."[150]

On a number of occasions FO workers and leaders expressed their criticism of the Marshall Plan. They stated they were grateful for the sacrifice American workers made to provide the counterpart funds (Turtledove took such expressions as a positive sign of Labor Information work), but they wanted to know why the U.S. could not prevent the *patronat* from stealing Marshall Plan benefits. Turtledove stated, somewhat resentfully, "Once again I was confronted with the difficulty of telling men earning fourteen thousand francs a month (with butter at seven-hundred and fifty francs a kilo) how much the Marshall Plan had done for France."[151]

Labor Information propaganda was thus a double-edged sword. It increased awareness of the Marshall Plan, especially with workers in non-Communist unions. Yet once these workers were better informed they often used their new knowledge to criticize the Plan for benefiting industrialists at the expense of workers. They thus arrived at the CGT criticisms of the Marshall Plan. Turtledove was clearly frustrated by the cycle:

> You cannot have it both ways: if it is the Marshall Plan that is to be given the credit for France's recovery, particularly its rise in production, then it must also be the Marshall Plan that must bear responsibility for the increasing maldistribution of income and wealth that has accompanied recovery.[152]

Rather than "preaching that Marshall Plan was all things to all men," Labor Information should make it clear that the French government decided where the money went.

Finally, according to Turtledove, the Labor Information program and the anti-Communist measures of the French government, combined with CGT miscalculations, had resulted in a drop in CGT membership. However, because the workers who left the CGT were joining neither FO nor the CFTC, Turtledove concluded that these workers "no longer wanted any truck with any more unions." The relative decline of the CGT was, therefore, a hollow victory. The role of the Marshall Plan was, at least ostensibly, to promote the growth of "free" labor unions, not to destroy organized labor in general. Yet far from promoting growth, Labor Information propaganda contributed to the apathy: "Distributing five hundred thousand pamphlets is meaningless unless someone reads them and understands them and *believes* them." Turtledove concluded that the billions of dollars comprising the Marshall Plan would be better spent in Oregon instead of France: "Let *us* have a Roman holiday before the debacle."[153]

What was the source of Turtledove's pessimism? One explanation is that his perspective, limited to non-Communist labor, reflected only the weaknesses and pessimism of a labor movement without purpose, a group that perceived themselves as betrayed by the promise of U.S aid. But there was an alternative to Turtledove's resignation. A rare trip by a freelance photographer to CGT paper mills provided a glimpse into a labor movement with a different perspective.

Georges Cony, a French-born American national, made the trip for the socialist newspaper *Le Populaire*. Cony went to Rouen to visit a large paper mill. He greeted the plant manager and asked to speak to the FO representative, a worker named Alvarez. He wanted permission to take photographs, but also to find out what they thought of the Marshall Plan and French reconstruction. The manager's reply startled Cony:

> Alvarez represents fifty-five workers in my plant. I don't think he is qualified to give the workers' point of view of the problems you are interested in; I would like you rather to talk to Lemoine, the CGT delegate. He is an intelligent guy, knows the problems well. I think he is more qualified, representing eleven hundred workers in my factory, to give you the workers' opinion than a man who represents fifty-five men.[154]

Cony hesitated, but then agreed to meet the CGT representative. He decided to be honest. He told Lemoine that he was working on pictures for a socialist newspaper, but they would also appear in U.S. publications for the ECA. Cony wanted to know how Lemoine felt about productivity. The CGT leader told Cony that the workers in the plant were fortunate to have a production bonus: "The production bonus means that workers are more interested in the work they are engaged in and in management's problems."[155] The CGT workers pressured management to maintain up-to-date machinery. Lemoine proudly showed Cony a new steambarker from the United States. "In this plant," he told Cony, "management is alert to get machinery up to date, work is easy from one end to the other."[156]

Cony then traveled to another paper plant in Navarre. Heartened by his previous encounter with the CGT, he asked the plant manager if he could speak with the CGT and the FO representatives. The former represented 608 workers, the latter 162 (which Cony considered to be unusually large).[157] By coincidence both representatives arrived to meet with Cony at the same time. After a long and "frank" conversation with the two Cony found that they "were in complete agreement on practically all problems."[158] They both favored lowering the workweek from fifty-two to forty hours and a one hundred franc hourly minimum wage. When Cony asked how the two unions could co-exist without problems, the representatives indicated their common interests. "Troubles start between federations on the national scale," replied Lebrun, the CGT representative. Before Cony left the plant Lebrun thanked him for sharing information about the Marshall Plan.

These conversations made a deep impression on the journalist. In his report he called for a complete reevaluation of the relationship between Labor Information and the CGT. "I am glad," he wrote, "that I was given the opportunity by this office to go there. It helped me to revise my judgments on many problems."[159] His most important change of heart was his attitude toward Technical Assistance (TA). He recommended that henceforth CGT members be included in TA visits to the United States.[160] He reminded the Labor Information staff that not all CGT members were Communists. He had talked with several CGT men who disapproved of the CGT's politics. When he asked one of them why he didn't leave, the worker replied: "The CGT is the first union of France. The CGT is far more active than other unions. The CFTC is no more independent—sold to the Church, and FO is worth nothing, zero added to zero."[161] Cony had learned more about French labor and its view of the Marshall Plan in the four days he spent talking with the CGT members in the paper mills of Rouen than he had in the previous year. He urged that more such meetings take place: "It is among those who do not read *Rapports, Reader's Digest,* or *Bulletin Syndical* that our propaganda should be done."

Finally, the trip had caused Cony to change his perception of the CGT. All too often, he pointed out, talking with FO members only confirmed the American belief that the CGT members were "monstrous animals with tortuous ways and means." Cony criticized Turtledove for not even making the effort to talk with the CGT, although Cony admitted that most Americans lacked the "tact and diplomacy" to make such contacts, in addition to language ability. Nevertheless, he was willing to accompany small teams of Americans in the future. As long as the teams were labeled "U.S. labor" and not "ECA" they would be favorably received by the CGT.[162] In short, more visits were needed that developed personal ties between workers. On a radio broadcast in 1949 the CFTC had, in fact, criticized the "tourist" visits of American labor officials; it suggested that labor officials stay with the families of French workers.[163]

Although Cony was worried that his remarks were "too revolutionary," the ECA reaction to Turtledove's report contained many of the same suggestions. However, the ECA rejected outright any suggestion of increased contact with the CGT. Jean Monnet and other French officials had also sought to include CGT members in productivity missions to the United States and they were frustrated by the categorical exclusion.[164] For the Labor staff of ECA Washington, the reports of Cony and Turtledove highlighted the need to increase direct U.S. labor contacts with FO.[165] The staff acknowledged that ECA affiliation was a possible check to effective labor relations in France. They suggested that confidential funds be used to send American workers and consultants to France, with counterpart funds used to cover local expenses; there would be no indication of affiliation with the ECA.[166]

This discussion resulted in Turtledove's proposal for "Operation Bootstrap."[167] The plan called for an extensive program of U.S. labor visits to France. "Operation Bootstrap" was important not for what it accomplished—it was never fully implemented—but because its premises illustrated the extent of U.S. labor pessimism. According to Turtledove, the negative anticommunism of the United States had not been able to promote a positive unionism. Concomitant with the decline of organized labor in France, the Fourth Republic itself no longer enjoyed widespread support or legitimacy:

> There is no political *dynamism* to be found in non-Communist labor. Over all, half the cause and half the result lies in the spiritual paralysis that is the most disturbing aspect of France today.... Politically, the only *dynamism* comes from the extremes of both right and left. If the danger of communism has decreased, thanks in considerable measure to the Marshall Plan, the danger of neo-Fascism, of a streamlined Vichy or a virtual dictatorship based on the necessity for "strong government" is mounting.[168]

The Fourth Republic was a "sick patient." For Turtledove, a "virile free trade union movement" would provide the greatest source of economic and political stability. In the absence of these conditions what could the United States expect? Had Turtledove followed the logic of his analysis to its conclusion the resulting sorites would have looked something like this:

> Democratic stability is the basis for the survival of the Fourth Republic
>
> Non-Communist organized labor is the basis for democratic stability

<u>American interventions in France weaken non-Communist organized labor</u>

American interventions in France weaken the basis for the survival of the Fourth Republic[169]

The problem with U.S. labor visits and initiatives such as "Operation Bootstrap" was twofold. First, and most obviously, the majority of American trade unionists who visited France were disappointed not only because the Marshall Plan had failed to help workers in a material sense, but also because it had failed to decrease the strength of the CGT. In addition, the negative conclusions of the American officials were often publicized, providing the PCF with extraordinary samples for counterpropaganda. In August 1950 John W. Livingston, the vice president of the UAW, visited Europe. He told a gathering of union officials and reporters: "The Marshall Plan is a miserable failure as far as Europe's common man is concerned. European workers have been underpaid while industrialists, benefiting from ECA funds, reap huge profits."[170] Livingston's statement was publicized not only in *L'Humanité,* but also in other major French dailies.[171]

Labor visits to France were just one measure aimed at strengthening "free" labor. French visits to America were also intended to further the same goal with the additional expectation that such visits would help increase productivity in France. According to American officials these visits would "produce and foster this 'virus' of productivity."[172] Other authors have examined the French experience of these visits.[173] My goal is to show how Labor Information used these visits as propaganda opportunities, and the difficulties that arose as a result. These visits represented a continued belief in the efficacy of "information techniques" to accomplish specific goals: the adoption of techniques and management models intended to increase productivity.

The first French team arrived in late 1949. The seventeen members were drawn from the electrical equipment industry and included members of the CGC, CFTC, and FO.[174] The team attended a three-week seminar on industrial relations in Philadelphia. They saw motion pictures, attended lectures, and talked with union officials and managers. In Philadelphia the ECA labor advisors addressed the group. Bert M. Jewell presented a lecture entitled: "The Meaning of Productivity in a Technological Nation." He assured the French that "there is nothing that the human hand can perform that cannot be better performed by a machine."[175] Jewell recognized that the workers feared increased mechanization would cost jobs. He sought to assuage this fear: "The impact of the machine on workers' jobs is controllable or reducible by management and union cooperation." Such assurances may have seemed rather hollow given the French context.

In May 1950, a French public works and road construction team arrived. In Maryland they spent the day on the State yacht, *Potomac,* with Governor William Preston Lane.[176] The ECA newsletter reported that the governor praised the long-standing friendship between France and the United States. According to the newsletter, the leader of the French team "responded for the group—with tears in his eyes."

Max Rolland, a French national working for Labor Information, accompanied many of the French teams on their tours of the United States as a translator and liaison. His reports gave a very different perspective on the French experience. After a visit to Detroit, Rolland wrote the assistant director of Labor Information to criticize the trips. He stated that for the labor representatives on the teams the trips were "big disappointments."[177] The teams visited very few union shops, and the few meetings with union officials that did occur were with "big shots," not rank-and-file members. American union leaders received the French formally, not as union brothers.

In Detroit a French team was unable to meet with Walter Reuther. An assistant of Reuther told the team that collaboration on productivity between employers and employees in the automobile industry was "all bunk."[178] Rolland stated that such public relations blunders were all too common. They only confirmed the general impression of the French visitors that "very often productivity is very high when there is no union." He continued: "We have not seen any instance of a union taking an active part in promoting high productivity."[179] To add insult to injury, the French managers on the team were equally unimpressed. Or rather, they were impressed by the anti-labor enthusiasm of American management: "They are discovering the U.S. through the eyes of managers who want to bust the unions or enslave them." French managers recognized the productivity of American plants, but concluded it resulted from ruthless action by management and the modernization that occurred during the Second World War.[180] American officials concluded that Rolland overstated the negative results of the technical-assistance visits, but any mistakes made were clearly the fault of Jewell and Golden and not indicative of more fundamental issues.[181]

In France, Labor Information sought the widest possible circulation for the stories of the Technical Assistance teams. Labor Information provided short press releases about the departure, composition, and return of French teams. These received relatively wide circulation in both the Parisian and regional press.[182] However, far more important were the stories written by French reporters or French members of Technical Assistance teams.

Writing in *Le Monde,* André Blanchet provided what was perhaps the most positive presentation of a French Technical Assistance team.[183] In posing the question of productivity, Blanchet gently criticized U.S. propaganda: "The idea of acting on French productivity through the means of mass-produced brochures and press campaigns would seem idealistic."[184] The Technical Assistance visits marked a more intelligent and rational approach at reaching the "specialists," on the one hand, but also for demonstrating the results of productivity to French workers. These visits gave French workers an opportunity to see neighborhoods where it was easier to count the houses without TV antennas than those with them.[185] American factories were extraordinary not only for the size, but also for their opulence. Drinking fountains, vending machines, and cafeterias were the rule, not the exception. Everything in Blanchet's presentation attested to the luxury and wealth of the United States, from the parking lots full of workers' cars to the clothes of the workers, and the cleanliness of factories.

As the Technical Assistance visits proceeded, an argument arose about the best way to handle their publicity. Mission France believed that Labor Information publicity was excessive. The Mission's labor adviser complained that the French trips to the U.S. had a "tour to Moscow" feel because reporters and photographers were omnipresent.[186] One French team specifically requested that no journalists accompany them. Other teams complained that they had been pressured to participate in photosessions and news conferences.[187]

The staff of Labor Information chided the French Mission for its sensitivity. The few complaints there were, stated Harry Martin, were either affectations of modesty or "Gallic flippancies."[188] In either case, the program and its attendant publicity need not be changed. The ECA Information Division in Washington supported Labor Information's position. It suggested that publicity for the visits be dramatically increased.[189] No consensus was reached on the matter, and the French Mission subsequently rejected (against the protests of ECA information) a proposal for a film of a visiting French team.[190]

By 1952, the ECA information office was in open conflict with several ERP country Missions. Some, including Mission France, had tempered their activities as a result of the generally hostile reaction productivity propaganda elicited. Robert Mullen, the director of ECA information, complained bitterly:

> In their over-sensitized fear of "intervening" in the internal affairs of other countries, too many Missions have acted as brakes upon the activities of forward looking Europeans who want to push the productivity movement.[191]

He complained that some Missions were engaged in passive, others in active, resistance to the promotion of productivity. Mullen was "baffled" by this recalcitrance. "Surely," he concluded, "[productivity] should be the first export item of our kind of civilization."[192]

The Demise of the Labor Information Program

Heightened productivity publicity coincided with increased disaffection by non-Communist labor. In 1952 the pilot foundry program collapsed when FO pulled its support.[193] The collapse of the foundry program reflected the general rejection of the productivity drive by French labor. FO and the CFTC had endorsed the productivity drive without enthusiasm in 1950 at the Rome meeting of the ERP International Trade Union Conference.[194] Speaking for FO, Léon Jouhaux stated, "It is not possible to conceive of a higher productivity without a raised standard of living, that is to say, a higher purchasing power of the working masses." The CFTC representative stated that "Capitalism does not always conceive the aim and the purpose of productivity in the same way that we conceive of it."[195]

The Korean War caused a deepening and widening of American propaganda in general, but it also increased French workers' anxieties about the prospect of World War Three and the impact of rearmament on their standard of living. Given this sentiment, Labor Information would have done well to moderate its voice, but it did not. In early 1951 the head of Labor Information described his program as "an information panzer force."[196] The Labor Information program for 1951 stated: "From the start of the fighting, Labor Information officers had taken it upon themselves, without waiting for directives, to throw the weight of their influence into the telling of the American story."[197] The stakes were high. Labor Information had to convince French workers that the Marshall Plan was not only beneficial to them, but rearmament would not decrease their standard of living. Labor Information rose to the challenge:

> The urgencies of international tension require ... that we must "sell" Europe on *itself,* on its own potential for survival and defense, on the practical aspects of building an integrated Europe with high productivity, low prices, a vast mass market, a better way of life, for the masses of the populace PLUS the essentials of defense.... This calls for most skillful propaganda in the world, *together with the bold action required to give meaning to that propaganda.*[198]

In a revealing comment the report stated: "It is imperative that Labor Information have a voice in the making of policy and its carrying out at all levels." No such voice was forthcoming. In fact, the State Department began to limit the voice of Labor Information by starting its own tentative propaganda efforts directed toward European labor.[199]

The lack of input Labor Information possessed on substantive policy issues was one reason non-Communist labor viewed the productivity drive as an "inflated balloon."[200] Even before the assistance of a dedicated program productivity had increased. In absence of collective bargaining and guarantees, increased productivity entailed only wider profit margins. To make matters worse, the label "productivity" was carelessly applied to instances that were certainly not conducive to its widespread acceptance. For example, *Le Monde* reported that productivity in French coal mines had resulted in a twenty-year trend of decreasing employment.[201]

The FO publication *La Révolution prolétarienne* provided a clear indication of French labor's negative view of productivity with the article "Down with Productivity!"[202] The major complaint of the article was that American propaganda presented productivity as a new idea. "The idea of productivity," the author pointed out, "is as old as the world; let's say, to be more exact, as old as management. Ever since there have been employers, the constant, daily concern of the employer has been to obtain a maximum number of products with a minimum number of workers." "Productivity" was put forward in the hope that it would be taken for something new. American propaganda ("slogans, clichés, and bla-bla-bla") was difficult to digest even for individuals who liked the United States.

Indeed, by 1952 the French were finding it hard to swallow much of the American presentation. The traveling exhibit that had been tirelessly plying the roads of France finally met its demise at the hands of, depending on one's perspective, a group of concerned citizens or a communist mob. The incident occurred in Oyonnax, in the department of Ain.[203] The director of the exhibit had followed the regular protocol of pre-notifying newspapers and officials. However, when the exhibit rolled into town on a Saturday the welcome was anything but warm. The morning edition of the local communist organ *Les Allobroges* (with a circulation estimated at eighty-eight thousand in 1953) had promulgated a call to action.[204] Schmitt, the exhibit's manager, arranged a hasty meeting with the mayor, a well-meaning socialist named Georges Mermet-Guyennet.[205] The mayor advised Schmitt to cancel the exhibit—the temperament of the Communists was simply too volatile. The exhibit was quietly but quickly secured in a room in the Hôtel de Ville.

At seven p.m. a group of several dozen men led by the head of the Oyonnax section of the Communist Party arrived at the Hôtel de Ville.

They were in no mood to parlay. After a brief struggle they broke down the doors and sought out the exhibit. They made short work of its material, smashing nineteen of its twenty panels. In addition to the panels, the group destroyed as much hardware as they could. The Mayor, working late that night, locked his office door and tried desperately to contact the CRS (Compagnies républicaines de sécurité, the national security police). As he struggled to place the call the Communists found him and, according to witnesses, "molested" him.[206] During the chaos Schmitt and the other members of the exhibit's staff fled to nearby Bourg-en-Bresse in fear for their lives.

The next day was quiet in Oyonnax. The exhibit lay smashed beyond recognition in the Hôtel de Ville. A convoy of trucks bearing over a hundred CRS troops arrived that morning. The mayor, evidently quite traumatized by the affair, exerted his authority as best he could. With a detachment of troops he arrested the Communist leader on the charge of "interfering with a municipal magistrate in the exercise of official duties."[207] No charges could be filed against *Les Allobroges* because it had called for merely a demonstration, not calculated acts of violence.

The American reaction was predictable. The chief of the Information Division told the Mission's head, "I think it would be useful to consider this, along with various other straws in the wind, as an indication that the Commies are now determined to see just how far they can go in the way of provocation."[208] Perhaps, but the charge of provocation more squarely applies to the American exhibit, which had been antagonizing local populations since its inception. In fact, the attack on the exhibit was an early indication that a wave of anti-Americanism was sweeping France. It was, after all, just over a week later that thousands of protestors would take to the streets of Paris to condemn the arrival of the new head of NATO, the American general Ridgway.

"A Crassly Materialistic People?"

By 1951 the frustration in the Labor Information Division and Mission France was palpable. Harold Kaplan, a Mission France information officer, summarized the standard French criticisms of the Marshall Plan: the average French citizen saw no change in their life as a result of U.S. aid; Marshall Plan funds benefited nationalized industries such as electricity and gas, but utility prices continued to climb; wages were too low; small enterprises were hurt by the Marshall Plan.[209] Kaplan was exasperated. "The French criticize the plan for failing to do what it could not possibly have done," he complained. "In effect, all that they say is that the Marshall Plan has failed to solve all of the pressing economic problems of France."

The problem was, as Turtledove had pointed out, that the work of Labor Information and Mission France had contributed to the perception that the Marshall Plan would fix the French economy. To make matters worse, the American message was often contradictory. Publications and radio programs said one thing, American union members another. Similarly, Labor Information called for higher wages while the ECA pushed for deflationary measures. The efforts of Mission France and Labor Information were the metaphorical rope of which they possessed more than enough to hang themselves. Only too late did they realize that their work did not reflect policy, or that it had cultural implications incidental to its intended goals.

In a self-reflective report, one staff member concluded, "Past Labor Information activities have placed us in a position where we must first prove our good faith."[210] The mistake had been to favor propaganda over conscientious attempts to reach French labor:

> The expensive, expansive, general rather than specialized, completely Americanized approach to an information, education and propaganda and counter-propaganda operation has shocked rank and file and militant cadremen alike by its obvious high cost and equally obvious lack of real content or immediate pertinence.[211]

The average French worker still had very little idea about what the Marshall Plan had actually done for France; most still held that it was only a means by which "Wall Street" dumped cheap surpluses on France. The final suggestion revealed the extent of the public-relations crisis: French workers, including the CGT, needed to be given subsidized tours of French Marshall Plan projects in order to show that they were real.[212]

Yet the same report also called for a renewed propaganda effort. It rehashed familiar arguments: "Free labor" was in a "deplorable condition"; FO and the CFTC had very little money and less equipment to mount a propaganda drive to reach their own members, let alone the CGT. Labor Information needed to immediately launch a "drastic program" to salvage the situation.[213] The program would include more posters and pamphlets for general use, and more subsidies to non-Communist French labor. It was not to be. Harry Martin had recently rejected a similar initiative from Washington. His blunt reply was: "We have gone with European Labor far beyond the point where this sort of thing has any general widespread usefulness."[214]

In early 1953 James C. Dunn, the new ambassador to France, implemented a drastic check on Labor Information activities. He concluded that overt aid to French labor was self-defeating, and any attempt to assist it in other ways was even more damaging.[215] Dunn's conclusion about American interventions in French labor echo Irwin Wall's later assessment that "the American role in France often appeared as intrusive at it was ineffective."[216]

In 1952 the director of Labor Information, Harry Martin, complained that the growing militarization of American aid risked further alienating French labor. The Mutual Security Agency (the successor of the Marshall Plan) budgetary program for fiscal year 1954 had recently been released. It emphasized the military uses of the funds to the detriment of broader "defense support" programs.[217] For Martin, this risked making the program even more unpalatable to workers than it already was. Their condition was still distressed and the money would be better spent, and have better propaganda value, in contributing to programs that would help workers, such as housing. Martin explained the consequences of the growing militarization of U.S. aid:

> We have already made the lesser, and explainable, mistake in previous years of moving too fast toward the military rationale. We are paying for that every day, already, in the tremendous upsurge in acceptance for the "Neutralist" viewpoint. Worse still, we have provoked the beginnings of a general wave of "Anti-Americanism" per se—i.e., simple and unreasoning hatred for the U.S.—which has nothing to do with, but is infinitely more dangerous than either Communism or Neutralism.[218]

For Martin, little could be done to stop the "disillusionment" of the European worker.[219]

In 1948 Labor's support for the Marshall Plan was seen as essential for the success of the program. Clearly at this point we can conclude this was not the case. The Marshall Plan continued to function fine despite massive worker indifference and intermittent CGT opposition. The original emphasis on labor support reflected the belief that war between the Soviet Union and the United States was imminent. American planners had nightmares of "commie" workers sabotaging war production at the factory or sending defective equipment in to battle.[220] The failure of the Marshall Plan to improve workers' standards of living was, therefore, a threat to security. One official offered this bleak assessment of the Marshall Plan's labor policies: "Guns should be produced but for the use of anti-Communists; it was not intended that guns and Communists be produced at the same time."[221]

Finally, we must briefly examine how the Labor Information program reinforced French stereotypes of American culture. Pamphlets, exhibits, trains, radio, movies, posters—American propaganda was ubiquitous.[222] The program did more than provoke anti-Americanism among French labor. The propaganda for the productivity drive, in

[handwritten: Marshall Plan Labor Information program failed; reinforced Fr stereotypes of Am]

particular, reinforced the French stereotype that America was a "mechanical civilization." Devoid of artists, chess professionals, or philosophers, it had nothing to offer the world except technical experts.

Even for those most sympathetic to U.S. policy, the productivity propaganda was excessive. An article about productivity disturbed one reader of *Rapports,* the official periodical of Mission France. In addition to practical questions about unemployment and retraining costs, the reader asked: "Don't modern machines and their precision have the tendency to estrange a worker from his labor?"[223] Another reader of *Rapports* asked for more articles about the cultural life of the United States: "Show that you have not only factories and specialists, show the work of intelligence not only the flat intelligence of utilitarianism, however important it may be for the amelioration of the standard of life."[224]

One French woman wrote the president of Corning Glass after visiting a display of glasswork at the Musée des Arts Décoratifs.[225] She congratulated him for the "harmony and beauty" of the display. The aesthetic beauty of the exhibit was a corrective to productivity propaganda: "Today we are assailed by and engulfed in the slogans of your propaganda bent toward increased productivity.... We are deluged with your technicians and your treatises on the art of production and efficiency." The glassworks, with their "pure and charming contours," had made it possible "for a great number of Frenchmen and Frenchwomen to see you in a different light, less forbidding and less utilitarian." In doing so it modified the impression—"so metallic, so exaggeratedly technical"—that most French had of the United States.[226]

American intellectuals were not silent about the contribution of U.S. propaganda in further erasing them from the French imagination. At the end of 1951 Charles Odegaard, the head of the American Council of Learned Societies, wrote the head of the USIS, Assistant Secretary of State Edward W. Barrett.[227] Odegaard complained that U.S. propaganda favored productivity and technical assistance at the expense of America's intellectual and artistic achievements. It was not enough to show the world that Americans could produce goods in mass quantities. More important was to show that other values, be they of a spiritual or intellectual nature, animated life in the United States. Odegaard's final question summarized the crux of American propaganda. He asked, "Is the emphasis of our own American programs abroad such as to help create what we do not in fact believe is a fair judgement of our culture; namely, that we are a crassly materialistic people?" For the Labor Information program, as with other U.S. programs, we can conclude yes.

Notes

1. *Transatlantic From the Office of ECA Labor Advisors,* vol. 2, no. 2 (November 1949).
2. Is it 1929 in France? Memo from Ken Douty to Barry Bingham, chief of Mission France, 7 February 1950, NARA, RG. 469, entry 1048, box 6.
3. Ibid.
4. Ibid.
5. Federico Romero, *The United States and the European Trade Union Movement, 1944-1951,* trans. Harvey Fergusson (Chapel Hill: University of North Carolina Press, 1992), 102; John Bledsoe Bonds, *Bipartisan Strategy: Selling the Marshall Plan* (Westport: Praeger, 2002).
6. Anthony Carew, *Labour Under the Marshall Plan: The Politics of Productivity and the Marketing of Management Science* (Detroit: Wayne State University Press, 1987), 80.
7. Jon V. Kofas, "U.S. Foreign Policy and the World Federation of Trade Unions, 1944-1948," *Diplomatic History* 26, no. 1 (2002): 21–60.
8. Romero, 92–95, 103–105.
9. Robert H. Zieger, *The CIO, 1933-55* (Chapel Hill: University of North Carolina Press, 1995), 265.
10. Robert H. Zieger, *The CIO, 1933-55,* 277; Jon V. Kofas, "U.S. Foreign Policy and the World Federation of Trade Unions, 1944-1948," 55.
11. Meeting with AFL, CIO and UMW Representatives, 4 January 1950. American Foreign Policy Center, Official Conversations and Meeting of Dean Acheson, 1949–1953.
12. Statement of CIO views on International Problems, 17 February 1950. American Foreign Policy Center, Official Conversations and Meeting of Dean Acheson, 1949–1953.
13. Ibid.
14. "The truth was there was no high-level labor input into ECA policy-making, and this stemmed from the vacuum at the top," Carew, *Labour Under the Marshall Plan,* 88.
15. Romero, *The United States and the European Trade Union Movement, 1944-1951,* 184.
16. Ibid., 204.
17. I am following here the general consensus of Carew and Irwin Wall. The involvement of the U.S. was a sufficient, but not necessary condition for the split in France labor; Carew, *Labour Under the Marshall Plan,* 228–229; Wall, *The United States and the Making of Postwar France, 1945-1954,* 103.
18. Memorandum for the File, Frank G. Wisner, Assistant Director for Policy Coordination, 16 November 1948, *F.R.U.S. Emergence of the Intelligence Establishment, 1945-1950* (Washington, D.C.: U.S. GPO, 1996), 732–733.
19. Wall, *The United States and the Making of Postwar France, 1945-1954,* 104–105.
20. Annie Lacroix-Riz, *La CGT de la liberation à la scission de 1944-47* (Paris: Editions Sociales, 1983), 343; Wall, 106–107.
21. "Labor View of France," *Trans-Atlantic From the Office of Labor Advisors* 1, no. 10 (April 1949), 3.
22. Ibid.
23. Kuisel, *Seducing the French,* 79.
24. There were two reasons for this. First, the presence of the U.S. (economic, military, cultural) was greater than that of the Soviet Union. Second, FO had no history independent of U.S. financial aid or the political pressure attached to it. However subservient the CGT was to the Soviet Union, it possessed a long and

venerated history. The CGT also obscured its ties to the Soviet Union and the PCF.

25. Romero, *The United States and the European Trade Union Movement, 1944-1951*, 185.
26. Richard F. Kuisel, "The Marshall Plan in Action," 336.
27. Ibid., 336.
28. Ibid., 337.
29. Charles S. Maier, "The Politics of Productivity: Foundations of American International Economic Policy After World War II," *International Organization* 31 (Autumn 1977): 607–633; reprint *The Cold War in Europe*, ed. Charles S. Maier (New York: Markus Wiener, 1991): 169–201 (page references are to reprint edition).
30. French Labor Leader Statements, 5 December 1950, NARA, RG. 469, entry 352, box 1.
31. Memo from Charles Edmundson to Roscoe Drummond, head of ECA Information, 9 September 1950, NARA, RG. 469, entry 1049, box 3.
32. Thomas Wilson, interview by Linda and Eric Christenson 23 April 1993 Washington, D.C., VHS recording Christenson Associates.
33. Memo from Robert R. Mullen to William Joyce, 16 October 1950, NARA, RG. 469, entry 302, box 11.
34. Draft Agenda of an Action Program for French Labor, NARA, RG. 469, entry 302, box 11. This report was circulated in December 1950.
35. Ibid.
36. Postwar inflation in France was one of the major problems identified by American economists. In general, ERP economic policy stressed deficit reduction and other deflationary measures. See Alan S. Milward, *The Reconstruction of Western Europe, 1945-1951* (London: Methuen & Co., 1984), 98–99; Chiarella Esposito, *America's Feeble Weapon: Funding the Marshall Plan in France and Italy, 1948-1950* (New Haven: Greenwood, 1994).
37. Draft Agenda of an Action Program for French Labor.
38. Productivity Exhibits and Demonstrations in the PCs [participating countries], from ECA administrator to all European Missions, 9 March 1951, NARA, RG. 469, entry 302, box 20.
39. Ibid. Emphasis in original.
40. Ibid.
41. Memo from T.W. Wilson to Henry Labouisse [Chief of Mission France], 13 November 1951, NARA, RG. 469, entry 1193, box 44.
42. Ibid.
43. Memo from Robert R. Mullen to William Foster, Donald Stone, 12 March 1951, NARA, RG. 469, entry 302, box 11.
44. Productivity Drive Information Program, 1 September 1951, NARA, RG. 469, entry 302, box 20.
45. Ibid.
46. Ibid.
47. Emphasis in original, Memo from Allan L. Swim, Chief, Operational Planning, Labor Information, to John Hutchison, Deputy Director, Labor Information, 15 June NARA, RG. 469, entry 1048, box 7. One of the reasons Labor Information, and the Information Division of the ECA, approached the propaganda of the productivity drive with such alacrity can be found in the interorganizational rivalries of the ECA with the State Department, and Labor Information with the Industry Division of the OSR. See Carew, *Labour Under the Marshall Plan*, 83–87.
48. A detailed discussion of this is Stephen Burwood's "American Labor and Industrial Unrest in France, 1947-1952" (Ph.D. diss., S.U.N.Y. Binghamton, 1990).

49. John Hutchison, interview by Linda and Eric Christenson, 29 June 1993, Sebastopol, California, VHS Recording, Christenson Associates.
50. Chronological Resume of Labor Exhibit, NARA, RG. 469, entry 1193, box 45.
51. Memo from Helen Kirkpatrick to Ian Fraser, 12 December 1950, NARA, RG. 469, entry 1193, box 45.
52. Comments on Exhibition, 18 October 1950, NARA, RG. 469, entry 1193, box 45.
53. Ibid.
54. Rapport: Exposition à Grenoble, 19 October 1950, NARA, RG. 469, entry 1193, box 45.
55. Ibid.
56. Ibid.
57. Ibid.
58. Ibid.
59. Key Areas of the French Communist Party, NARA, RG. 469, entry 1048, box 6; see also François Goguel, *Chronique électorales la quatrième république* (Paris: Presses de la Fondation nationale des sciences politiques, 1981), 100–101.
60. Rapport: Exposition à Marseille, 18 November 1950, NARA, RG. 469, entry 1193, box 46.
61. Ibid.
62. Wall, *The United States and the Making of Postwar France, 1945-1954,* 108–109.
63. Ibid., 109.
64. Report on Union Attitudes on Mission Information Work, 2 January 1951, NARA, RG. 469, entry 1193, box 54.
65. Letter from Robert Faherty to Harry Martin, 11 June 1951, NARA, RG. 469, entry 1048, box 6.
66. Two French Mission Labor Information Projects, report from Harry Martin to Robert R. Mullen, 2 May 1951, NARA, RG. 469, entry 1048, box 6.
67. Letter from Robert Faherty to Harry Martin, 11 June 1951.
68. ECA France Information Division, Exhibits Program 1951, NARA, RG. 94, entry 2462, box 34.
69. Letter from Robert Faherty to Harry Martin, 21 February 1951, NARA, RG. 469, entry 1048, box 6.
70. Two French Mission Labor Information Projects.
71. Ibid.
72. Ibid.
73. ECA Mission to France Monthly Report, September 1951, NARA, RG. 469, entry 1193, box 49.
74. Success of the *Bulletin syndical,* 19 June 1951, NARA, RG. 469, entry 1048, box 6.
75. Report and analysis of distribution of *Bulletin Syndical,* January 1952, NARA, RG. 469, entry 1193, box 54.
76. Ibid.
77. Report on the ECA Press, André Drom, 22 May 1951, NARA, RG. 469, entry 1048, box 7.
78. Ibid.
79. Memo from Robert Faherty to Pat Frayne, 30 November 1950, NARA, RG. 469, entry 1193, box 54.
80. Memo from Robert Faherty to Imprimerie JEP, 2 February 1951, NARA, entry 1193, box 54.
81. Two French Mission Labor Information Projects.
82. Memo to Pat Frayne from Robert Faherty, 6 December 1950, NARA, RG. 469, entry 1193, box 54.
83. Ibid.
84. Report on Union Attitudes on Mission Information Work, 2 January 1951.

85. Letter from M. Couladoux to M. Douty, 8 October 1951, NARA, RG. 469, entry 1193, box 54.
86. Report and Analysis of distribution of *Bulletin Syndical,* January 1952, NARA, RG. 469, entry 1193, box 54.
87. Ibid.
88. *Bulletin Syndical,* March 1953, NARA, RG. 469, entry 1193, box 54.
89. "Joe Smith, travailleur," NARA, RG. 469, entry 1193, box 54.
90. Report on the ECA Press.
91. ECA Special Mission to France Monthly Report for February 1950, NARA, RG. 469, entry 1048, box 8.
92. Fourth quarterly Report, 1950, Information Division of ECA Mission to France, 2 January 1951, NARA, RG. 469, entry 1193, box 51.
93. Report on ECA Press.
94. Report on Union Attitudes on Mission Information Work.
95. Letter from Helen Kirkpatrick, Chief, Information Division, Mission France, to A. Malterre, Secretary-General of CGC, undated, NARA, RG. 469, entry 1193, box 49.
96. Proposed program for Radio, Labor Information, 15 February 1951, NARA, RG. 469, entry 302, box 12.
97. *Rapports: France—Etats-Unis,* No. 46, January 1951, provided a broadcast schedule.
98. This was emphasized in the memo: Productivity Exhibits and Demonstrations in the Participating Countries, from ECA Administrator to all European Missions, 9 March 1951, NARA, RG. 469, entry 302, box 20.
99. *Le Monde,* 5 September 1951.
100. Letter from Harry Martin to Barry Bingham, 20 March 1950, NARA, RG. 469, entry 1052, box 4.
101. Ibid.
102. Letter from W.C. Guasmann, special adviser to the director of Labor Information, to Harry Martin, undated [but from the two-week sojourn of the Train in Paris during October], NARA, RG. 469, entry 1049, box 3.
103. The Train of Europe, 10 January 1951, NARA, RG. 469, entry 1051, box 19.
104. Monthly Report Information Division ECA Special Mission to France, October 1951, NARA, RG. 469, entry 1194, box 49.
105. Letter from W.C. Guasmann, special adviser to the director of Labor Information, to Harry Martin.
106. *Oeust-Matin,* 22 October 1951.
107. The OEEC hoped for a reincarnation of the train in 1952, but the U.S. embassy in France declared that no U.S. propaganda or sponsorship could be given to it; memo from Charles K. Moffly, Acting Public Affairs Officer, U.S. Embassy Paris, to Frank L. Dennis, Director, Office of Information, Special Representative in Europe, NARA, RG. 469, entry 1193, box 45.
108. *Le Monde,* 12 October 1951.
109. Monthly Report Information Division ECA Special Mission to France, October 1951, NARA, RG. 469, entry 1194, box 49.
110. Letter to Thomas K. Hodges, Chief, Research and Analysis Section, Mission France, from Marriane Crites, 15 October 1951, NARA, RG. 469, entry 1051, box 24.
111. Ibid.
112. *Trans-Atlantic: From the Office of Labor Advisors, ECA Labor News Letter,* vol. 3, no. 6 (March 1951), 12–13.
113. Transcript of French version of film *Productivity, Key to Plenty,* NARA, RG. 469, entry 1051, box 21. The original, English language version of the film was produced in 1949; NARA, Motion picture films, 16mm, RG. 200, FC collection, item #4943.

114. Commercial Films for Distribution thru Unions and Progressive Organizations, Labor Information, 19 December 1950, NARA, RG. 469, entry 1193, box 49.
115. Ibid.
116. Letter from Sally Ann Cist, Acting Films Officer, Labor Information, to Harry Martin, 21 March 1951, NARA, RG. 469, entry 1051, box 21.
117. Commercial Films for Distribution thru Unions and Progressive Organizations.
118. From Paris To Secretary of State, 13 November 1950, NARA, RG. 469, entry 236, box 96.
119. Commercial Films for Distribution thru Unions and Progressive Organizations.
120. Letter from Lothar Wolff, Motion Picture Officer ECA-OSR, to André Tadie, 25 August 1950, NARA, RG. 469, entry 1193, box 49.
121. Letter from Sally Ann Cist to Harry Martin, 7 March 1951, NARA, RG. 469, entry 1051, box 21.
122. The film was shot in Isbergue with the cooperation of FO workers. Letter to T.W. Wilson from H. Kaplan, su: jour de peine, 1 February 1952, NARA, RG. 84, entry 2462, box 36.
123. Ibid.
124. Ibid.
125. Kuisel, "The Marshall Plan in Action," 348.
126. Productivity Drive Information Program.
127. Letter from H. Kaplan to Albert Hemsing, 23 September 1952, NARA, RG. 84, entry 2462, box 36.
128. Ibid.
129. The program collapsed because FO pulled its support. Richard F. Kuisel, "The Marshall Plan in Action," 350; Letter from Harold Kaplan to Films Branch, 19 November 1952, NARA, RG. 84, entry 2462, box 36.
130. Richard F. Kuisel, "The Marshall Plan in Action," 353.
131. Emissions radiophoniques sur la productivité, SGCI, F60 *ter* 394.
132. Commission de l'information et de la propaganda, compte rendu, 16 October 1951, SGCI, F60 *ter* 394.
133. Ministre plenipotentiaire à Tunis to Robert Schuman, 28 March 1950, Ministère des Affaires Etrangères, Papiers Bruneau.
134. Jean Mons to Robert Schuman, 11 April 1950, Ministère des Affaires Etrangères, Papiers Bruneau.
135. Affaires Etrangères—direction d'Afrique—to Paris, Ministère des Affaires Etrangères, Papiers Bruneau.
136. Note pour le Ministre, 18 April 1950, Ministère des Affaires Etrangères, Papiers Bruneau.
137. Richard F. Kuisel, *Seducing the French,* Chapter 4: "Missionaries of the Marshall Plan"; "The Marshall Plan in Action"; "L'American way of life et les missions françaises de productivité," *Vingtième Siècle,* No. 17 (January–March 1988): pp. 21–38.
138. Richard F. Kuisel, "The Marshall Plan in Action," 343.
139. "Team Reports on France," *Trans-Atlantic From the Office Labor Advisors,* vol. 2, no. 11, 4.
140. St. Malo FO School Trip, Report on, NARA, RG. 469, entry 1048, box 8.
141. Ibid.
142. Ibid.
143. Ibid.
144. Their report to the ECA concluded: "The real hourly wage of male workers is thirty five percent less than in 1938. The Marshall Plan has brought real prosperity to all but the French workers. There is nothing to prevent the direct benefits of increased production made possible by the Marshall Plan aid from

going entirely to the employer. In one plant where a five hundred percent increase in productivity resulted from ECA help the workers are receiving exactly the same wages as before. Workers without exception are uninformed of the mechanics of the plan and they are totally unaware of the benefits, if any, to them." NARA, RG. 469, entry 1048, box 7. See also Burwood, 293.

145. Report on trip to Marseille, 15 March 1950, NARA, RG. 469, entry 1048, box 8.
146. Ibid.
147. Ibid.
148. Ibid.
149. Ibid.
150. Ibid.
151. Ibid.
152. Ibid.
153. Ibid.
154. Letter to Harry Martin, Bill Gaussman, Hugh Sutherland from George Cony, December 1950, NARA, RG. 469, entry 1048, box 8.
155. Ibid.
156. Ibid.
157. Ibid.
158. Ibid.
159. Ibid.
160. American immigration policy refused entry to anyone with Communist affiliation but this was moot because the CGT stayed away from the program, Kuisel, *Seducing the French,* 79.
161. "Report on trip to Rouen," from Georges Cony to Harry Martin, 12 October 1950, NARA, RG. 469, entry 1052, box 4.
162. Letter to Harry Martin, Bill Gaussman, Hugh Sutherland from George Cony, December 1950.
163. Transcript of La Ronde des Nations, 6 May 1949, SGCI, F60 *ter* 393.
164. Terushi Hara, "Productivity Missions to the United States: the Case of Post-War France," in Dominique Barjot, ed., *Catching Up with America: Productivity Missions and the Diffusion of American Economic and Technological Influence after the Second World War* (Paris: Presses de l'Université de Paris-Sorbonne, 2002), 175.
165. Labor and Economic Conditions in France, letter from Donald C. Stone to William H. Foster, 29 March 1950; Letter from Donald C. Stone to Bert M. Jewell and Clinton S. Golden, 25 March 1950; NARA, RG. 469, entry 302, box 11.
166. Labor and Economic Conditions in France, letter from Donald C. Stone to William H. Foster, 29 March 1950.
167. Operation Bootstrap, from H.L. Turtledove to Harry Martin, 1 April 1950, NARA, RG. 469, entry 302, box 11.
168. Ibid.
169. The intermediate conclusion is: non-Communist organized labor is the basis for the survival of the IVth Republic.
170. Quotation from Associated Press newswire, 15 August 1950, quoted in telegram from London embassy to ECA administrator, 15 August 1950, NARA, RG. 469, entry 302, box 11.
171. *L'Aube,* 19 August 1950, *Le Figaro,* 21 August 1950, *Le Populaire,* 22 August 1950. The story was also carried by American newspapers, *New York Times,* 15 August 1950.
172. Quoted in Kuisel, *Seducing the French,* 80.
173. In addition to Kuisel's treatment, see: Barjot Dominique and Chrisophe Réveillard, eds., *Catching up with America;* Matthias Kipping, "Operation Impact: Con-

verting European employers to the American Creed," in *The Americanization of European Business: the Marshall Plan and the Transfer of U.S. Management Models,* eds. Matthias Kipping and Ore Bjarner (London: Routeledge, 1998): 55–73; Henri Morsel, "La mission de productivité aux États-Unis de l'industrie française de l'aluminium," *Histoire, Economie, Société* 18, no. 2 (1999): 413–418.

174. "First French Team Here," *Trans-Atlantic: From the Office of Labor Advisors,* vol. 1 no. 2 August 1949.

175. Ibid.

176. "Governor Fetes French Workers," *Trans-Atlantic: From the Office of Labor Advisors,* vol. 2 no. 8 May 1950.

177. Letter from Max Rolland to John Hutchinson, forwarded to A.W. Harriman, 11 May 1950, NARA, RG. 469, entry 928, box 25.

178. Memo to Boris Shiskin from Deputy U.S. Special Representative (Katz), 5 June 1950, NARA, RG. 469, entry 914, box 2.

179. Letter from Max Rolland to John Hutchinson, forwarded to A.W. Harriman.

180. Ibid.

181. Memo to Boris Shiskin from Deputy U.S. Special Representative (Katz), 5 June 1950.

182. These press releases were regularly run in the *Dépêche du Midi, Le Figaro, Le Monde, Les Echos,* in addition to pro-American publications such as *Réalités, Sélection du Reader's Digest,* and, of course, *Bulletin syndical* and *Rapports.* Distribution of press releases are contained in the Monthly reports of the Information Division of Mission France, NARA, RG. 469, entry 1193, box 49.

183. "Les Leçons de la productivité américaine," André Blanchet, *Le Monde,* 11–12, 14 October 1950.

184. "Les Leçons de la productivité américaine," by André Blanchet, *Le Monde,* 11 October 1950.

185. Ibid.

186. Publicity on French Technical Assistance Teams During Visits in the U.S., 18 October 1950, NARA, RG. 469, entry 1048, box 7.

187. Letter from Ken Douty to Harry Martin, 16 November 1950, NARA, RG. 469, entry 1048, box 7.

188. Letter from Harry Martin to Ken Douty, 26 October 1950, NARA, RG. 469, entry 1048, box 7.

189. Letter from Robert R. Mullen to Harry Martin, 27 October 1950, NARA, RG. 469, entry 1048, box 7.

190. Letter from Ken Douty to Helen Kirkpatrick, 22 November 1950, NARA, RG. 469, entry 1048, box 7.

191. Letter from Robert Mullen to Robert Oliver, 18 January 1952, NARA, RG. 469, entry 302, box 2.

192. Ibid.

193. Richard F. Kuisel, "The Marshall Plan in Action," 349.

194. *Report of Third International Trade Union Conference* (ECA: Washington, 1950).

195. Ibid.

196. ECA's Labor Information Program for 1951, Labor Information, February 1951, NARA, RG 469, entry 302, box 12.

197. Ibid.

198. Ibid.

199. Letter from Robert Oliver, Labor Advisor ECA, to William C. Foster, ECA Administrator, 2 January 1951; letter from Milton Katz, Special Representative in Europe, to William C. Foster, 20 December 1950; NARA, RG 469, entry 302, box 11.

200. The statement was off the record by an FO official, "FO and productivity round up," letter from Max Rolland to Harry Martin, 17 December 1951, NARA, RG. 469, entry 1048, box 7.
201. Ibid.
202. *La Révolution Prolétarienne,* December 1951.
203. This narrative is based on the account of J.R. Schmitt, the director of the exhibit: Destruction of Labor Exhibit, NARA, RG. 84, entry 2462, box 34.
204. Average daily circulation of the French Provincial newspapers for the months of January and April 1954, American Foreign Policy Center Archive, Confidential U.S. State Department Central Files: France, Internal Affairs, 1950–1954.
205. Ibid.
206. Ibid.
207. Ibid.
208. Communist attack on labor exhibit, 19 May 1952, NARA, RG. 84, entry 2462, box 34.
209. Letter from Harold Kaplan to R.C. Wood, 8 February 1951, NARA, RG. 469, entry 1193, box 49.
210. General analysis and recommendations regarding Labor Information program, ECA Mission France, Hugh Sutherland and David Safer, Special Media, Labor Information, NARA, RG. 469, entry 1048, box 6.
211. Ibid.
212. Ibid.
213. Ibid.
214. Letter from Harry Martin to Ward Melody, 23 April 1952, NARA, RG. 469, entry 302, box 12.
215. Dunn's crackdown on U.S. propaganda occurred at the same time the USIA was in formation. Dunn's expectation was that it would become the only voice for U.S. propaganda. The Foreign Information Activities of the Department of State, Annex II Labor Information; Letter from William Koren, Public Affairs Officer, USIS, American Embassy, Paris, to Mary Vance Trent, 4 August 1952, NARA, RG. 84, entry 2462, box 10.
216. Wall, *The United States and the Making of Postwar France, 1944-1954,* 299.
217. Letter from Harry Martin to Frank Dennis, Director Office of Information, NARA, RG. 469, entry 302, box 7.
218. Ibid.
219. In some cases, however, the workers were not becoming disillusioned—they were voting for the CGT. Elections for council delegates in the Renault factory were held in mid-1951. The CGT polled over twenty thousand votes, almost 75 percent of the vote. The CFTC and FO barely registered, earning only 9.5 and 5 percent respectively. Eighty seven percent of the workforce voted in the election. In fact, absenteeism at the Renault factory votes had dropped consistently since 1948. The Renault factory offered an exception to the worker apathy that U.S. aid and propaganda generated.
220. In the words of Harry Martin: "Guns, we must have. A lot more guns. Armies, we need. I shudder when I consider our collective weakness, militarily, on this continent. But no Army is worth a tinker's damn if it is composed of soldiers who hate the entrails of their allies, carrying guns that have been deliberately made defective by our former friends among the disillusioned workers, firing bullets that have been deadened by the saboteurs who once stood on our side in the fight against aggression." Letter from Harry Martin to Frank Dennis, Director Office of Information, NARA, RG. 469, entry 302, box 7.
221. Summary Notes of the Meeting of the Deputy Mission Chiefs and Program Officers, 12 September 1951, NARA, RG. 469, entry 928, box 2.

222. See *Journal Officiel,* 13 September 1951, for a debate about American productivity propaganda.
223. *Rapports,* No. 68 (November 1952).
224. *Rapports,* No. 53 (August 1951).
225. Letter from Mme. de Vandenay Tharand to M. Houghton, Corning Glass, 24 July 1951, NARA, central decimal files of the State Department, 59, 511.512/10-2551.
226. Ibid.
227. Letter from Charles E. Odegaard to Edward W. Barret, 25 October 1951, central decimal files of the State Department, 511.512/10-2551.

Chapter 5

THE MAKERS OF STORIES

Our first duty then, it seems, is to set a watch over the makers of stories, to select every beautiful story they make, and reject any that are
not beautiful. Then we shall persuade nurses and mothers to tell those
selected stories to the children. Thus will they shape their souls with
stories far more than they can shape their bodies with their hands. But
we shall have to throw away most of the stories they tell now.

Plato, *The Republic,* book II

In 1948 the Communist intellectual Georges Soria published an apoc-
alyptic warning about the dangers the Marshall Plan posed to France.[1]
According to Soria, the Marshall Plan threatened France's economy
in a number of ways. It impeded the development of the French industry (particularly aeronautical) and hurt French agriculture by
glutting the market with American surpluses; American capitalists in
the service of the "great trusts" traveled around Europe like so many
vultures buying up weakened European companies; French companies, "forced" to purchase raw material from American suppliers,
struggled to raise profits. The Marshall Plan was an oppressive yoke.
Even more alarming, however, was the cultural presence that the
Marshall Plan allowed the United States to establish in France. "Today," warned Soria, "every aspect of national life is subject to American pressure." American films, publications, and other cultural goods
not only hurt French industry, according to Soria they also constituted
"mental imperialism," an attack on the very spirit of the nation.[2]

French intellectuals had traditionally played the role of gatekeep-
ers and arbiters of public taste. Some historians argue intellectuals
such as Soria opposed mass culture, in theory more democratic than
high culture and a source for youth rebellion, because it threatened
their influence and stature.[3] However, this chapter argues that the

---

explicit political content of American mass culture during this period suggests that something more was at stake. Nation-states are created and sustained through cultural hegemony. By examining some key periodicals and publications this chapter looks at the control, production, and dissemination of images and ideas that provided an understanding and outlook about the social changes affecting France during the Fourth Republic. Who would provide this orientation? Who, that is, would control the "makers of stories" while telling their own?

Although government assistance to the U.S. culture industry was broadly (and unevenly) distributed, my focus here is on print media. Publications provide a unique insight into the American cultural presence in France. At a time when television was in its infancy, newspapers, journals, and popular magazines provided the cheapest and most accessible source for news and information. Print media was also a more common source for information than radio. According to Philippe Roger, the French edition of *Reader's Digest,* newspapers, detective stories, and Marshall Plan publications served as the most common source for French knowledge about the United States during this period.[4] As the number of recent works on the subject illustrates, film also provides a lens through which we can study Americanization.[5] However, my interest in this chapter is on Mission France, the primary agent of the Marshall Plan in the country, and its role in promoting American films in France was secondary. Although Mission officials followed the fortunes of Hollywood exports (the Motion Picture Association of America) with interest, the Embassy and the State Department were the primary interlocutors. In any case, intervention by Mission France was problematic because negotiations often stuck on the issue of converting American movie profits from francs to dollars, which was hardly in line with the goal of the Marshall Plan to close the dollar gap.[6]

In this chapter I examine publications to illustrate the origins, form, and extent of American assistance, and to provide examples of aid that did, or did not, contribute to American hegemony. I first examine the publications of Mission France, most notably *Rapports France—Etats-Unis,* but I also examine book and pamphlet programs. *Sélection du Reader's Digest,* the French edition of *Reader's Digest,* and the French publication *Réalités* provide examples of private publications that received assistance from Mission France. Aid from Mission France to private publications was often reciprocal. In seeking assistance from the American government, publishers argued that their products contributed to American policy goals by presenting American society favorably and by fighting communism.

This chapter also examines efforts by French politicians to limit the presence of foreign publications. I show how the United States colluded with sympathetic French politicians to weaken legislation. Print media is an important, perhaps primary constituent of civil society. The programs that promoted American publications in France illustrate fundamental aspects of Americanization.

Reader's Digest and other mass cultural goods were economic ventures, so it is necessary to indicate how these complemented or differed from other government promotions. The presence of American print media should be understood in the context of general efforts by American industry and the American government to expand their markets and influence in postwar France. As such, it is important to first consider some economic criticisms of the Marshall Plan.

As we have seen, one of the most common criticisms of the Marshall Plan was that it dumped American surpluses on the French market. In truth, however, American exports to Europe declined during the Marshall Plan years.[7] Agricultural goods were an important exception to this trend. Congressional measures ensured that food purchases through the Marshall Plan would be made in the American market.[8] Soria and other Communists also charged that the Marshall Plan was intended to prevent a post-War recession in the American economy. However, the Marshall Plan appeared to have little effect on either preventing or ending the American recession of 1949. Nor were the consequences particularly burdensome for European economies. Although European exports to the United States dropped in these years despite the Plan's efforts, this was offset by an increase in intra-European trade.[9]

Contrary to Soria and others, the ERP did not result in increased American investment in France. Relative to its GNP and, more importantly, its trade surplus with Europe, American investment in Europe was at a low point.[10] Direct American investment in the metropole at the close of the Marshall Plan amounted to $280 million, while investments in the colonies totaled $50 million.[11] American investors expressed concern about the political stability of Western Europe, the convertibility of profits, and currency devaluation.

Although the Marshall Plan did not increase American investments in or exports to Europe, or prevent the recession of 1949, it was certainly not because of a lack of effort on the part of the American government. For example, during the recession the Office of the Special Representative (OSR) instructed all ERP Missions to encourage purchases from sectors of the U.S. economy with unemployment in excess of 12 percent.[12] Missions were instructed to approach governments with lists of "preference market areas." The OSR recognized that

the Missions had limited control over what the participating countries purchased, but it hoped that they could influence where they
purchased.[13]

Marshall Plan legislation also contained specific measures to encourage American investment in Europe. Section 111 (b)(3) of the
Economic Cooperation Act guaranteed the convertibility of profits
up to 100 percent of the original dollar investment for approved projects. There were two drawbacks, however. The participating countries had to grant their approval and the guaranty did not protect
against currency devaluation.[14] Media industries were singled out
for assistance because of their potential to contribute to the propaganda efforts of the United States. The Informational Media Guaranty program (IMG) supplemented the original program in 1949. The
overt purpose of the IMG was to "obtain the widest possible circulation in Europe of informational media conveying a true understanding of American institutions and policy."[15] The IMG covered four
areas: magazines, books, motion pictures, and newspapers and news
agencies. It was especially important for film companies because
their product was made in the U.S. and only rented in Europe, thus
making them ineligible for the original guaranty program. Moreover
films, like other projects, were still subject to local approval. It is no
surprise that the Motion Picture Export Association was not wholly
satisfied with the original arrangement.[16]

Despite these programs, the reticence of investors frustrated
American officials. Senators on the Committee on Foreign Relations
accused the head of the ECA, Paul Hoffman, of failing to encourage
American investment in Europe.[17] Both Hoffman and Barry Bingham
of the French Mission testified that the guaranty programs were in
place, only willing investors were lacking. The ECA could do nothing
about that.[18] Congress had originally envisaged $300 million in guar-
antees for 1948-1949. The total guarantees actually utilized during the
Marshall Plan, however, amounted to only $40 million.[19] The IMG was
a significant portion of the overall guarantees, but the majority of this
was paid in West Germany where convertibility was a serious problem. During its first year 90 percent of the IMG guarantees were paid
to projects in West Germany.[20]

Thus, despite common perceptions the Marshall Plan was not the
engine of economic imperialism it was often held up to be. Granted,
structures and policies were in place that favored American interests, but as with other aspects of American influence, there were limits on their exercise and effectiveness.[21]

Nevertheless, there were exceptions to these general trends,
and it is important to be as specific as possible. Dollar figures do not

always tell the whole story. It is difficult to compare the overwhelming presence of American mass culture and the entry of many U.S. corporations with the dollar amounts invested. The latter was not indicative of the former. For example, Coca-Cola required minimal foreign direct investment to begin operations in France.[22] While the United States government championed free trade with Western Europe it also provided assistance and, via the State Department, leverage that was often decisive in securing American companies a large share of foreign markets. *Reader's Digest* is an example of this pattern.[23] Often the initiative for aid came from the private sector. The State Department willingly assisted endeavors that contributed to the American propaganda struggle against communism, from combating Communist critiques of American society to proselytizing for the American way of life. American companies worked in concert with State Department and ECA programs that were already extensive.

Rapports France–Etats-Unis and the Publications of Mission France

During the Marshall Plan years the highest circulation American publication in France was the Mission France monthly magazine, *Rapports: France–Etats-Unis (Rapports)*. Indeed, with a monthly printing in excess of one million copies by 1952 it was one of the most widespread publications in France. Its purpose was to serve as an official American source for stories about the Marshall Plan, life in the United States, and international affairs. During the final months of the war the American publication *Voir* had served a similar purpose. Yet there was an important difference between the two. *Rapports*—financed by counterpart funds—was free. *Voir,* in contrast, was a joint commercial venture with the French government. From its inception in January 1945 *Voir* proved to be a popular magazine. By the time it ceased publication ten months later it was turning a quarterly profit of $236,000.[24] As the American cultural attaché, William R. Tyler, explained: "We have reached the stage where a government publication ... is in fact competing with other illustrated reviews which are of local origin."[25] This raised difficult issues for the French and American government, and *Voir* ended circulation in October. Much to the chagrin of American officials a French publisher began selling a replica soon after. The content was wholly different but the name and style were duplications of the American publication. The publisher withdrew the French *Voir* following an official protest by the American embassy.[26]

Rapports, which began print in February 1950 and replaced the smaller *L'Aide américaine à la France,* was meant to fill the void left by the disappearance of *Voir.* Mission France produced a number of pamphlets but *Rapports* was a proper magazine. Its appearance, like that of *Voir,* resembled other mass circulation American magazines. The sixty-four-page (on average) magazine featured numerous articles; photographs, eventually in color; letters to the editor; and other regular features. The editing and composition of the magazine was carried out at the offices of the French Mission under the direction of Harold Kaplan, with the assistance of a French staff. French visitors to American exhibits or fairs could request copies by filling out a short form, but Mission France also distributed *Rapports* widely through FO and other pro-American organizations. Every issue contained a subscription card. Soon after the appearance of *Rapports* Mission France began receiving large numbers of cards and requests for the magazine. By October 1950, the *Rapports* mailing list was already approaching the half-million mark.[27]

A July 1952 report by Mission France provided a content analysis of articles appearing in *Rapports.* The "topic" column created by Mission France provides an important example of Mission France's propaganda goals for *Rapports.*

Table 5.1 Designation of Articles for *Rapports*[28]

# of Articles	Topic
66	On France in the form of pep talks
64	On France in the form of needlers—factual articles on various aspects of French life (example: the bad state of highways) which deftly prod readers to call for improvement
63	Miscellaneous on France
69	Miscellaneous on the U.S.
19	Pro-U.S. policy
7	Promoting Voice of America
24	French-American cooperation
43	Americana
21	Franco-American cultural ties

What was the nature of the articles in these categories? True to the American goal of countering French misperceptions, every issue of *Rapports* published at least one general article about American soci-

Rapports was US propaganda w/ high circulation in France

ety. "Universities in American life" showed the French reader that Americans had easy access to affordable higher education.[29] "What does a young American girl dream about?" showed that American girls were no different from French girls: they dreamed about family and home, and possibly womanly careers.[30] The article "American women at work" by Freida S. Miller showed that American working women remained mindful of maintaining a clean home and family dinners.[31] To counter stereotypes that the United States lacked cultural institutions the article "Images of American museums" showed that even remote areas of the country possessed museums with impressive collections.[32] Race relations in the United States, a common object of Communist and non-Communist criticism, received treatment in just one issue of *Rapports:* James Baldwin's article "The black problem in America" (*Le problème Noir en Amérique*).[33]

Although these articles perhaps helped achieve general policy goals such as improving Franco-American relations, *Rapports* included articles that targeted specific objectives of Mission France. Increased productivity, as we saw, for both agriculture and industry was a major objective of American policy. During the first two years of *Rapports* every issue included an article that either addressed productivity directly or treated it in a more general context, such as an October 1950 article about the Technical Assistance program. *Rapports* encouraged agricultural productivity through articles about artificial insemination, hybrid corn, and fertilizers. Productivity articles appeared less frequently during 1952, likely in response to the French backlash, but the topic still appeared in every other issue.

Another policy objective of Mission France that received a good deal of treatment in *Rapports* was the promotion of American tourism in France. In the July 1950 *Rapports* the article "The tourist and you: counsels and suggestions" appeared. It informed readers that American tourists came to France to enjoy its rich cultural heritage and the warm hospitality of the French. The article also suggested that the French provide assistance and understanding in areas where the American tourist might be lacking, such as wine lists and other French dining customs. The article "When American youth come to breathe the air of Paris" stressed the cultural betterment young Americans received by visiting Paris.[34]

study abroad

Finally, *Rapports* included articles by American officials that were explicitly anti-Communist. This was in line with the American policy of addressing Communist criticisms of the United States and the Marshall Plan. Milton Katz, the successor of Averell Harriman as head of the OSR, contributed the article "Democracy in action against reactionary Communism."[35] Other articles dealt with Soviet seizures of

Czechoslovakian industries, labor camps in the Soviet Union, and "The great struggle of the Russian peasantry."[36]

Despite the predominance of articles relating directly to American policy, *Rapports* was in many ways a French magazine. Although it was an official publication of Mission France more than a dozen French authors contributed. Each issue contained on average between two and three articles by French authors. Some French contributors wrote pro-American articles about aspects of American culture and industry. Articles such as "The United States mobilizes its prodigious resources," "The Rockefeller Foundation," and "The life of workers in the United States" gave readers a French perspective on life in America. These contributions expressed the general modus operandi of Mission France's information division: pro-American propaganda by French sources was more effective than pro-American propaganda by Americans. In this respect, *Rapports* resembled the highly successful American newspaper the *Neue Zeitung* studied by Jessica Gienow-Hecht, which the Office of Military Government in Germany published from 1945 to 1947.[37] However, unlike *Neue Zeitung* editorial control of *Rapports* never left the hands of American officials in Mission France; the French contribution was limited to articles.

The French contributors to *Rapports* also wrote articles about France, usually linking them with a story about the Marshall Plan or French reconstruction. Every issue contained at least one such article. Typical of these were the articles "The Schuman Plan and what it will do for Europe," "Renault exports," "Toulouse, old city new problems," and "Scientific research in France."[38] Another common theme by French contributors dealt with Franco-American cultural exchanges. Articles such as "Degas in New Orleans," "Victor Hugo in America," and "Pierre Houdon, the first French artist in the United States" were regular features.[39]

Rapports was arguably the most successful propaganda program of Mission France. In private French officials commented enthusiastically about it. In November 1951 the American cultural attaché in Paris reported that René Pleven, then prime minister, and his wife had told him that *Rapports* was "some of the best" propaganda carried out by the United States.[40] Paul-Louis Bret, the former director of Agence Havas and Agence France Presse and a UNESCO official from 1950 to 1952 also commented favorably. He told Mission France officials that on a recent trip to Lyon he had been struck by the importance of *Rapports* for local agricultural and industrial directors.[41] "Its appearance and style prevent any boredom," he explained, "and its substance is also good."[42] Bret ultimately contributed an article to the May 1952 issue.

According to Mission France, demand for *Rapports* was widespread. By June 1950, only five months after its appearance, the magazine had received 309,000 mail-in subscriptions.[43] From May to June alone requests had increased by 130,000.[44] At the close of 1950 Mission France reported that it received two thousand written requests for *Rapports* every day.[45] Circulation crossed the half-million mark. A year later, with daily requests now averaging fifteen hundred per day, Kaplan commented: "The magazine has become a remarkably effective instrument of American policy in France."[46] In July 1952 *Rapports* reached its highest circulation. Mission France mailed one million copies monthly and distributed another hundred thousand at fairs and exhibits.[47]

In addition to the Prime Minister, who else read *Rapports*? In consultation with the French polling firm IFOP, Mission France conducted studies of the magazine's readership from 1951 to 1953. A 1951 analysis of the subscription cards provided a class-based breakdown of the readership.[48] In proportion to total population, workers and farmers were underrepresented. Civil servants, "liberal professions," and the self-employed were overrepresented. Only 1 percent of *Rapports* readers thought the Marshall Plan was harmful to France, compared to 16 percent of the French population as a whole.[49] One in five readers agreed that the Marshall Plan served French interests at great expense to the U.S.; three quarters of *Rapports* readers thought the Marshall Plan served both French and American interests. In 1953 IFOP polled 824 *Rapports* subscribers. The upper classes remained overrepresented, but gains had been made among workers.[50] Two-thirds of those polled expressed support for U.S. policies in Europe. Seven in ten found the magazine to be a useful source of information about the U.S. One in five readers thought the magazine was excessively pro-American. Overall, the readers rated *Rapports* a fifteen on a scale of one to twenty. Mission France officials were especially pleased to discover that most readers shared *Rapports* with others: six in ten loaned the magazine to others while four out of five discussed it with others. *Rapports* subscribers were also likely to read *Sélection du Reader's Digest.*[51]

However, because *Rapports* was free and Mission France never cancelled subscriptions unless requested it is impossible to take the circulation figures at face value. Mission France may have shipped a million copies per month, but were a million per month read? The evidence suggests that actual readership of the magazine decreased as its circulation numbers increased. As we have seen, the daily requests received by Mission France declined from two thousand per day in 1950 to fifteen hundred in 1951. This number, although extraordinary, should also be taken with a grain of salt. Some of these cards no doubt did represent a sincere and continuing interest in *Rapports* but it is difficult to tell how many. As a matter of policy Mission France mailed *Rapports,* issue after issue, to all who requested it only once.[52] All that can be said with confidence is that the subscription cards do represent visitors to American exhibits who requested a free subscription to *Rapports.* How many of these subscribers merely requested the magazine because it was free or out of curiosity? The 1951 survey provides some indication. Fifty-eight percent of the respondents to the survey responded that they had read "at least one" article from either the September or August issue. Six percent of the respondents reported that they had not even opened the magazine.[53] In 1952 an attempt was made to cull the mailing list. Mission France inserted a prepaid postcard in each issue it mailed.[54] Readers merely had to return the postcard to indicate a continuing desire to receive *Rapports.* The Labor Information division had used the same method with its publication *Bulletin syndicale.* The results for *Rapports* were similarly disappointing. Mission France received so few replies that it concluded the mailing had been sabotaged: "Many of the cards were said to have been removed by Communists handling the mail."[55] As *Rapports* increased in circulation its budget also increased and doubts remained whether the circulation figures provided an accurate reflection of the impact of the magazine. One American official complained that he had purchased a fish wrapped in the latest issue of *Rapports.*[56]

By late 1951 *Rapports* accounted for half of the information budget of Mission France.[57] At a time when the Mission France budget was contracting, the magazine's million-plus circulation called for increased expenditures. The production cost in 1952 was 13.75 cents per issue. The yearly expenditure in counterpart funds amounted to a staggering $1.8 million.[58] Harold Kaplan stated that *Rapports* was too heavy a burden for Mission France to carry.[59] Nevertheless, American officials were loath to drop a publication they considered effective. The head of Mission France, Henry Labouisse, told ECA officials it would be "highly regrettable" to drop *Rapports* because it possessed "at least several million readers."[60] Officials were also reluctant to drop the magazine because of their previous experience with *Voir.* In the politically charged atmosphere of the Cold War a *Rapports* clone by Communists had the potential to cause considerable damage to French public opinion.

Labouisse suggested three ways in which *Rapports* could be made a "permanent institution" of American policy in France. A first option was for the USIS to take over its publication and continue to

Rapports ended 1953

distribute it free of charge. This, however, was unlikely given the budget of the USIS in France, which was significantly smaller than that of Mission France. According to Kaplan, the necessary decrease in printing was sure to be catastrophic.[61] Another option was to publish *Rapports* on a "semi-commercial" basis. The USIS would still control the content of the magazine but the printing and distribution would be given to a French company (a *société fermière*). This option presented immense legal and public relations problems. It was not at all clear that the French government would condone such a program or that French publishers would complacently accept the appearance of the American publication.[62] Finally, Labouisse suggested contacting an American foundation for support. Both the Ford and Rockefeller foundations were active supporters of State Department projects. Yet given the cost of *Rapports* this also seemed unlikely.[63]

Given the lack of options, Labouisse made the formal decision to end *Rapports* in mid-1952.[64] He explained, "As France recovers her place in the world (and, by the same token, her nationalistic reflexes) I do not believe that it will be regarded as proper that the U.S. government should continue to distribute more than a million copies of *Rapports* each month." The last issue appeared in May 1953. A final effort to privatize the magazine occurred when Paul Winkler, the American owner of the international distribution agency Opera Mundi, expressed a desire to take over *Rapports*.[65] The American secretary of state, John Foster Dulles, rejected this last bid, however. He doubted the American embassy could maintain editorial control, and in any case Winkler was "unsuitable" for such a liaison. Ultimately, liquidating *Rapports* was preferable to the risks inherent in any of the suggested alternatives.[66]

With the end of *Rapports* the United States lost an important propaganda tool in France. Although it is unlikely that the circulation figures reflected the actual readership, *Rapports* still reached a large audience. It is doubtful that many Communists read the magazine. As the studies of the readership indicated, in many instances *Rapports* was preaching to the converted. However, it is possible to exaggerate the extent of this. Some readers were critical of *Rapports* for its lack of objectivity; others saw it primarily as a source for information about the United States. *Rapports* was attractive for more than its anticommunism. It was free, stylish, and modern, and it offered numerous articles about France and the United States by French writers (albeit many that amounted to "needlers" or "pep talks"). At a time when the price of newsprint in France was high and wages low *Rapports* may have appealed to many who simply wanted a free, well-written monthly magazine.

Although *Rapports* was its primary publication, Mission France produced a number of other pamphlets that served similar purposes. Like *Rapports,* they were circulated in the millions. During 1950 Mission France printed over ten million copies of various pamphlets and brochures.[67] Some of these were specialized, either topically or geographically. For example the pamphlet *The tourist and you* closely resembled the *Rapports* article of the same name. The Labor Information division and the agricultural exhibit also distributed specialized pamphlets. Pamphlets such as *The Marshall Plan and the southwest* and *The new destiny of the Rhône* promoted regional Marshall Plan projects. Mission France printed a quarter million of both these pamphlets.

Most pamphlets printed by Mission France addressed a general audience and sought to provide basic information about the Marshall Plan. Of these the most common was *The ABC's of the Marshall Plan,* which was distributed from 1949 to 1951. Subscribers to *Rapports* also received a free copy of the pamphlet in the mail. *ABC's* provided a brief history of the Marshall Plan, from George C. Marshall's speech at Harvard to the passage of the Economic Cooperation Act ("Congress, aware that peace could not be maintained without global economic stability, voted the necessary credits").[68] The pamphlet went on to provide an explanation of counterpart funds and the dollar amount of aid voted for 1949. A map of France provided the location of Marshall Plan projects using a pictorial key (lightning bolts represented power projects, tractors represented agricultural projects).

Another general pamphlet produced by Mission France was *What you should know about the Marshall Plan.* This nineteen-page pamphlet appeared as a supplement to the 8 February 1949 *Le Parisien Libéré,* a mass circulation daily. On a two-page spread a smiling Uncle Sam said "Help yourself and Uncle Sam will help you!" Illustrations of a cheery cowboy paying taxes destined for France or giving dollar bills to Marianne (the symbol of the French Republic) appeared throughout the pamphlet. Although things were better in France since the start of the Marshall Plan, the pamphlet informed, "It would be a mistake to think the Marshall Plan is all powerful." Indeed, readers were told that the most serious problems of France concerned "salaries and prices, respect for the law, and political stability." These priorities reflected the official line of the U.S. government vis-à-vis inflation, the black market, and the fragility of center-right coalitions. These problems could not be solved "from without" because these were "national problems, problems of authority and government."

A continual policy goal of Mission France propaganda was to counter French stereotypes about the United States and to address Communist criticisms of American society. The seventy-nine-page pamphlet *A glance at the United States* attempted to provide a near total catalogue of the American way of life. Distributed in excess of two hundred thousand in 1951, it provided information about the geography, government, population, and history of the United States.[69] Other sections dealt with music, literature, the arts, living standards, agriculture, industry, trade unions, "American women," mineral resources, and other topics. The pamphlet contained dozens of photographs. The most striking aspect of the pamphlet was its recourse to hyperbole. Virtually every photograph was of an extremely large object, or the largest of a given kind of object. One photo showed a group of researchers standing around the Palomar telescope, "the biggest in the world." Another showed an aerial view of Boulder Dam, "one of the biggest in the world." The section on geography showed a picture of the Grand Canyon. Aerial shots of Manhattan (with the highest building in the world in clear view) and Yankee Stadium showed what a big city New York was. Other figures and statistics emphasized the superabundance and size of the United States. Factories were large—the River Rouge Ford plant was the largest—as was car production. But workers' salaries were equally large, or certainly big enough to buy a car to drive on America's wide roads. Public schools were shown to be both big and numerous.

The picture presented by these pamphlets was simply too rosy to be accepted as a full and fair picture of the United States. French commentators repeatedly pointed out such flaws in American publications. The Spanish commentator Julian Marias explained Europeans' perception of American grandeur in this way:

> In certain respects the greatness of the United States is undeniable and is not denied, or at least infrequently. But this is understood to be merely a quantitative greatness and so suggests nothing really new or compelling[70]

In addition to providing general information about the United States the pamphlet program of Mission France also responded to the State Department's call for a "psychological offensive" in 1950.[71] Several hard-hitting pamphlets were prepared for distribution through either France—Etats-Unis or Jean-Paul David's Paix et Liberté.[72] In theory this would not make the pamphlets attributable to the United States government. *Who runs the U.S.?* addressed the criticism that "Wall Street" controlled American government. *Does the Soviet want peace?* provided a criticism of Soviet peace propaganda and *Free or slave labor* compared the condition of workers in "free" and "totalitarian" states. *Women of the U.S.* provided detail about the American housewife, farmer's wife, and factory worker or businesswoman at home and at work.[73] As with other pamphlets, the subscription list for *Rapports* was used for an initial mailing. Mission France also assisted the conservative daily *Le Figaro* with the production of a commercial anti-Communist publication in 1951. A French consultant to the Labor Information Division provided information to his uncle, Henri Masson-Forestier, the business manager at *Le Figaro*.[74] The pamphlet contained maps depicting the regional strength of the French Communist Party and it also "revealed" Communist publications and front organizations.

Books supplemented the American program of pamphlets and magazines in an important way. American propaganda specialists such as William C. Johnstone, who viewed books as essential weapons for psychological warfare, fueled this expansion.[75] The program was also a reaction to extensive Communist book publishing and distribution programs.[76] According to Reinhold Wagnleitner, worldwide American book exports increased tenfold from 1949 to 1963.[77] Overall, the majority of guarantees issued under the IMG went to book publishers, beginning with 55 percent in 1949 and climbing gradually but steadily in subsequent years.[78] By the time the IMG ceased in 1967 it was responsible for the distribution of 134 million copies of American books in fifty-six languages.[79]

Mission France oversaw the translation and distribution of hundreds of American books in France. Demand was great. USIS libraries and France—Etats-Unis centers needed translated texts, but French universities also lacked U.S. texts. Louisiana State University began a donation program to universities in Lille, Poitiers, Bordeaux, and Lyon.[80] A more pressing concern for psychological warriors was the acquisition of American books in translation to stock the shelves of USIS information centers. The USIS and Mission France purchased books from French publishers for placement in these centers, but also for donation to French schools, universities, and municipal libraries. The "presentation program" donated more than one hundred thousand books during 1951.[81]

The donations were certainly valuable for public relations purposes, but the titles given ("American classics" and scientific texts) lacked the hard-hitting anticommunism that satisfied the "psychological objectives" of Mission France and USIS propaganda work.[82] Pro-American, anti-Communist texts simply did not exist in French or were not satisfying to American officials. As a result, in early 1951 Mission France and the USIS began a translation program of anti-Communist and pro-American texts. Using counterpart funds, Mission France offered subsidies to French publishers to translate books and, more importantly, provided the cost of printing.[83] The initial program called for twenty-five titles per year that contributed to policy objectives by either attacking communism or providing explanations about American culture and institutions.

Some of the notable anti-Communist books to make their appearance under this program included Hannah Arendt's *The Origins of Totalitarianism* and Craig Thompson's *Police State*.[84] The program also subsidized the publication of texts by Russian émigrés, such as *The Iron Curtain* by Igor Gouzenko, *Escape from the Soviets* by Tatiana Tchernavin, and Victor Kravchenko's *I Chose Freedom*. William Tyler, the American cultural attaché in Paris, favored the translation of titles that combated the "cultural barbarian myth."[85] *Art and Life in America* by Oliver W. Larkin and *American Music* by W.L. Landowski both appeared in France as a result of the translation program.

Tyler also used his influence to insure that only suitable publications benefited from U.S. assistance. In 1950 he rebuffed efforts by Claude Gallimard and Marcel Duhamel to intervene on the behalf of *la Série Noire*. Began in 1945, this series of inexpensive detective stories published American authors or French authors under an American-sounding pseudonym (Serge Laforet, for example, published under the name Terry Stewart).[86] Yet by 1950 the series was under sustained attack from intellectuals, such as Jean-Paul Sartre, and the Communist Party. Gallimard was concerned that it would be subject to censorship because of the law of 16 July 1949 which protected children from violent publications.[87] Gallimard and Duhamel thought Tyler could influence the Press Commission favorably on their behalf. Tyler expressed his sympathy but told them he could do nothing. However, to Mission France, Tyler reported that he was struck by the vitriol directed at *la Série Noire,* and he concluded that since no American company was involved (only authors) officials could follow a path of nonintervention. He remarked that should *la Série Noire* disappear it would take a large amount of "light" American fiction with it.[88]

From *Rapports* to *Reader's Digest:* Mission France's Aid to Private Publications

In addition to its own publications Mission France provided assistance to private magazines and publications in France. *Sélection du Reader's Digest,* the French edition of *Reader's Digest,* received assistance that aided its sales in France to the detriment of French competitors. Mission France also assisted the French magazine *Réalités* by funding reporters' trips to the United States and providing information and feedback. In return for assistance these magazines provided a steady flow of pro-American articles for French readers. Other magazines also assisted the American effort. *Life,* for example, provided a traveling photographic exhibit.

Sélection du Reader's Digest first appeared in France in March 1947. The timing was propitious. International tensions were relatively low compared to what they would be in another year. According to Thierry Cottour, the sacrifices made during the war were still fresh in the memory of the French, and American products were in demand.[89] Of course, *Sélection* also had a significant material advantage because of its parent company Reader's Digest Association in Pleasantville, New York. Paper production and stock in France was one-third the prewar level. *Sélection,* however, could use paper imported from the United States. Of the first fifty-three tons of pulp used for the initial runs of *Sélection*, only thirty-five originated in France.[90]

Official negotiations with the French government to gain permission to publish *Sélection* centered on two issues: the transfer and conversion of *Sélection* profits to the United States and competition with French publications. Given the acute shortage of dollars, French officials asked for a limit on profit transfers. Reader's Digest agreed without protest. Unconverted francs were used to expand operations in France, Belgium, and Switzerland. Indeed, the Paris office became the central office for continental distribution.[91]

The issue of competition with French periodicals was also easily solved. Reader's Digest officials simply argued that *Sélection* would be a French magazine. DeWitt Wallace, the founder of *Reader's Digest,* relied on a group of competent officials to conduct dealings with the French. Paul W. Thompson, a retired American general who had participated in the Normandy landings, led the negotiating team.[92] Wallace's brother-in-law, Samuel Barclay Acheson, the director of international editions (who was also a Doctor of Theology), also contributed to the negotiations. Thompson assured officials from the Services de la presse and the prime minister's staff that *Sélection* would have an editorial staff drawn from "the most outstanding personalities of French literature."[93] In addition, Thompson stated that the goal of the magazine was to use articles from the greatest French authors, and that the magazine would remain politically neutral. "The entire direction of the magazine," he explained, "will be virtually French and it will be able to survive in France practically on its own means." Yet all of the articles in the first *Sélection* were recycled from the American *Reader's Digest.* A condensed translation of Rémy's (Gilbert Renault) *Mémoires d'un agent secret de la France libre* that had previously appeared in *Reader's Digest* reappeared in its original version for *Sélection.*[94] French officials accepted Thompson's assurances and cleared *Sélec-*

tion for publication. It is also likely that in 1947 the French government did not want to risk starting a dispute with *Reader's Digest* while it was in the process of negotiating with the U.S. for economic aid.

Beginning in late 1947 *Sélection* mounted an extensive advertising campaign and in late 1948 it crossed the printing milestone of a million copies. In 1947 *Le Monde* reported that *Sélection* was a stunning success.[95] The cover of the first *Sélection* showed Notre Dame de Paris in springtime, and successive covers also favored nationalistic themes: Joan of Arc, the Tour de France, and the Tricolor. André Siegfried provided a dedication that filled the inside front and back covers of the first issue. There was, he explained, something young and exciting about *Sélection* that reflected the curiosity of its editors. This member of the French Academy also recommended reading *Sélection* for its condensed treatment of books. "I believe," concluded Siegfried, "that Kant himself, the recluse of Koenigsberg, would read *Reader's Digest* if he were alive today." In fact, *Sélection* had the endorsement of two members of the French Academy. Jules Romains, also writing on the inside cover, expressed his hope that the publication would be successful in France. Whatever the effects of such blessings by the French Academy, *Sélection* was a hit. By 1954 it possessed an astounding half-million mail subscribers.[96] *Sélection* dominated its French rivals. Two French publications, *Constellation: Le monde vu en Français* and *Ecclesia,* copied the format and style of *Sélection* but failed to attract either the buyers or subscribers to match *Sélection.*

The attacks against *Sélection* indicate that like Hollywood or Coca-Cola, it became a symbol of American cultural and economic penetration. Jean-Paul Sartre's review *Les Temps modernes,* Emmanuel Mounier's *Esprit,* and many others attacked it as emblematic of America's cultural invasion of France.[97] Georges Soria derided it for promoting "frivolism and eroticism."[98] *Sélection,* like American movies, according to the Communist writer, presented the United States as a land where everyone was born with a car next to their baby crib and a bathroom in pink marble, but it did little to reveal the complexities of life or the problems the country faced.[99]

Cottour suggests a number of reasons for the success of *Sélection.* Relative to other magazines, *Sélection* was inexpensive at just twenty-five francs per issue. *Esprit,* the intellectual monthly, cost seventy-five francs. The highbrow *Réalités* cost one hundred and fifty francs per issue. The price of *Sélection* did increase to seventy francs per issue by 1951 but this was still reasonable and color photos and illustrations were added. *Sélection* also had an advantage because of the financial resources of Reader's Digest Association. The parent company purchased a building on the prestigious boulevard St. Germain.[100] Reader's Digest also gave *Sélection* an advantage in marketing and technical expertise that other competitors had to acquire through experience. Officials from Pleasantville made a number of trips to Paris during the first years of *Sélection* to ensure that the operation proceeded smoothly.[101] The pocket-sized format of *Sélection* was also unique and may have contributed to its popularity.[102] Contrary to Thompson's professed neutrality, *Sélection* was virulently anti-Communist. This was inevitable given that reprints from *Reader's Digest* were the major source of articles. But *Sélection* also created a niche by publishing brief and nonspecialized articles about science and medicine. *Sélection* was careful to print articles that retained an appeal to both sexes. The condensed readings were also a draw. Finally, *Sélection* benefited from the marketing of the New York firm J. Walter Thompson. The direct, personable approach of *Sélection* was unlike any other periodical in France. When prices rose, subscribers received an explanation of the reasons why. When a subscription ran out, *Sélection* sent the next issue free as a "reminder." However, even given these explanations Cottour is still struck by the achievement of *Sélection*, calling its success "an aberration."[103]

The records of Mission France indicate another reason for *Sélection*'s dominance in the French market. In late 1951 Paul W. Thompson wrote the head of Mission France, Henry Labouisse, with an unusual request. Thompson's letter began with a moving description of the role *Sélection* played in the fight against communism:

> The first number of *Sélection* appeared in March of 1947, at a time when, you will recall, France was a battlefield on which Democracy was locked in a life-and-death struggle against a strong and militant communism. In those critical pre-ECA days the owners of Reader's Digest thus risked prestige and private money on a venture attended by obvious risks. In fact, *Sélection* was heartily welcomed by the French public, and its circulation rapidly rose beyond the one million copies per month level. I like to think that this mass appearance of a typical American publication on the French scene at that critical time contributed to the subsequent action of the French people in rejecting communism.[104]

Thompson then requested the list of *Rapports* subscribers, which he understood to be in excess of eight hundred thousand. The list was especially attractive, he explained, because many on it were rural inhabitants. They would be likely to purchase subscriptions to *Sélection* not only because of their pro-American tendencies (in theory those who requested *Rapports* were pro-American), but also because of the difficulty in obtaining international reading material in small towns and villages.[105]

Sélection got Rapports subscriber list to increase pro-America sales

Thompson's letter was marked with a sense of urgency. Access to the *Rapports* list offered the best possible means to increase sales and "contribute to the objectives" of the United States at the same time. He pointed out that 90 percent of the magazine's sales occurred on the newsstand. Paying subscribers amounted to fewer than two hundred thousand. According to Cottour, *Sélection* faced a crisis in the early months of 1952.[106] Sales had declined in the previous two years and the magazine staff was anxious to increase the number of paying subscribers to stay profitable.

The head of Mission France immediately forwarded the request to Washington. Labouisse stated that there were drawbacks and advantages to the proposal; given the potential legal issues he wanted to defer to the judgment of the legal advisors. Richard Bissell, the deputy ECA administrator, replied within a week that it would be impossible to give the list to Reader's Digest.[107] Labouisse informed Thompson of the decision and suggested that he take up the matter with the office of General Counsel in Washington.[108]

Undeterred, Thompson renewed his request a year later. This time, however, Mission France endorsed the proposal, calling *Sélection* a "valuable supplement to official information activities."[109] The conditions for the release were stringent.[110] Reader's Digest agreed to pay all fees for duplication. Furthermore, the mailings would have to be done in blocks of three hundred thousand covering three months and distributed over a wide area to avoid saturation. No link between *Sélection* and the U.S. government could be revealed or implied. Thompson accepted the conditions immediately and the first mailing went out in the spring of 1953.[111]

Why did U.S. officials reverse their decision? It is unclear what had changed in a year—perhaps persistent lobbying by Thompson, perhaps a desire on the part of the embassy to increase the flow of general, pro-American material in France from nongovernment sources. Venona Project declassifications provide another possible, albeit speculative, reason for the American reversal. These documents identify André Labarthe, the director of *Constellation,* as a soviet agent (code name: Jérôme) during the Second World War.[112] Early in the war Labarthe, a former Socialist deputy, held the position of director general of French armament and scientific research. The Venona documents naming Labarthe were deciphered in 1948 at the earliest, but perhaps much later. Thus, it is possible that Labarthe had been identified during the period of the *Reader's Digest* request. If this was the case, Thompson's argument that assistance to *Reader's Digest* would help defeat communism in France would have gained greater saliency among American officials.

Did the *Rapports* list make the difference between success and failure for *Sélection?* It is hard to say. Cottour, without access to American archives, contends *Sélection* was worry-free beginning only in
1954 when it possessed a numerically solid subscription base. The
Rapports list certainly had the potential to account for the increase
in subscriptions from 1953 to 1954. According to the terms for the
release of the list, Reader's Digest was responsible for supplying
Mission France with the names of individuals from the *Rapports* list
who purchased subscriptions to *Sélection.* Unfortunately, this document no longer exists, or remains undiscovered in the archives. At
the time the request was made the sales of *Sélection* were in decline,
but the magazine was hardly on the brink of folding. To be sure, one
of the advantages of *Sélection* was that its parent company could
shrug off short-term losses while funding advertising campaigns and
subscription drives. Reader's Digest also qualified for guaranties
from the IMG which defrayed production and distribution costs.[113]
Nevertheless, obtaining the names and addresses of over a million
potential subscribers, many of whom were ideal targets for subscription sales, was certainly a luxury the French competitors of
Sélection did not enjoy. The *Rapports* list provides the most obvious
explanation for the dramatic increase in *Sélection*'s subscription
sales. One notable correlation is that the IFOP poll indicating overlap between *Rapports* and *Sélection* readers was taken after the first
mailing. The *Rapports* list combined with other forms of assistance
like the IMG program and the power of a multinational corporation
ensured that *Sélection* would have a distinct material advantage over
its competitors. *Constellation* and *Ecclesia* had done their best to im-
itate the style of the American magazine, but they could duplicate
neither the breadth of U.S. governmental assistance, nor the resources
of Reader's Digest in Pleasantville.

Mission France provided assistance to other private periodicals
that supported the objectives of the United States. The expensive, elite-
oriented *Réalités* was one such magazine. Unlike *Sélection, Réalités*
was French produced and French owned. Founded in 1946, *Réalités*
achieved a circulation of one hundred and fifty thousand by 1953, modest by the standard of better-known periodicals. Nevertheless, costing
the equivalent of $1.25 per issue, *Réalités* had an average reader who
was well off. The editor and founder, Alfred Max, described *Réalités*
as "a well-edited magazine on the American pattern" that provided perspectives on current events, personalities, art and decoration, travel,
and economics.[114]

Réalités was a glossy, slick magazine. It was slightly larger than
8½" by 11" and possessed abundant color photographs. The table of

contents presented the regular features under the rubric "current politics and Parisian life." They included a column about current theatre, cinema, and other cultural events; an editorial; *réalités du monde*—a synopsis of international politics; and a four-page spread of photographs of notable politicians and intellectuals. Each issue also contained a literary insert. A typical issue contained advertisements for Frigidaires, transatlantic air travel, cognac, pianos, and electronic calculating machines.

The articles of *Réalités* appealed to an upper-class audience. Editorials by Raymond Aron and articles supporting European unification gave it an "Atlanticist" character. In some cases *Réalités* was pro-American for what it did not say. An article by Henri Perruchot on the defense of the French language cited failing orthography, punctuation, and grammar as the clearest indicators of "decadence."[115] Perruchot did not mention the increasing use of anglicisms, a practice such writers as René Etiemble would later vituperate against. *Réalités* was also explicitly pro-American. The article "How the richest foreigners dress in Paris" contained a full-page picture of Mrs. David Bruce (David Bruce was then head of Mission France but would soon take over the Embassy) in an evening dress.[116] The author noted she preferred the designers Christian Dior and Jean Dessès. When it came to economic issues *Réalités* catered to the *patronat,* but also called for some liberalization in trade practices and labor relations. An article from the same issue, "How the Marshall Plan functions," responded to criticisms that the process of obtaining counterpart funds was too bureaucratic. Such controls were necessary, the author suggested, because the United States had a right to be sure the money was not spent "in vain." Another article argued in support of Keynesian economics: "Already in partial use in the United States and England, it limits crises, maintains full employment, and increases individual consumption in constantly expanding economy."[117]

Réalités did not avoid sensitive issues such as rearmament and military spending. The March 1950 article "American Strategy" explained that the United States had moved away from a nuclear "push-button" strategy to one predicated on "realism" and "equilibrium."[118] This included stationing U.S. troops in France. Aron was a regular contributor of both editorials and articles. In a May 1950 editorial he argued that "peace, perhaps, is the Cold War." In another editorial he argued that the United States offered the only effective check to Soviet expansion.[119]

On occasion Mission France offered direct assistance to *Réalités.* In September 1952 the editors asked Mission France for assistance with an upcoming issue devoted to life in the United States. Specifically, *Réalités* asked for financial assistance and logistical support for an extended visit to the United States by two reporters and a photographer.[120] Mission France and the State Department not only granted this request, they also agreed to fund an extensive poll by IFOP that would appear in the same issue.[121] "It is difficult," concluded William R. Tyler, the American cultural attaché, "to see how this issue could fail to influence French opinion along the lines which USIS France is striving to direct it."[122] The assistance given remained hidden. The *Réalités* team spent several weeks in the United States and the product of the trip appeared as the September 1953 issue, "America as the French see it." The articles were immediately made available to *Sélection* and an abridged translation appeared in *U.S. News and World Report.*[123]

A substantial portion of the issue was devoted to "the Negro question." American publications rarely responded to French criticisms of racial inequality in the United States. The French reporters, however, made it a point to investigate these criticisms. In addition to revealing the authors' own assumptions about race, their conclusions were among the most strident pro-American opinions written by a French source during this period:

> Our first impression was that the insoluble theoretical aspects of the question are not translated violently into daily life, mainly because of the Negro's disarming good will and his incurable optimism. Later on, but only later, did we discover that the real answer is that the Negroes have already won their battle. Time is on their side; the era of martyrs and mass protests *useful* to their cause has definitely ended…. The American Negro has won his fight. He has won on all fronts but in different degrees with certain inconsistencies and absurdities resulting quite often from the simple fact that evolution over recent years has been much too rapid.[124]

The authors admitted that racism still existed in Mississippi and that the outcome there might be unclear for another few years, but the problems arose only from a few "unreconstructed rebels." In an effort at self-reflexivity, the authors compared American racism with French elitism: "Suddenly we remembered our good friends, I., Q., and R., navy officers, who were boasting back in 1946 that they had never shaken hands with a sailor in their lives." The State Department was so impressed with the way *Réalités* had "tackled the Negro question" that they sought to make a pamphlet out of the article for global distribution. This was rejected by the Embassy in Paris, however, because such a pamphlet would have revealed the links between *Réalités* and the U.S. government.[125]

"America as the French see it" provided positive comment on almost all the areas of American life subject to comment by French critics. An examination of the breadth and depth of religious faith in the United States, for example, countered French criticisms that the United States was morally vapid. Detailed interviews with factory workers and union officials countered criticisms that American capitalists were all-powerful. Such interviews were also valuable, from an American point of view, because they showed the French *patronat* that cooperation with non-Communist trade unions was possible and economically viable.

There can be little doubt that *Réalités* attracted readers who, by virtue of economic and social standing, were sympathetic to the United States. Nevertheless, many of the letters to the editor published by the magazine expressed ambivalence toward the United States. That is, if, following Aron, many readers thought association with the North Atlantic Treaty and the United States offered the best security against Soviet expansion, they were less clear that French culture benefited as a result of such ties.[126] The millions of dollars spent on pro-American propaganda failed to decrease French ambivalence toward the United States. Indeed, as I have argued, U.S. government programs strengthened French ambivalence more often than not. Some articles also made clear that support for American economic and foreign policy—however conditional—should not be confused with supporting the American way of life. An article in the August 1950 issue on comparative standards of living made this clear: "Spiritual values apart, there is still much to do in France if we want to acquire a material well-being of the same order as the most industrialized countries."

Cooperation with private publications generally benefited the propaganda efforts of Mission France. *Réalités* and *Sélection* provided private outlets for American material at a time when the French public was weary of political propaganda by the United States and the Soviet Union.[127] Yet there was a risk in trusting private industry to conduct propaganda. Helen Kirkpatrick and William R. Tyler vetted propaganda material originating from Washington as much as possible, but control over private publications escaped them. The editorial by Henry Luce in the January 1953 issue of *Life* illustrated how relations with private publications could and did break down.

The infamous editorial, entitled "France: New Government," appeared in the American edition on 26 January 1953. Noting that the average life span of French government was four and half months, Luce offered this "unintellectual" analogy of French government:

> The building where the National Assembly convenes is really a theater with a stage instead of a speaker's rostrum. The show on the stage is

produced and played in by the current premier and cabinet ministers: the members of the Assembly make up the audience. The show always opens with a rollicking farce involving Marianne—the beautiful girl who symbolizes the Republic—and the Prime Minister and cabinet members who rush around and hide behind and under things whenever there's a knock on the door.[128]

Following this and other interruptions in the play, the State Department, played by W.C. Fields, placed a billion-dollar note in Marianne's garter. The editorial expressed hope that French citizens would work to change "the number one obstacle" to European unity: the habits and machinery of French politics.

Official French reaction was swift. The French ambassador, Henri Bonnet, communicated an official note of protest on 28 January.[129] The U.S. ambassador in Paris, James C. Dunn, thought the editorial was "particularly unfortunate" because French officials interpreted it as an indication of the new Eisenhower administration's perception of France (some French commentators noted the links between Luce, Eisenhower, and the propaganda specialist C.D. Jackson). Yet Dunn thought that the French outcry was a product of the current "psychological climate" rather than any long-term disaffection with American policy.[130]

Other American officials were not as sanguine. One USIS official provided a catalogue of current issues that the editorial had exacerbated: the negative French reaction to the trial of the Rosenbergs; the persecution of Charlie Chaplin; the debate on the European Defense Community; the U.S.'s use of the U.N. to "meddle" in north Africa.[131] *Life* and Mission France had been working on a number of projects prior to the editorial's appearance. The most visible project was a traveling exhibit, "*Life* Memorable Photographs." In the days following the appearance of the editorial, translations appeared in dozens of regional and national newspapers.[132] French reaction to news of the editorial was so negative that the showing of the *Life* exhibit was cancelled in Lyon, Lille, Rouen, and Marseille, as a result of both official French requests and decisions by regional USIS officers.[133]

Writing in *Le Figaro*, François Mauriac provided the most acerbic commentary.[134] His commentary was all the more notable because neither Mauriac nor *Le Figaro* were known for their anti-Americanism. Mauriac accused Americans of measuring the greatness of a nation only in terms of its material prosperity. As such, American commentators had little authority to comment on another nation's political morality. In any case, it was the United States' own morality of isolationism that torpedoed the League of Nations after the First World War ("where thirty Frenchmen died for every American death").

Mauriac found the vulgarity and tastelessness of the editorial especially disturbing. It indicated a pathological weakness in the American psyche, perhaps sexual repression, and a distinct lack of nobility unbefitting a nuclear power. Finally, Mauriac noted that France was currently involved in a bloody war on behalf of the shared values of Western Civilization: "It is not for France alone that French and Vietnamese die every day." Perhaps the editors of *Life* were also critical of this "dirty war," but Mauriac knew that the Pentagon had a different view of it.

Many French commentators reacted to the editorial by declaring that relations with the United States were irretrievably damaged even prior to Luce's piece. Writing in *La Tribune* (Saint Etienne), Michel Soulié declared,

> The article in *Life* rings the death knell on the policy inaugurated by the Marshall Plan. It must be taken seriously, if not tragically. It is not enough to reply to it by protestations of wounded national pride; one must recognize it for what it is and prepare accordingly for the future.[135]

La Dépêche du Midi (Toulouse) noted that the French were gradually coming to view anti-Americanism as "one of the most elementary principles of life in general." The American cultural attaché in Washington, Charles K. Moffly, concluded, "It is clear that the *Life* editorial ... has markedly contributed to French resentment."[136]

Bandes desinées: "De-Americanization"?

The impact of American periodicals such as *Life, Sélection du Reader's Digest,* and derivative French periodicals such as *Réalités* provide examples of the strength of the American cultural presence in France. Yet Pascal Ory and, more recently, Thierry Crépin have attempted to provide counterexamples to this hegemony.[137] Examining comic strips (*bandes dessinées*) from 1945 to 1950, Ory and Crépin conclude that they are an instance of *désaméricanisation,* or "de-Americanization."[138] Prior to the war the American-owned King Features dominated the French comic book market. Its chief representative, Paul Winkler, also ran an international distribution company based in Paris, Opera Mundi, which in turn was linked to the Hearst publishing empire. King Features' leading publication in 1939 was *Le Journal de Mickey Mouse* with a circulation just under four hundred thousand.[139] Other American comics such as *Tarzan, Felix le chat, Charlie Chan,* and *Guy l'éclair* (Flash Gordon) contributed to American dominance.[140] Yet following the war, Ory contends, American comic books never regained

their prewar hegemony. Instead, a "Franco-Belgian" school successfully challenged American dominance with *Le Journal de Tintin* and *Le
Journal de Spirou*. Ory suggests two reasons for this reversal. Aes-
thetically, American comic strips were less appealing than new
comics from Belgium. The other reason was the law of 16 July 1949,
on Publications for Youth. This censored children's publications
that depicted crimes, violence, or moral debauchery.[141] In addition
Crépin suggests that the two Belgian comics successfully adapted to
this new law and appealed to the Catholic culture of their French
readers.[142]

Although the law was not directed against American publications
per se, Crépin and Ory argue that the overseeing commission (La commission de surveillance et de contrôle des publications destinées à
l'enfance et à l'adolescence) used this prohibition (article two) as a
protectionist device against American comics.[143] It is no surprise that
American comics received such treatment. Aside from any commercial interests in prohibiting American comics, French critics across
the political spectrum blamed American culture for corrupting the
youth of France. Indeed, given the increase in youth delinquency, in
both France and the United States, perhaps only Hollywood received
more blame for the perceived moral decline.[144] Nevertheless, the
analyses of Crépin and Ory are in need of revision. They overesti-
mate the decline of American comics. Furthermore, they neglect the
influence of Mission France and the U.S. government in weakening
the legislation.

In early 1948 representatives from Opera Mundi and Hearst contacted the Embassy regarding the proposed legislation on children's
publications.[145] The most alarming component of the proposed law
was article twelve, which set a 25 percent maximum content of foreign material for all children's publications. American publishers argued that this would set a dangerous precedent. It would eventually
allow, they suggested, for future regulation of American books and
newspapers. Furthermore, in their eyes the limitation was politically
inspired because foreign material from any other country but the
United States was negligible.[146] Winkler assured the Embassy that
Opera Mundi publications, and American comics in general, were of
the highest moral character. He had no objection to banning depic-
tions of moral debauchery in children's publications and he included
examples of violent and sexual content from the Communist comic
Vaillant. The Blum-Byrnes accords regulating American movies in
France had just been renegotiated on stricter terms, and measures
against American publications may have seemed like the next logical target.[147]

Colonel Félix, the president of the National Assembly's press committee and a deputy of marked pro-American sympathies, did not support the original proposal banning foreign material.[148] However, the measure did receive support from the Ministry of Education and a number of Socialist and MRP deputies.[149] American officials commiserated with Winkler that Communists were manipulating these deputies.[150] However, the text of the proposal indicated that something else was at stake: "If educational goals guide the majority of French editors whose publications are directed at children such is not the case for foreign editors who see children only as clients, and as a means to increase profits."[151] The American cultural attaché suggested that direct approaches be made to leaders of the moderate Mouvement républicain populaire (MRP) because they "did not realize" that the measure was a Communist-inspired attempt to ban American publications.[152]

Felix reportedly told Tyler that an official intervention by the American embassy would provide him with the necessary leverage to kill the measure (article twelve) before it came to a vote.[153] Winkler and the embassy suffered a setback when Paul Gosset, an MRP deputy who supported limitations on American comics, replaced Colonel Felix as head of the press committee.[154] Winkler himself lobbied energetically and he informed Tyler that he had obtained an "informant" in the Council of the Republic (the French upper house) who had provided him with a blueprint on how to kill the measure.[155] Rather than directly approaching non-Communist deputies in the Assembly, Winkler's informant told him that direct intervention by the U.S. embassy would lead the Minister of Justice (and the keeper of the Seals), André Marie, to remove the questionable paragraphs entirely before the law left the Council of the Republic. The Assembly would accept this change on a second reading because it would not risk its majority over the issue.

Less than a week after receiving Winkler's blueprint, the American embassy filed an official "verbal note" of protest with the minister of foreign affairs, Maurice Schumann.[156] The American ambassador, David Bruce, stated that article twelve was redundant in light of article two, which regulated publications based on moral content. Bruce reminded the foreign minister that article twelve was also a breach of the 1947 Geneva agreement concerning trade and informational exchange. In the Assembly André Marie had already cited the risk of reprisals against French products by the United States.[157] Schumann wrote André Marie to demand the abrogation of article twelve shortly after he received Bruce's message.[158] In March the Council of the Republic removed article twelve as Winkler had predicted.[159] The law was then passed without article twelve, but the Communists abstained because it was now clear that a "right-wing" interpretation of article two had the potential to censor Communist publications.[160]

Winkler and the American Embassy had effectively bypassed Communist and non-Communist deputies in the National Assembly who supported limiting American comics based on nationalistic principles. Yet the Assembly soon made another attempt to "set a watch over the makers of stories." The sponsors this time were four Socialist deputies who in 1950 put forward the Deixonne proposition (named after one of the deputies) that set a 75 percent minimum of French content in children's publications.[161] With Communist support the measure had a good chance of passing. Winkler once again rallied support from the Council of the Republic, the American Embassy, and private groups. He beseeched the head of the American Federation of Labor, J. Lovestone, to intervene on his behalf with Léon Blum. "The Socialist group of the French Assembly," he explained, "seems to be maneuvered, undoubtedly without its leaders being aware of it, by Communist interests."[162] The American Embassy retransmitted its verbal note to the Minister of Foreign Affairs.[163] The Deixonne proposition, like article twelve, was rejected by the Council of the Republic.[164]

The State Department and Winkler had successfully lobbied for the removal of article twelve, but did article two function, as Ory and Crépin suggest, as a protectionist measure against American publications? It did, but it is unclear that it, alone, was a sufficient obstacle to American publications. Crépin's analysis of the meetings of the oversight commission demonstrates that the members of the commission viewed their "moral duty" to protect French youth as more important than their role in restricting free trade.[165] In fact, French resistance to American comics predated the Law of July 16. In early 1948 Winkler had sought assistance from the American embassy to regain French authorization to publish *Le Journal de Mickey*.[166] Authorization was not granted until 1952 by which time the Belgian *Tintin* had established itself. And yet within a year of its appearance *Le Journal de Mickey* obtained a circulation in excess of six hundred thousand—hardly an indication of an aesthetic preference among consumers for French publications.[167] To be sure, American comics were subject to censorship as a result of article two, but so were many French publications.

Rather than a case of "de-Americanization," the debate surrounding the Law of July 16 revealed the extent of American influence in French politics. Winkler and American officials immediately identified article twelve as the greatest danger, and their efforts to have it removed were successful. As for article two, American officials showed little interest in opposing it because it did, after all, have the potential to censor publications by the Communist party. Ultimately, few French politicians disagreed on the need to "set a watch over the makers of stories." The only question was which storyteller represented the greatest threat: the United States or the Soviet Union. For the center-right governments of the Fourth Republic the answer was, clearly, the Soviet Union and the Communist Party of France. As for the Communists, they were quite right to view Opera Mundi as an agent of the United States. Shortly after the law was passed, Opera Mundi agreed to a request from the State Department to circulate an anti-Communist article, "Moscow's Phony Peace Campaign," to its agencies throughout Europe, South America, and Asia.[168]

The Invasion of American Mass Media

[handwritten marginal note: too much Am. media in France]

In 1952, after four years of Marshall Plan aid and in the midst of increasing military aid (the Mutual Defense Assistance Program) the head of Mission France's information division, Harold Kaplan, briefed American officials.[169] Kaplan catalogued the various projects carried out by the seventy American information officers with the assistance of some two hundred French staffers. From publications to exhibits, from cooperating with the Voice of America to newsreel showings, the programs of Mission France reached, or at least attempted to reach, every village and town in France. Yet Kaplan advised that the information and propaganda work be dramatically reduced. If this recommendation was not in itself startling, the reasons behind it were. According to Kaplan, there was simply too much U.S. material, from too many sources, both public and private. They had reached the point of "an excessive American presence in this country."[170] He developed this thesis in detail:

> Much of the presence results from the impact of commercial, educational, and other private organizations, and as such is largely beyond our control. American fiction, Hollywood, *Reader's Digest,* the great press and photo agencies, have created a situation absolutely unprecedented in French history. The French have had great periods of curiosity and preoccupation with respect to foreign civilizations ... but there has never been anything comparable to the present invasion of American mass media.... The danger which remains, along with some unimaginable picture of America which emerges from the cacophony, is the sheer oppressiveness of mass and volume on a people who, for centuries, have conceived of *rayonnement* as an essentially outward-going movement.[171]

As we saw, it was Mission France that assisted *Reader's Digest* in achieving dominance in the French market. It was Mission France that worked with French editors to produce *Réalités* "on the American pattern." Perhaps Kaplan was not insensitive to the irony. In the long run, he suggested, the best that could be hoped for was that the merits and drawbacks of all this material would cancel each other.

Historical scholarship now rightly emphasizes the cultural component of American expansion in Europe. Reinhold Wagnleitner, for example, argues that the support given to American culture was not a minor element of U.S. economic, military, and political strategy. Government aid to the U.S. culture industry was so extensive, he suggests, because American culture offered the best means of establishing a Pax Americana.[172] American companies used anticommunism as a means to convince the American government that they were worthy of receiving aid. For private ventures, however, political commitment often defers to commercial interests. In many cases the assistance provided arose on an ad hoc basis (such as the use of the *Rapports* list). In other cases the initiative came from Mission France or the USIS. The overall picture of intervention must take into account improvisation and inconsistency. Above all, the "invasion" did not attain all the political goals of Mission France even if the commercial ventures succeeded.

The publications considered here provide insight into the nature of Americanization. Most importantly, these publications demonstrate the importance of understanding the impact of political economy. *Voir* and *Rapports* achieved wide popularity not only because French readers liked them, but also because they were free (or inexpensive in the case of *Voir*). Postwar France was a country not only of limited resources, but also of limited media and consumer goods. The United States had the will and the means to fill the vacuum. In turn, the popularity of *Voir, Rapports,* and *Sélection* prompted French imitation. Once established, American publications became indicators and symbols of the economic, political, and cultural presence of the United States in France. *Réalités,* so congenial in outlook to U.S. policy, also copied the form of American mass culture. Imitation was not limited to pro-American publications either. The Communist comic *Vaillant,* for example, not only used the American innovation of text balloons, it possessed the gritty feel and look of American comics and movies.

This is not to suggest that American mass print culture was uncontested or universally adopted, but only to note that American political and economic penetration as a result of the Marshall Plan enabled and facilitated cultural penetration on equal or better terms with local products. In general, vigilant opposition by the United

States to restrictive trade practices and an umbrella of investment incentives and guaranties created conditions conducive to expansion abroad. *Sélection* illustrated this dynamic. It would be inaccurate to suggest that *Sélection* achieved dominance because French consumers preferred it to *Constellation* and *Ecclesia*. This assumes that *Sélection* operated under the conditions of a free market, which was not the case. It had access to advantageous resources and information provided by the U.S. government. The isolated subscribers to *Sélection* were not exercising a choice between it and French competitors. Political economy, in this case and others, determines the choices available to consumers.

Rapports and *Sélection* were two of the most widespread magazines in France during the Marshall Plan. How did these explicitly pro-American publications affect its French readers? Influence and reception are certainly two of the most difficult processes for historians to measure. Nevertheless, there are theoretical tools available that allow for at least some tentative answers to this question. This chapter has illustrated the political economy of Americanization vis-à-vis *Rapports, Sélection,* and book publications. To this we can add Joanne P. Sharp's analysis and reading of the "imaginary geography" created by *Reader's Digest*.[173] For Sharp, the anticommunism of *Reader's Digest* had implications for its readers' identities. Its politico-religious discourse created a "moral geography" of the world that projected and reflected American values.[174] Central to this geography was the division of the world into American and Soviet. This binary, "them" and "us," reinforced a pro-American, anti-Communist identity. Through this binary DeWitt Wallace articulated his own beliefs about religion, the role of government, race, gender, and society. According to Sharp, *Reader's Digest* empowered its readers in a carefully constructed way. The imaginary geography helped place the individual within the global context of the struggle between the American way of life and communism, and it gave prescriptions for action and stories of the consequences of inaction and failure.[175] Sharp points out that in this way, political issues resonated with individuals who had "little or no direct relationship with them."[176] What beliefs or actions did *Reader's Digest* help promote in its devoted readers? Sharp compares its impact to fear and paranoia caused by Orson Welles's 1938 broadcast of *War of the Worlds*.[177]

Sharp does not suggest that there was only one possible way to read the magazine; she concedes that individuals engaged with *Reader's Digest* in different ways.[178] However, an infinite number of readings were not possible either. The format of the articles, the use of "you" and "I" to draw in the reader, its appeal to authority and the air of objectivity and other characteristics of the magazine, along with factors like education, socialization, and language rules, delineated the boundaries of "normal" meaning. "Each reading may be unique," Sharp explains, "but only in a trivial sense as it relates to the issues discussed here."[179] There exists, in other words, a "mass subject" that arises from the discursive conditions of the public sphere.[180]

Sélection and *Rapports* illustrate an important relationship in our understanding of Americanization and globalization. The flow of information, people, capital, and culture, as we have already seen, is an important aspect of globalization. The extent to which these processes undermine the sovereignty of the nation-state is a central question in current debates about the legitimacy of the nation-state and its relationship to globalization.[181] Benjamin Barber, for example, argues that transnational capital, communication and information networks undermine the sovereignty of strong states.[182] The France of the Marshall Plan years was hardly self-sufficient. American pamphlets and publications, public and private, were unprecedented peacetime interventions by the United States into the very subjectivity of another public. Through *Sélection, Rapports,* millions of pamphlets, and other publications the United States represented a political authority within France distinct from the government of the Fourth Republic. During the Marshall Plan the Fourth Republic delegated, surrendered, or quite simply lacked the authority to control political debate or the articulation of political choices within its own borders.[183]

Thus, the expansion of American mass culture raised fundamental issues in France. As Kaplan indicated, the issue was not only the "invasion" of American mass media, but also what this said about the French state and culture. Plato's warning about the makers of stories was particularly applicable to French politicians during the Marshall Plan years. The success of the publications discussed in this chapter shows that Americanization, like globalization, was not an inevitable, natural process. Rather, it was the result of political economy and the quiescence of pro-American politicians. Opposition to American publications and comics, Coca-Cola, or the Blum-Byrnes accords on the cinema reflected domestic political divisions in France, but it was also an attempt by French politicians to accommodate the abdication of sovereignty with the tradition of a *voluntariste* state.

Am media penetrated France because they were cheap, and because US political + economic policies facilitated them

Notes

1. Georges Soria, *La France deviendra-t-elle une colonie américaine?* préface Frédéric Joliot-Curie (Paris: Éditions du Pavillon, 1948).
2. Ibid., 187.
3. See, for example, Richard Pells, *Not Like Us,* 238.
4. Philippe Roger, *Rêves et cauchemars américains,* Chapitre II, "Comment les français connaissent-ils les États-Unis?"
5. See, for example, Patricia Hubert-Lacombe, *Le Cinéma Français dans la guerre froide* (Paris: L'Harmattan, 1997); Jean-Pierre Jeancolas, "L'Arrangement Blum-Byrnes à l'épreuve des faits: les relations (cinématographique) franco-américaines de 1944-1948," *Bulletin de l'Association française de récherche sur l'histoire du cinéma,* no. 13, (Décembre 1993): 3–49; Richard F. Kuisel, "The Fernandel Factor: the Rivalry between the French and American Cinema in the 1950s," unpublished paper; Fabrice Montebello, "Hollywood Films in a French Working Class Milieu: Longwy, 1945-1960," in David Ellwood and Rob Kroes, eds., *Hollywood in Europe: Experiences of a Cultural Hegemony* (Amsterdam: VU University Press, 1994): 213–246; Jens Ulff-Møller, *Hollywood's Film Wars with France: Film-Trade Diplomacy and the Emergence of the French Film Quota Policy* (Rochester: University of Rochester Press, 2002).
6. Telegram from Dean Acheson, U.S. Secretary of State, to American Embassy, Paris, 7 March 1952, NARA, central decimal files of the State Department, 851.452/2-1352.
7. Alan Milward, *The Reconstruction of Western Europe, 1945-51* (London: Methuen & Co., 1984), 91.
8. Milward, *The Reconstruction of Western Europe, 1945-51,* 121; see also "American Surplus," *Financial Times,* 22 March 1950.
9. Milward, *The Reconstruction of Western Europe, 1945-51,* 347–349.
10. Ibid., 93.
11. Gérard Bossuat, *La France, l'aide américaine et la construction européene, 1944-1954* (Paris: Comité pour l'Histoire Economique et Financière de la France, 1992) 1: 374.
12. Telegram from OSR to all Missions, 30 November 1949, NARA, RG. 469, entry 921, box 1.
13. Ibid.
14. Bossuat, *La France, l'aide américaine et la construction européene, 1944-1954,* 1: 375.
15. Foreign Aid Appropriation Act of 1949 (public law no. 793, 80th Congress), NARA, RG. 469, entry 1037, box 1.
16. Reinhold Wagnleitner, *Coca-Colonization and the Cold War,* 244.
17. Extension of European Recovery hearings, 21 February 1950, U.S. Senate Committee on Foreign Affairs.
18. Bingham suggested that American investors still saw the "France of 1947," but that the perception was slowing changing. Extension of European Recovery hearings, 21 February 1950.
19. Bossuat, *La France, l'aide américaine et la construction européene, 1944-1954,* 1: 375.
20. Memo from Harriman to Mellen, Status of IMG program as of 31 December 1949, NARA, RG. 469, entry 928, box 25.
21. Milward, *Reconstruction of Western Europe, 1945-51,* 125.
22. Kuisel, *Seducing the French,* 53–55.
23. Hollywood also provides an example of this. Wagnleitner argues that during the Allied occupation the Austrian government was "completely subordinate" to the American film industry, 265.

24. Memo from Tyler to State Department, 3 August 1945, NARA, RG. 84, entry 2462, box 1.
25. Ibid.
26. Memo from Tyler to State Department, 26 June 1946, NARA, RG. 84, entry 2462, box 1.
27. Telegram from U.S. Embassy Paris to Secretary of State, 18 October 1950, NARA, central decimal files of the State Department, 511.5121/10-1850.
28. *Rapports* magazine, report to head of Mission France, Henry Labouisse, 5 July 1952, NARA, RG. 84, entry 2462, box 4.
29. *Rapports,* May 1950.
30. *Rapports,* June 1950.
31. *Rapports,* March 1950.
32. *Rapports,* May 1951.
33. *Rapports,* September 1951.
34. *Rapports,* September 1950.
35. *Rapports,* January 1951.
36. *Rapports,* January 1951, June 1950, and April 1951, respectively.
37. Jessica Gienow-Hecht, "Art is Democracy and Democracy is Art: Culture, Propaganda, and the *Neue Zeitung* in Germany, 1944-1947," *Diplomatic History* 23, no. 1 (Winter 1999): 21–43.
38. *Rapports,* July 1951, April 1950, October 1952, and May 1953, respectively.
39. *Rapports,* August 1952, July 1952, and August 1951, respectively.
40. Memorandum of conversation with M. René Pleven, 18 November 1951, NARA, RG. 84, entry 2462, box 35.
41. Letter from Paul-Louis Bret to Mission France, 24 February 1952, NARA, RG. 469, entry 1193, box 54.
42. Ibid.
43. ECA Special Mission to France, monthly report for June 1950, NARA, RG. 469, entry 1048, box 8.
44. ECA Special Mission to France, monthly report for May 1950, NARA, RG. 469, entry 1048, box 8.
45. 1950 Report of the Information Division, ECA Mission to France, NARA, RG. 469, entry 1193, box 45.
46. Memorandum from Kaplan to Thomas F. Wilson, 18 October 1951, NARA, RG. 469, entry 1193, box 54.
47. *Rapports* magazine, report to head of Mission France, Henry Labouisse, 5 July 1952.
48. A survey of the readership of *Rapports—France-Etats-Unis,* ECA Special Mission to France, NARA, RG. 84, entry 2462, box 4.
49. Ibid.
50. Telegram from MSA France to Secretary of State, highlights IFOP poll of 824 *Rapports* readers, 11 July 1953, NARA, RG. 84, entry 2462, box 4.
51. Seventeen percent reported "often," twenty percent reported "sometimes," telegram from MSA France to Secretary of State, highlights IFOP poll of 824 *Rapports* readers.
52. Memorandum from Kaplan to Thomas F. Wilson, 18 October 1951.
53. A survey of the readership of *Rapports—France-Etats-Unis.*
54. *Rapports* magazine, report to head of Mission France, Henry Labouisse, 5 July 1952.
55. Ibid.
56. Interview with Julian Stein, Mission France information division, 4 November 1997. Other officials took this as an indication that *Rapports* was enjoying a wide circulation. Wrapping fish in newspaper was a common practice in Europe until

the late 1970s (based on the author's experience) and did not necessarily reflect distaste for the publication.

57. Memorandum from Kaplan to Thomas F. Wilson, 18 October 1951.
58. *Rapports* magazine, report to head of Mission France, Henry Labouisse, 5 July 1952.
59. Memorandum from Kaplan to Thomas F. Wilson, 18 October 1951.
60. Memorandum from Henry Labouisse to T.W. Wilson, 13 November 1951, NARA, RG. 469, entry 1193, box 54.
61. Memorandum from Kaplan to Thomas W. Wilson, 18 October 1951.
62. Memorandum from Henry Labouisse to T.W. Wilson, 13 November 1951.
63. Letter from Thomas W. Wilson to Ford Foundation, 5 January 1952, NARA, RG. 469, entry 1193, box 54.
64. Telegram from Labouisse to Secretary of State, 11 July 1952, NARA, RG. 469, entry 236, box 97.
65. Telegram from USIS Paris to Secretary of State, 23 June 1953, NARA, RG. 84, entry 2462, box 4.
66. Telegram from John Foster Dulles to USIS Paris, 7 July 1953, NARA, RG. 84, entry 2462, box 4.
67. 1950 Report of the Information Division, ECA Mission to France, NARA, RG. 469, entry 1048, box 8.
68. A copy of *L'ABC's du Plan Marshall* can be found in NARA, RG. 469, entry 1193, box 45.
69. Tirages, distributions, et attributions année 1951, Mission France, NARA, RG. 84, entry 2462, box 38.
70. Julian Maris, "From Spain," in *As Others See Us: The United States Through Foreign Eyes,* ed. Franz Joseph (Princeton: Princeton U.P., 1959), 26.
71. Psychological Offensive, memo from Paris to State Department, NARA, central decimal files of the State Department, 511.51/10-1650.
72. Memo from USIS Washington to ECA/F-USIS joint staff meeting, 16 October 1950, NARA, RG. 469, entry 1193, box 44.
73. The American cultural attaché, William R. Tyler, had ultimate control over the distribution of the pamphlets and it was he who had originally suggested using the "front" organizations. Psychological Offensive, memo from Paris to State Department, NARA, central decimal files of the State Department, 511.51/10-1650.
74. Memo from Jacques Masson-Forestier to Harry Martin, 28 May 1951, NARA, RG. 469, entry 1048, box 7.
75. See, for example, quote by Lovestone, 46.
76. Marc Lazar, "Les <<batailles du livre>> du Parti Communiste Français (1950-52)," *Vingtième Siècle,* No. 10, April-June 1986: 37–49.
77. Wagnleitner, 149; see also Pells, 243–244.
78. W. McNeil Lowery and Gertrude S. Hooker, "The Role of the Arts and the Humanities," in *Cultural Affairs and Foreign Relations,* ed. Paul J. Braisted (Washington, D.C.: Columbia Books, 1968), 67.
79. Wagnleitner, 149.
80. USIE semi-annual evaluation report (1 January to 30 June 1951), NARA, central decimal files of the State Department, 511.51/6-1350–511.51/12-2951.
81. Cultural relations and informational work, foreign service inspection report, December 1951, NARA, RG. 84, entry 2462, box 13.
82. Ibid.
83. Subsidies to French book publishers, 29 January 1951, NARA, RG. 84, entry 2642, box 38.
84. Book translation program, State Department circular, 29 April 1953, NARA, RG. 84, entry 2642, box 3.

85. USIS semi-annual evaluation report for period 1 June to 30 November 1952, NARA, RG. 84, entry 2462, box 45.
86. Roger, 62.
87. Résumé du rapport, undated memo from Librairie Gallimard to William R. Tyler, NARA, RG. 84, entry 2462, box 35; see also Roger, 276.
88. Letter from W.R. Tyler to Brown, 21 June 1950, NARA, RG. 84, entry 2462, box 35.
89. Thierry Cottour, "Un géant au format de poche. L'arrivée du Reader's Digest en France (1946-1954)," Mémoire de D.E.A., Institut d'études politiques de Paris, October 1992, 57.
90. Ibid., 70.
91. Ibid., 68.
92. Ibid., 66.
93. Quoted in Cottour, 69.
94. Ibid., 82, 85.
95. *Le Monde*, 4 April 1947.
96. Cottour, 190.
97. Cottour, 141; see also Roger, 222.
98. Soria, 186.
99. Ibid., 187.
100. Cottour, 180.
101. Ibid.
102. Ibid., 90.
103. Ibid., 199.
104. Text of letter transmitted from ECA France to ECA Washington, 28 December 1951, NARA, Rg. 469, entry 1193, box 51.
105. Ibid.
106. Cottour, 165–166.
107. Telegram from Washington to MSA Mission France, 5 January 1952, NARA, Rg. 469, entry 1193, box 51.
108. Letter from Henry Labouisse to Paul W. Thompson, 7 January 1952; letter from Paul W. Thompson to Henry Labouisse, 8 January 1952; NARA, RG. 469, entry 1193, box 51.
109. Telegram from Paris to Secretary of State, 9 January 1953, NARA, central decimal files of the State Department, 511.5121/1-953.
110. Letter from Henry Labouisse to Paul W. Thompson, 24 April 1953, NARA, RG. 469, entry 1193, box 51.
111. Letter from Paul W. Thompson to Henry Labouisse, 27 April 1953, NARA, RG. 469, entry 1193, box 51.
112. NSA—The VENONA Home Page, http://www.nsa.gov/docs/venona/index.html, see the releases for July and August 1940, and July 1941.
113. OSR Information Division, guaranties branch, country subject files, NARA, RG. 469, entry 1037, box 4.
114. Letter from Alfred Max to Hodding Carter, 13 November 1953, NARA, RG. 469, entry 1193, box 54.
115. *Réalités*, no. 72, January 1952.
116. *Réalités*, no. 36, January 1949.
117. *Réalités*, no. 50, April 1950.
118. *Réalités*, no. 49, February 1950. This article appeared at a time when many Neutralists argued that France would be reduced to a nuclear wasteland, or not defended at all.
119. *Réalités*, no. 62, March 1951.
120. Memo from USIS Paris to USIS Washington, Report on special issue of French magazine *Réalités* on the U.S., NARA, RG. 84, entry 2462, box 4.

121. Philippe Roger examines this poll in detail, pp. 44–53; see also Kuisel, *Seducing the French,* 29, 244, n. 39.
122. Memo from USIS Paris to USIS Washington, Report on special issue of French magazine *Réalités* on the U.S.
123. Letter from Alfred Max to Hodding Carter, 13 November 1953.
124. *Réalités,* no. 34, September 1953.
125. Memo From USIA Paris to USIA Washington, 4 March 1954, NARA, RG. 84, entry 2462, box 4.
126. *Réalités,* no. 49, February 1949.
127. See the series, "France in the propaganda crossfire," in *Le Monde,* 12, 13, 14, 17, 18, and 19 June 1952.
128. *Life,* 26 January 1953.
129. Telegram from American Embassy, Paris, to Secretary of State, 30 January 1952, NARA, RG. 84, entry 2462, box 14.
130. It is unclear to what Dunn was referring, simply because there were so many immediate points of contention between France and the United States.
131. Memo from Charles K. Moffly to all consulates in France, 31 January 1953, NARA, RG. 84, entry 2462, box 14.
132. *La Journal de la Corse,* 29 January 1953; *L'Espoir de Nice,* 28 January 1953; *Midi-Libre* (Montpellier), 1 February 1953; *La Marseillaise,* 29 January 1953; *Combat,* 26 January 1953; *La Croix,* 27 January 1953.
133. Letter from Ann H. Eskin to John L. Brown, NARA, RG. 84, entry 2462, box 4.
134. *Le Figaro,* 27 January 1953.
135. *La Tribune,* 29 January 1953.
136. Memo from Charles K. Moffly to all consulates in France, 1 January 1953.
137. Pascal Ory, "Mickey Go Home! La désaméricanisation de la bande dessinée (1945-1950)," *Vingtième Siècle,* Octobre 1984: 77–88; Thierry Crépin, *"Haro sur le gangster!" La moralization de la presse enfantine, 1934-1954* (Paris: CNRS, 2001).
138. Pascal Ory, "Mickey Go Home! La désaméricanisation de la bande dessinée (1945-1950)," 77–88.
139. Ory, 78; Crépin, 69.
140. Roger, 63.
141. *Journal Officiel,* 19 Juillet 1949; See also Richard I. Jobs, "Tarzan under Attack: Youth, Comics, and Cultural Reconstruction in Postwar France," *French Historical Studies* vol. 26, no. 4 (2003): 687–725.
142. Crépin, Chapitre IX, "L'accommodement des éditeurs belges."
143. Crépin, 438; Ory, 84.
144. See, for example: "Comics," *L'Humanité,* 9 July 1949, 23 April 1952; "L'angoissant question des journaux d'enfants," *Ce Soir,* 24 March 1948; *Le Figaro,* 11 March 1948; Roger, 63–65. Such criticisms of American comics were not limited to France either. In Austria Walt Disney successfully fought censorship of Mickey Mouse (Wagnleitner, 103–104).
145. Letter from Delman, Opera Mundi, to John H. Tobler, American Embassy, 22 March 1948; Letter from Douglas H. Schneider to John H. Tobler, 19 March 1948, NARA, RG. 84, entry 2462, box 4.
146. Letter from Delman, Opera Mundi, to John H. Tobler, American Embassy, 22 March 1948.
147. Jeancolas, 33–41.
148. Telegram from American Embassy to State Department, 23 November 1948, NARA, RG. 84, entry 2462, box 4.
149. Ory, 81.
150. Memo concerning proposed legislation limiting American comic strip material in French children's publications, NARA, RG. 84, entry 2462, box 4.

151. Quoted in Ory, 81.
152. Telegram from American Embassy to State Department, 23 November 1948.
153. Ibid.
154. Crépin, 175; Telegram from American Embassy to State Department, 23 November 1948.
155. Letter from Paul Winkler to William Tyler, 5 February 1949, NARA, RG. 84, entry 2462, box 4.
156. American Embassy, Paris, to Minister of Foreign Affairs, 11 February 1949, NARA, RG. 84, entry 2462, box 4.
157. *Journal Officiel,* 27 January 1949.
158. Schumann discussed this in a letter to M. Xavier Duguet, Président du Syndicat National des Agences de Presse, 23 February 1949, NARA, RG. 84, entry 2462, box 4. According to Winkler, this was "obviously the result of the verbal note," letter to William R. Tyler, 5 April 1949, NARA, RG. 84, entry 2462, box 4.
159. Crépin, 295.
160. Ory, 83.
161. Ibid.
162. Letter from Paul Winkler to J. Lovestone, 17 March 1950, NARA, RG. 84, entry 2462, box 4.
163. American Embassy, Paris, to Minister of Foreign Affairs, 9 March 1950, NARA, RG. 84, entry 2462, box 4.
164. Ory, 83; Crépin, 315.
165. Crépin, 345, 439.
166. Letter from Paul Winkler to Douglas Schneider, 11 March 1948, NARA, RG. 84, entry 2462, box 4.
167. Crépin, 439.
168. Telegram from American Embassy, Paris, to Department of State, 12 August 1949, NARA, RG. 84, entry 2462, box 4.
169. Memo from Harold Kaplan to Achilles, Labouisse (chief of Mission France), Moffly, Timmons, Tyler (cultural attaché), and Wallner, 22 October 1952, NARA, RG. 469, entry 1193, box 51.
170. Ibid.
171. Ibid.
172. Wagnleitner, *Coca-Colonization and the Cold War,* 2.
173. Joanne P. Sharp, *Condensing the Cold War: Readers Digest and American Identity* (Minneapolis: Minnesota University Press, 2000).
174. Ibid., 169.
175. Ibid., 36.
176. Ibid., xiv–xv.
177. Ibid., 163–164.
178. Ibid., 46.
179. Ibid., 45.
180. Michael Warner, "The Mass Public and the Mass Subject," in *Habermas and the Public Sphere,* ed. Craig Calhoun (Cambridge: The M.I.T. Press, 1992): 381–382.
181. Edward S. Cohen, "Globalization and the Boundaries of the State: A Framework for Analyzing the Changing Practice of Sovereignty," *Governance: An International Journal of Policy and Administration,* vol. 14, no. 1 (January 2001): 75–97.
182. Barber, *McWorld vs. Jihad,* 12, 80.
183. Cohen, 76. He emphasizes the role of states in boundary maintenance and the control of aspects of social life within their borders.

CONCLUSION

"Is space sufficient to create culture?" the good Brazilian professor asks me. It's a meaningless question. But these spaces are the ones that will gain from technical progress. The faster the airplane flies, the less important are France, Spain, and Italy. They were nations, now they are provinces, and tomorrow they will be the world's villages. The future is not ours, and there's nothing we can do against this irresistible movement.

Albert Camus, *American Journals*

In early 1950 a team of French mountaineers left the offices of the French Alpine Club at No. 7 rue La Boétie. Their objective was the summit of the Himalayan peak Annapurna and the glory of the first ascent of an eight thousand meter peak. On 3 June 1950, after months of hardship, the expedition's leader Maurice Herzog and the veteran climber Louis Lachenal planted the tricolor atop the summit. The duo almost perished in their effort and they suffered permanent disfigurement from frostbite. In the words of one French alpinist: "All France knows the price that had to be paid."[1] Their conquest attracted worldwide attention and made the team national heroes. Coming just five years after the end of the war, the team's effort lifted French national pride, if only briefly.

And yet even in the remotest regions of the earth France could not escape the cultural presence of the United States. Shortly after entering the village of Manangbhot the French team was surrounded by villagers. Herzog provided this description of the encounter:

The villagers gathered round gesticulating:
"American?"
"No, French."
"Yes, French."
As if this were conclusive proof, they nodded approval: "American!"

Notes for this section begin on page 239.

"No, there are Americans, and there are Englishmen, but we are French."
"Oh yes! But you're Americans all the same!"[2]

As Camus observed, the world was indeed getting smaller.

The Marshall Plan's contribution to this process was significant.
Or, from another perspective, the Marshall Plan confirmed the influence—already global—of the United States. Transatlantic tourism
for the middle class was one way that it decreased distances. Another was the aid it gave to reconstruction and modernization. The
electrification of rural France was an important element of the Monnet Plan, which was underwritten to a large degree by Marshall Plan
funds. Where electrification went, telephones, radios, and soon tel-
evisions followed. And, in the long run, where television and radio
went, so did American mass culture.

Reflecting on the public diplomacy of the U.S. during the Marshall
Plan, two general issues warrant further attention. First, I will offer
my own assessment of the U.S. public diplomacy. I will also indicate
the lessons American officials drew from their experience in France.
What were the implications of their experience for the overall conduct of American public diplomacy? A second issue is the relationship between the U.S. public diplomacy, Americanization, and official
and unofficial French reaction.

Assessing the Public Diplomacy of the United States

The Marshall Plan failed to achieve all its goals in France, whether
political, economic, or cultural. However, this study has argued that
the failure to achieve its goals did not necessarily reduce the impact
of the Marshall Plan's public diplomacy. Indeed, I have argued that
one of the reasons for the failure of much of its cultural and information programs was because their impact was too great. U.S. public
diplomacy created a myth surrounding the Marshall Plan. Yet even
many of those who believed in the myth were disappointed with the
results. It created expectations that the United States was unable to
fulfill. The public diplomacy of the Marshall Plan must be counted
as one of its least successful elements. As we saw, officials in the Labor Information division ultimately concluded that the presence of
Marshall Plan material and officials were often liabilities rather than
assets for gaining the support of workers. Similarly, Helen Kirkpatrick,
the head of Mission France's information division for most of the
Marshall Plan years, sought to remove the U.S. label from much of its
output. Her work with William R. Tyler at the embassy to create the
Association France–Etats-Unis was one such effort to create "gray"

(not attributed to the U.S.) information material. After years of public diplomacy in France these officials concluded that the most effective U.S. program was the least visible one.[3]

Perhaps the most important lesson is that U.S. public diplomacy during the Marshall Plan was incapable of contributing to short-term policy goals. This realization was implicit in many of the arguments made by Tyler in support of educational exchanges, support for the arts, and other projects designed to increase mutual understanding between French and Americans in the long term. Measuring the efficacy of these programs is difficult and anecdotal. This and the lack of a government tradition of support for the arts and culture made gaining support for these programs difficult, although Soviet sponsorship of the arts goaded the U.S. government into supporting them during the Cold War.

Ultimately, many of the French visitors to American fairs, or those who received pamphlets and other material, construed the American effort merely as a propaganda drive. This was, after all, a population that had only recently been liberated from German efforts to influence public opinion. Insofar as the French population assessed the American effort as propaganda, it was doomed to failure. This was true not only for exhibits, including the ones destroyed, but also for the high-culture programs of the United States such as the "Masterpieces of the Twentieth Century" exhibit in Paris. When the American material was not identified as propaganda the reception was generally warmer. This helps explain the late successes—in terms of popularity not policy—of American exhibits when Mission France switched from providing Marshall Plan pamphlets to presenting American consumer goods. Did U.S. public diplomacy at least consolidate support among pro-American groups in France? In some cases perhaps. However, the inability of Labor Information to gain support from the rank-and-file members of FO and the CFTC was a crucial failure in this respect.

In 1953 the new U.S Ambassador to France, James Clement Dunn, issued a definitive statement on the U.S. information policy in France.[4] Dunn criticized what he identified as a "unilateral" approach to information work. American material, according to Dunn, was the product of an "information factory" that produced huge volumes of material for worldwide distribution. Physical analogies about "targets" reinforced the distance—geographic as well as psychological and cultural—between the producers of this material and the populations in question. Dunn observed that Western Europeans, in general, distrusted official material and publications. He suggested that the increasing tempo of the Cold War had placed a fundamental con-

Ambassador
critical —
have —
US
propaganda

straint on the effectiveness of information work. The official auspices
of their information work were seen not as signs of integrity and authority but rather the clearest indication that their work was partisan and therefore as prejudiced as Communist material. This problem
was further exacerbated because the U.S. Congress would only fund
information work if it could be justified as "a sharp-edged psychological instrument." The results were programs and material that
were rigid and stereotyped. According to Dunn, most Europeans believed that the understanding of Americans was limited to an "anticommunism of a rather elementary and immature kind."[5]

Dunn's memo, which was also sent to William Fulbright and the
senate committee conducting a review of U.S. information policy, recommended that information work be curtailed and be replaced by a
renewed emphasis on cultural relations. He explained, "The current
emphasis has resulted in creating a general impression of the United
States as a country obsessed with propaganda and political warfare
to the relative exclusion of those values common to Western civilization and to the free world, which we share with other countries."[6]
Dunn's analysis and conclusions confirmed what Kirkpatrick and
Tyler had been arguing since 1950. The lessons learned in France
were now placed firmly in the center of the debate about the future
nature of U.S. public diplomacy.

A major weakness of U.S. public diplomacy was its attempt to
address too many major issues at the same time. Simultaneously it
sought to respond to Communist charges, promote the American way
of life, inform the public about the Marshall Plan, increase French industrial productivity, and build support for crucial U.S. interests such
as rearmament and NATO. In this way the American effort in France
was similar in intent to the domestic consensus-building programs
in the U.S. such as the Freedom Train, conceived and backed by the
Advertising Council.[7] However, the application of such a consensus-
building program in a foreign country was altogether different. It is not
even clear that these goals were mutually attainable. Mission France
officials, for example, worried about the consequences on public
opinion of identifying the Marshall Plan with rearmament. Labor officials pointed out that demonstrations of American productivity often
increased apprehension about the American way of life. Similarly,
American tourism was more successful as an economic enterprise
than it was in promoting Franco-American understanding. It would
have taken more than specialists sensitive to French culture to achieve
the rather grand and multiple goals of U.S. policy.

The host of institutions and organizations devoted to public diplomacy only made matters worse. It was one thing for Mission France,

the ECA in Washington, the USIS, the Office of the Special Representative, and Labor Information to disagree on policy. It was quite a different matter, and much worse, that each possessed the resources and means to conduct public diplomacy independent of the other organizations. It was only after a concerted campaign that Kirkpatrick and Tyler achieved partial success in excluding what they considered to be the most offensive voices, such as the ECA information office in Washington, from France. But there was another voice that neither of them could silence: the American Congress. An analysis of Communist pamphlets and newspaper articles concluded that direct, accurate quotations of American senators and representatives were the major source for Communist attacks on American policy.[8] Speeches by Senator McCarthy were a favorite, but in general there was never a shortage of bellicose or isolationist statements to be had. A French official in Washington concluded that most senators operated under the assumption that criticism of the United States was possible only after one had been "duped" by Communist propaganda.[9] The Communist strategy was shrewd. It recognized that France was but one priority among many for the United States. The U.S. had other priorities, such as West German rearmament, which could be used to argue that France's interests were not taken seriously.

American officials in France had to cope with not only France's unique political culture but also the vicissitudes of U.S. policy. Public diplomacy did not occur in a policy vacuum. American policy often appeared to be inconsistent, and it changed over time. Thus, for example, Europeans—especially the French—subjected to American exhortations to expand free trade pointed to the U.S.'s own protectionist policies. The targets of American policy changed too. Thus the shift toward rearmament along with the reestablishment of U.S. military bases profoundly affected American information work. Similarly the original purpose of U.S. information work was to show a "full and fair" picture of the United States. By 1950, with the onset of the Korean War, it was no longer sufficient merely to tell the story of America. Communist attacks had to be met with a "Campaign of Truth" that attacked the Soviet Union directly. Nor should we forget that in the era of mass communication domestic policies affect world opinion. Whether it was Senator Joseph McCarthy's persecution of Communists and alleged Communists, the trial of the Rosenbergs, or racism and civil rights abuses, the domestic policies of the United States impacted how it was perceived abroad, especially when they contradicted the mythic image being promulgated by U.S. public diplomacy.

A novel aspect of American public diplomacy was its incorporation of commercial interests. This relationship was problematic, but

U.S. public diplomacy cooperated with private enterprise

in general both the private sector and American officials were pleased with the results. The relationship between public diplomacy and private enterprise was closest in print media, for example *Sélection du Reader's Digest,* and film. The ECA was also quick to find policy value in commercial activities such as tourism. Finally, the U.S. emphasis on productivity and the American way of life furthered connections with private industry by presenting consumer goods at American exhibits. In many cases consumer goods were central to American displays. In this sense, the film *Productivity: Key to Plenty* was a tour de force. It illustrated the unique relationship between consumer goods and American public diplomacy. The message of the film was clear: Americanization simply made life easier and more enjoyable. It threatened neither traditional gender roles nor cultural values. The prescriptions of the film were equally simple. The American way of life could only occur in "free"—non-Communist—societies that embraced productivity. Attempts by the Labor Information division to Americanize the French *patronat* and the spread of American periodicals with the assistance of Mission France, to take only two examples, further illustrate how cultural interventions were indissoluble from economic and foreign policy goals.

The links between American public diplomacy and private enterprise weakened the American effort.[10] A common perception of the Marshall Plan in France was that it was an imperialistic tool to aid the expansion of American business. This view was not limited to Communists or labor. Some French businesses objected to the American economic "invasion" that accompanied U.S. aid. Indeed American business did become more visible during the Marshall Plan.[11] Coca-Cola, Hollywood, and *Reader's Digest* were examples of visible American commercial interests that advanced their market shares in these years in the name of supporting U.S. foreign policy. *Reader's Digest* provided a steady flow of pro-American articles at the same time as it drove its French competition into the ground. Official material from the U.S. was suspect because the French viewed it as propaganda. Unofficial material such as that provided by *Reader's Digest* was not necessarily more palatable because its very existence in France could be seen as an indication that the Marshall Plan favored American business.

The public diplomacy of the Marshall Plan emanated from lofty premises and aspired to grand goals of European transformation. It held that through the Marshall Plan the United States could reorder European society including institutions like labor relations and the family farm as well as basic values and attitudes. American policy makers thought they could cure social conflict as they improved economic performance. On the ground, however, the public diplomacy not only failed to "reform" French thought and habits, it also tended to reinforce stereotypes and created a backlash of public opinion.

What lessons did France learn from their experience of Marshall Plan public diplomacy? French politicians adapted where they could. Both the International Film Festival at Cannes and the programs to promote transatlantic tourism were examples of French cultural policy that arose in the midst of the American presence. As the first chapter showed, however, the Fourth Republic was unable to prevent the U.S. from using Article VIII to justify a massive propaganda campaign within its borders.

U.S. public diplomacy in France during the Marshall Plan did not strengthen the legitimacy of the Fourth Republic, and it may have even contributed to its perceived weaknesses. As Walter Hitchcock has argued, the foreign policy successes of the Fourth Republic, and even its domestic economic successes, did not confer legitimacy in the eyes of most French citizens.[12] U.S. public diplomacy programs raised questions of sovereignty and legitimacy, and the ubiquity of American mass culture (whether as a part of public diplomacy or independent of it) increased the apprehension of many French officials. Cultural protectionism must be understood in this light. Thus even though Benjamin Barber dismisses cultural protectionism he acknowledges that democracies are built "slowly, culture by culture," in other words, historically.[13] The democratic institutions of a nation-state such as France and the nature of its civil society are shaped by their cultural origins. France's culture and history is integral to French democracy.

In this vein it is worth examining Lionel Jospin's, then prime minister, 1997 call for an ambitious program to put France "on line."[14] He described the emergence of an "information society" as a natural consequence of the "globalization of information flows." Jospin pointed out the active support of the United States in aiding technological growth to refute the "irreversible retreat of the state" thesis. "Information is becoming strategic wealth," he explained. Most importantly, Jospin called for the digitization of France's cultural patrimony and the development of France's cultural presence on the new information networks. He continued:

> Our patrimony is an achievement of France. This is the way to show its value.... We must defend a cultural exception, with the same determination which we have exercised in the past on behalf of our audiovisual achievements.

Thus, Jospin reinforced the protectionist stance of the French State, calling for the protection of a "cultural exception." Tensions remain

between an integrationist, essentialist conception of French culture
and one based on multiculturalism. Recent support for regional culture and the government's celebration of the multicultural euphoria
following the 1998 World Cup and 2000 European Championship vic-
tories gave hope that the latter will prevail. The popularity of Jean-
Marie Le Pen during the presidential election of 2002 can be read
more pessimistically.[15]

Jospin's speech underscored the persistence of nation-states
in trying to control the terms under which their citizens confront
modernity. Herman Lebovics argues that such protectionism arises
from the assumption of French politicians that culture is crucial to
the legitimacy and survival of the nation.[16] This premise, which Lebovics traces back to François I, culminated in the work during the 1960s
of France's first Culture Minister, André Malraux. "Malraux established," explains Lebovics, "the principle that the state has a respon-
sibility to the cultural life of its citizens, just as it does—at a different
level of funding—to their education, health, and welfare."[17]

Simply put, culture does matter. When democratic states practice
cultural protectionism more is at stake than the defense of exclusion-
ary conceptions of national identity. French education, for example
the history of the Revolution or reading Rousseau, is an exposure to
both French culture *and* French democracy. When McWorld, to use
Barber's term, changes the reading habits and print culture of France
it is not only stifling cultural diversity but also affecting the nature
of public discourse, of memory, and hence of democratic practices.

Thus, the impact of the U.S. program must not be measured only
in terms of whether it achieved stated objectives. The Labor Information program, for example, did not increase worker support for
productivity or the Marshall Plan in general. Yet U.S. labor policy in
France did make an indelible mark by strengthening divisions in
French labor. Anti-Communist labor remained weak, and it often failed
to be a good "pupil," but for ECA officials weakening labor across
the board was preferable to allowing the CGT to exist unchallenged.
American hegemony was manipulated, but we should not lose the
forest for the trees. The U.S. got what it wanted in most cases, and
strategic policy defeats were rare.

The legitimacy of States, particularly democracies, depends on
their ability to provide meaning and orientation amid change and
strife. Therefore, it is misleading to read French resistance to American culture as hypocritical or based solely on cultural essentialism.
The United States offered its culture, the American way of life, as
both the cause and the explanation for changes taking in place in
postwar France. The consistency and strength of this message stood

in sharp contrast to the weaknesses and crises of the Fourth Republic. It is not surprising, therefore, that French politicians like Robert Schuman were interested to know how other countries addressed the spread of American culture. Americanization in both the material and semiotic sense posed a very real threat indeed to the ability of the French via their democracy to control their cultural future.

Notes

1. Lucien Davies, President of the French Alpine Club, preface to Maurice Herzog, *Annapurna,* trans. Nea Morin and Janet Adam Smith (New York: Dutton, 1952), 15.
2. Herzog, 82.
3. Candid views regarding psychological impact in France of U.S. foreign economic policy, memo by Harold Kaplan, undated 1953, NARA, RG. 84, entry 2462, box 32.
4. The Foreign Information Activities of the Department of State, circular from James C. Dunn to Department of State, 10 February 1953, NARA, RG. 84, entry 2462, box 10.
5. Ibid.
6. Ibid.
7. Robert Griffith, "The Selling America: The Advertising Council and American Politics, 1942-1960," *Business History Review* 57 (Autumn 1983), 388–393.
8. Communist propaganda—general lines, analysis by Jacques Masson-Forestier, research assistant Labor Information, June 1950, NARA, RG. 469, entry 1029, box 17.
9. Memo from Jean Daridan, chargé d'affaires de France aux Etats-Unis, to Robert Schuman, Foreign Minister, 26 January 1951, Ministère des Affaires Etrangères, série B-Amérique 53 "Propaganda politique des Etats-Unis à l'étranger."
10. An important exception to this is the cooperation of the U.S. government, business, and foundations. See Volker Berghahn, *America and the Intellectual Cold Wars in Europe* (Princeton: Princeton U.P., 2001).
11. Milward, 91.
12. Hitchcock, 204.
13. Barber, 278.
14. Jospin gave the speech at the University of Communication at Hourtin, 25 August 1997. Transcript and translation provided by Jack Kessler for H-Net French History discussion group, 16 September 1997.
15. See the dossier, "The French Elections of 2002" *French Politics, Culture, and Society* 21, no. 1 (Spring 2003): Pierre Martin, "L'Éléction présidentielle et les élections législatives françaises de 2002" and Sophie Meunier, "France's Double-Talk on Globalization."
16. Herman Lebovics, *Mona Lisa's Escort: André Malraux and the Reinvention of French Culture* (Ithaca: Cornell University Press, 1999).
17. Lebovics, 201.

BIBLIOGRAPHY

Archival Sources

National Archives and Records Administration, College Park, Maryland

Record Group 469, Records of the Economic Cooperation Administration
Record Group 306, Records of the United States Information Agency and its predecessors
Record Group 84, Post Reports
Record Group 59, Records of the Department of State
Central Decimal Files of the Department of State

National Security Archives at George Washington University, Washington, D.C.

Smith-Mundt Collection

Archives du Ministère des affaires étrangères, Paris

Série B Amérique, 1944-52, États-Unis
Série B Amérique, 1952-63, États-Unis
Papiers Bruneau
Cabinet du Ministre A. Pinay

Archives Nationales, Paris

F60 Archives of the President du Conseil
F60 *ter* Comité Interministérial pour les Questions de Coopération Economique Européene
80 AJ Commissariat Archives
AB XIX 4349-4350 - Fonds André Monnier 1943-1948

American Foreign Policy Center, Louisiana Tech University, Ruston, Louisiana

President Harry S. Truman's Office Files, 1945–1953
The Harry S. Truman Oral Histories Collection
Confidential U.S. State Department Central Files: France, Internal Affairs, 1945–1949

Confidential U.S. State Department Central Files: France, Internal Affairs, 1950–1954
Confidential U.S. State Department Central Files: France, Foreign Affairs, 1945–1949
Confidential U.S. State Department Central Files: France, Foreign Affairs, 1950–1954
Official Conversations and Meetings of Dean Acheson, 1949–1953

Oral Histories at the George C. Marshall Foundation, Lexington, Virginia

Paul Douglas, Finance Section, Mission France
Jacques Habert
Arthur Hartman, Finance Section, Mission France
Daniel Horowitz, Labor Attaché, Department of State
John Hutchison, Labor Information Division
Joan McMenamin, ECA
Waldemar Nielsen, Chief, Information Division, OSR
Julian Stein, Information Division, Mission France
Julian Street, Office of Travel Development, OSR
James West, Information Division, OSR
Herbert Weiner, International Labor Affairs, Department of State
Thomas Wilson, Special Consultant to the Special Representative in Europe

Official Documents and Publications

Cahiers Français d'information
Etudes et conjoncture. Ministère de finance et des affaires économiques.
Foreign Relations of the United States
Journal Officiel
L'Aide américaine à la France
Rapports: France–Etats-Unis
Report of Third International Trade Union Conference. ECA: Washington, 1950.
Transatlantic From the Office of ECA Labor Advisors
Travel in Europe: A Selective Reading List. Washington, D.C.: Library of Congress—European Affairs Division, 1950.
Foreign aid appropriation bill for 1949. Hearings before the subcommittee of the Committee on Appropriations, House of Representatives, Eightieth Congress, second session. Robert P. Williams, editor. G.P.O., 1948.
Economic Cooperation Administration. Hearings before the Committee on Appropriations, United States Senate, Eightieth Congress, second session on Economic Cooperation Administration, 1948.
Foreign aid appropriation bill, 1950. Hearings before the Committee on Appropriations, United States Senate, Eighty-first Congress, first session, on H.R. 4830. G.P.O., 1949.

Economic Cooperation Administration. Hearings before the Committee on
Foreign Relations, House of Representatives, Eighty-first Congress.
G.P.O., 1951.
United States Senate. Committee on Appropriations. Foreign-aid program
in Europe. Report of the Investigations Division of the Committee on
Appropriations, United States Senate, relative to activities of the
foreign-aid program in France and in the regional offices of the MSA in
Paris. G.P.O., 1953.

Journals and Articles

Abbink, John. "Tourism and Its Discontents: Suri-tourist encounters in
Southern Ethiopia." *Social Anthropology* 8 (2000): 1–17.
Antonio, Robert J. and Alessandro Bonanno. "A New Global Capitalism?
From 'Americanism and Fordism' to 'Americanization-Globalization.'"
American Studies 41, no. 2/3 (2000): 33–77.
Belmonte, Laura A. "A Family Affair? Gender, the U.S. Information Agency,
and Cold War Ideology, 1945-1960." In *Culture and International History,*
eds. Jessica C.E. Gienow-Hecht and Frank Schumacher, New York:
Berghahn Books, 2003: 79–93.
Black, Annabel. "Negotiating the Tourist Gaze." In *Coping With Tourists:
European Reactions to Mass Tourism,* ed. Jeremy Boissevain, New York:
Berghahn Books, 1996: 112–143.
Bowen, Ralph. "American Cultural Imperialism Reconsidered." *Revue
française d'études américaines* 24–25 (May 1985): 179–193.
Caruthers, Susan. "Not Like the U.S.? Europeans and the Spread of American
Culture," *International Affairs.* vol. 74, no. 4 (October 1998), 883–892.
Chapman, Herrick. "Modernity and National Identity in Postwar France."
French Historical Studies 22, No. 2 (Spring 1999): 291–314.
Cohen, Edward S. "Globalization and the Boundaries of the State: A
Framework for Analyzing the Changing Practice of Sovereignty."
Governance: An International Journal of Policy and Administration, vol.
14, no. 1 (January 2001): 75–97.
De Grazia, Victoria. "Americanization and Changing Paradigms of Consumer
Modernity: France, 1930-1990." *Sites* 1, no. 1 (1997): 191–213.
———. "Americanism for Export." *Wedge,* 7–8 (Winter-Summer 1985): 74–81.
———. "Mass Culture and Sovereignty: The American Challenge to
European Cinema, 1920-1960." *Journal of Modern History,* no. 61
(March 1989): 53–87.
Depkat, Volker. "Cultural Approaches to International Relations: A
Challenge?" In *Culture and International History,* eds. Jessica C.E.
Gienow-Hecht and Frank Schumacher, New York: Berghahn Books,
2003: 175–197.
Desson, Guy. "Après le vote de la Loi d'Aide: la leçon des chiffres," *Le Film
Français,* 31 Juillet 1953.

Dunch, Ryan. "Beyond Cultural Imperialism: Cultural Theory, Christian Missions, and Global Modernity." *History and Theory* 41 (October 2002): 301–325.

van Elteren, Mel. "Conceptualizing the Impact of U.S. Popular Culture Globally." *Journal of Popular Culture* 30, no. 1 (Summer 1996): 47–89.

Ellwood, David W. "Anti-Americanism in Western Europe: a Comparative Perspective." The Johns Hopkins University Center Bologna Center *Occasional Paper European Studies Seminar,* no. 3 (April 1999).

Endy, Christopher. "Travel and World Power." *Diplomatic History* 22, no. 4 (Fall 1998): 565–594.

Enzensberger, Hans Magnus. "A Theory of Tourism." *New German Critique,* no. 68 (Spring-Summer 1996): 117–135.

Fantasia, Rick. "Everything and Nothing: The Meaning of Fast-Food and Other American Cultural Goods in France." *Tocqueville Review,* XV 2 (1994): 57–88.

Furlough, Ellen. "Making Mass Vacations: Tourism and Consumer Culture in France, 1930s to 1970s." *Comparative Studies in Society and History* 40, no. 2 (April 1998): 247–286.

———. "Selling the American Way in Interwar France: *Prix Uniques* and the Salons des Arts Ménagers," *Journal of Social History* 26, no. 3 (Spring 1993): 491–519.

Freund, Charles. "In Praise of Vulgarity." *Reason* 33, no. 10 (March 2002): 24–36.

Gienow-Hecht, Jessica C.E. "Shame on *US*? Academics, Cultural Transfer, and the Cold War—A Critical Review." *Diplomatic History* 24, no. 3 (2000): 465–494.

———. "Art is Democracy and Democracy is Art: Culture, Propaganda and the *Neue Zeitung* in Germany, 1944-1947." *Diplomatic History* 23 (Winter 1999): 21–43.

Grainge, Paul. "Global Media and the Ambiguities of Resonant Americanism." *American Studies International* 39, no. 3 (October 2001): 4–24.

Griffith, Robert. "The Selling of America: The Advertising Council and American Politics, 1942-1960." *Business History Review* 57 (Autumn 1983): 388–412.

Guerlain, Pierre. "The Ironies and Dilemmas of America's Cultural Dominance: a Transcultural Approach." *American Studies International* 35 (June 1997): 30–51.

Jameson, Frederic. "Globalization and Political Strategy." *New Left Review* 4 (July/August 2000): 49–68.

Jeancolas, Jean-Pierre. "L'arrangement Blum-Byrnes à l'épreuve des faits: Les relations (cinématogrpahiques franco-américaines de 1944 à 1948." *Bulletin de l'Association française de recherches sur l'histoire du cinema* 13 (1992): 3–49.

Jobs, Richard I. "Tarzan under Attack: Youth, Comics, and Cultural Reconstruction in Postwar France." *French Historical Studies* 26, no. 4 (2003): 687–725.

Kofas, Jon V. "U.S. Foreign Policy and the World Federation of Trade Unions, 1944-1948." *Diplomatic History* 26, no. 1 (2002): 21–60.

Koshar, Rudy. "'What ought to be seen': Tourists' Guidebooks and National Identities in Modern Germany and Europe." *Journal of Contemporary History* 33, no. 3 (1998): 323–340.

Kroes, Rob. "American Empire and Cultural Imperialism: A View From the Receiving End." *Diplomatic History*, vol. 23, no. 3 (Summer 1999): 463–477.

Kuisel, Richard F. "What Do the French Think of Us? The Deteriorating Image of the United States, 2000-2004." *French Politics, Culture and Society* 22, no. 3, (Fall 2004): 91–119.

———. "Americanization for Historians." *Diplomatic History* 24, no. 3 (2000): 509–515.

———. "L'American way of life et les missions françaises de productivité." *Vingtième Siècle* 17 (January-March 1988): 21–38.

Lazar, Marc. "Les <<batailles du livre>> du Parti Communiste Français (1950-1952)," *Vingtième Siècle* 10 (April-June 1986): 37–49.

Leonard, Mark. "Diplomacy by Other Means." *Foreign Policy* 132 (September/October 2002): 48–56.

Maier, Charles S. "The Politics of Productivity: Foundations of American International Economic Policy After World War II." *International Organization* 31 (Autumn 1977): 607–633.

Moen, Eli and Harm G. Schröter. "Americanization as a Concept for a Deeper Understanding of Economic Changes." *Entreprises et Histoire* 19 (1998): 5–13.

Morsel, Henri. "La mission de productivité aux États-Unis de l'industrie française de l'aluminum." *Historie, Econonmie, Société* 18 (1999): 413–418.

Norval, Aletta J. "Hybridization: the Im/Purity of the Political." In *Sovereignty and Subjectivity,* eds. Jenny Edkins, Nalini Persram, Véronique Pin-Fat. Boulder: Lynne Rienner, 1999: 99–114.

Nouailhat, Yves-Henri. "Aspects de la politique culturelle des Etats-Unis à l'égard de la France de 1945 à 1950." *Relations internationales,* Spring 1981: 77–88.

Ory, Pascal. "Mickey Go Home! La désaméricanisation de la bande dessinée (1945-1950)." *Vingtième Siècle* (Octobre 1984): 77–88.

Peer, Shanny. "Marketing Mickey: Disney Goes to France." *Tocqueville Review* XIII, No. 2 (1992): 127–142.

Rosenberg, Emily S. "Consuming Women: Images of Americanization in the 'American Century.'" *Diplomatic History*, vol. 23, no. 3 (Summer 1999): 479–497.

Sablosky, Juliet Antunes. "Recent Trends in Department of State Support for Cultural Diplomacy: 1993-2002." *Cultural Diplomacy Research Series* 2003, Center for Arts and Culture, www.culturalpolicy.org.

Tuch, Hans N. "American Cultural Policy Toward Germany." In *The United States and Germany in the Era of the Cold War, 1945-1990,* ed. Detlef Junker, Cambridge: Cambridge U.P., 2004. Vol. 2: 274–279.

Wagnleitner, Reinhold. "The Empire of Fun, or Talkin' Soviet Union Blues: The Sound of Freedom and U.S. Cultural Hegemony in Europe." *Diplomatic History,* vol. 23, no. 3 (Summer 1999): 500–524.

Warner, Michael. "The Mass Public and the Mass Subject." In *Habermas and the Public Sphere,* ed. Craig Calhoun, Cambridge: The M.I.T. Press, 1992: 377–401.

Books, Theses, and Dissertations

Aldrich, Richard J. *The Hidden Hand: Britain, America, and Cold War Secret Intelligence.* New York: The Overlook Press, 2001.

Alves, Teresa, et. al. *Ceremonies and Spectacles: Performing American Culture.* Amsterdam: VU University Press, 2000.

Ang, Ien. *Watching Dallas: Soap Opera and the Melodramatic Imagination.* Trans. Della Couling. London: Meuthuen, 1985.

Aron, Raymond. *The Dawn of Universal History: Selected Essays From a Witness of the Twentieth Century.* Ed. Yair Reiner. Trans. Barbara Bray. New York: Basic Books, 2002.

Barber, Benjamin. *McWorld vs. Jihad: How Globalism and Tribalism are Reshaping the World.* New York: Ballantine Books, 1995.

Barjot, Dominique, ed. *Catching up with America: Productivity Missions and the Diffusion of American Economic and Technological Influence after the Second World War.* Paris: Presses de l'Université de Paris-Sorbonne, 2002.

Barjot, Dominique and Christophe Réveillard, eds. *L'américanisation de l'Europe occidentale au XXᵉ siècle.* Paris: Presses de l'Université de Paris-Sorbonne, 2002.

Baudrillard, Jean. *Amérique.* Paris: Grasset & Fasquelle, 1986.

Bender, Thomas, ed. *Rethinking American History in a Global Age.* Berkeley: University of California Press, 2002.

Benjamin, Walter. *The Arcades Project.* Trans. Howard Eiland and Kevin McLaughlin. Cambridge: Harvard University Press, 1999.

Berghahn, Volker. *The Americanisation of West German Industry, 1945-1973.* New York: Cambridge University Press, 1986.

———. *America and the Intellectual Cold Wars in Europe.* Princeton: Princeton U.P., 2001.

Bischof, Güntur, et al. *The Marshall Plan in Austria.* New Brunswick: Transaction Publishers, 2000.

Boissevain, Jeremy, ed. *Coping With Tourists: European Reactions to Mass Tourism.* New York: Berghahn Books, 1996.

Bonds, John Bledsoe. *Bipartisan Strategy: Selling the Marshall Plan.* New York: Praeger, 2002.

Boorstin, Daniel. *The Image: A Guide to Pseudo-Events in America.* New York: Harper, 1964.

Bossuat, Gérard. *Les aides américaines, économiques et militaires à la France, 1938-1960: Une nouvelle image des rapports de puissance.* Paris: Comité pour l'histoire Economique et financière de la France, 2001.

———. *La France, l'aide américaine et la construction européene, 1944-1954.* Paris: Comité pour l'Histoire Economique et Financière de la France, 1992.

Bourdieu, Pierre. *The Logic of Practice.* Trans. Richard Nice. Stanford: Stanford University Press, 1990.

Bourdieu, Pierre and Loïc J.D. Wacquant. *An Invitation to Reflexive Sociology.* Chicago: University of Chicago Press, 1992.

Braisted, Paul J. ed. *Cultural Affairs and Foreign Relations.* Washington, D.C.: Columbia Books, 1968.

Brogi, Alessandro. *A Question of Self-Esteem: the United States and the Cold War Choices in France and Italy, 1944-1958.* Westport: Praeger, 2002.

Burwood, Stephen. "American Labor and Industrial Unrest in France, 1947-1952." Ph.D. dissertation. S.U.N.Y. Binghamton, 1990.

Carew, Anthony. *Labour Under the Marshall Plan: The Politics of Producitivity and the Marketing of Management Science.* Detroit: Wayne State University Press, 1987.

Chabert, Pierre. *Le tourisme américain et ses enseignements pour la France.* Paris: Librarie Hachette, 1918.

Chilcolte, Ronald H. *The Political Economy of Imperialism: Critical Appraisals.* London: Rowan and Littlefield, 2000.

Clease, Armand and Archie C. Epps, eds. *Present at Creation: the Fortieth Anniversary of the Marshall Plan.* New York: Harper and Row, Ballinger Division, 1990.

Coleman, Peter. *The Liberal Conspiracy: The Congress for Cultural Freedom and the Struggle for the Mind of Postwar Europe.* New York: Free Press, 1989.

Compagnon, Antoine and Jacques Seebacher, eds. *L'Esprit de l'Europe, Tome 3: Goûts et Manières.* Paris: Flammarion, 1993.

Cottour, Thierry. "Un géant au format de poche. L'arrivée du Reader's Digest en France (1946-1954)." Mémoire de D.E.A., Institut d'études politiques de Paris, October 1992.

Cowen, Tyler. *Creative Destruction: How Globalization is Changing the World's Culture.* Princeton: Princeton UP, 2002.

Crépin, Thierry. *"Haro sur le gangster!" La moralization de la presse enfantine, 1934-1954.* Paris: CNRS, 2002.

Creton, Laurent. *Histoire économique de cinéma français: Producution et financement, 1940-1959.* Paris: CNRS Editions, 2004.

De Beauvoir, Simone. *After the War: Force of Circumstance, Vol. I: the autobiography of Simone de Beauvoir.* Trans. Richard Howard. New York: Paragon, 1992.

Eichengreen, Barry. *Europe's Post-War Recovery.* Cambridge: Cambridge U.P., 1995.

Ellwood, David and Rob Kroes, eds. *Hollywood in Europe: Experiences of a Cultural Hegemony.* Amsterdam: VU University Press, 1994.

Esposito, Chiarella. *America's Feeble Weapon: Funding the Marshall Plan in France and Italy, 1948-1950.* New Haven: Greenwood, 1994.

Fanon, Frantz. *The Wretched of the Earth.* Trans. Constance Farrington. New York: Grove Press, 1963.

Frank, Robert and René Girault, eds. *La puissance française en question (1945-1949).* Paris: Publications de la Sorbonne, 1988.

Frankel, Charles. *The Neglected Aspect of Foreign Affairs: American Educational and Cultural Policy Abroad.* Washington, D.C.: Brookings Institution, 1966.

Gienow-Hecht, Jessica C.E. *Transmission Impossible: American Journalism as Cultural Diplomacy in Post-War Germany, 1945-1955.* Baton Rouge: Louisiana State University Press, 1999.

Gienow-Hecht, Jessica C.E. and Frank Schumacher, eds. *Culture and International History.* New York: Berghahn Books, 2003.

Gillingham, John. *Coal, Steel, and the Rebirth of Europe, 1945-1955.* Cambridge: Cambridge UP, 1991.

Girault, René and Maurice Lévy-Leboyer, eds. *Le Plan Marshall et le relèvement économique de l'Europe.* Paris: Comité pour l'histoire économique et financière, 1993.

Goguel, François. *Chronique électorales la quatrième République.* Paris: Presses de la Fondations nationale des sciences politiques, 1981.

Gordon, Philip H. and Sophie Meunier. *The French Challenge: Adapting to Globalization.* Washington, D.C.: Brookings Institution Press, 2001.

Gramsci, Antonio. *Cultural Writings.* Eds. David Forgacs and Geoffrey Nowell-Smith. Trans. William Boelhower. Cambridge: Harvard U.P., 1985.

Gray, John. *Al Qaeda and What It Means to Be Modern.* New York: The New Press, 2003.

Grémion, Pierre. *Intelligence de l'anticommunisme: Le Congrès pour la liberté de la culture à Paris.* Paris: Fayard, 1995.

Guback, Thomas H. *The International Film Industry: Western Europe and American Film Since 1945.* Bloomington: Indiana University Press, 1969.

Guilbaut, Serge. *How New York Stole the Idea of Modern Art: Abstract Expressionism, Freedom, and the Cold War.* Tran. Arthur Goldhammer. Chicago: University of Chicago Press, 1983.

Haddow, Robert H. *Pavilions of Plenty: Exhibiting American Culture Abroad in the 1950s.* Washington: Smithsonian Institution Press, 1997.

Haines, Gerald K. *The Americanization of Brazil: A Study of U.S. Cold War Diplomacy in the Third World, 1945-1954.* Wilmington: Scholarly Resources, 1997.

Hecht, Gabrielle. *The Radiance of France: Nuclear Power and National Identity after World War II.* Cambridge: M.I.T. Press, 1998.

Hitchcock, William I. *France Restored: Cold War Diplomacy and the Quest for Leadership in Europe,* Charlotte: University of North Carolina Press, 1998.

Hixson, Walter L. *Parting the Curtain: Propaganda, Culture and the Cold War, 1945-1961.* New York: St. Martin's Griffin, 1997.

Hobsbawm, Eric and T. Ranger, eds. *The Invention of Tradition.* Cambridge: Cambridge University Press, 1983.

Hogan, Michael J. *The Marshall Plan: America, Britain, and the Reconstruction of Western Europe, 1947-1952.* Cambridge: Cambridge University Press, 1987.

Höhn, Maria. *GIs and Fräuleins: the German-American Encounter in 1950s West Germany.* Chapel Hill: University of North Carolina Press, 2002.

Horkheimer, Max and Theodor W. Adorno. *Dialectic of Enlightenment.* Ed. Gunzelin Schmid Noerr. Trans. Edmund Jephcott. Stanford: Stanford University Press, 2002.

Hubert-Lacombe, Patricia. *Le Cinéma Français dans la guerre froide.* Paris: L'Harmattan, 1996.

Jameson, Fredric and Masao Miyoshi, eds. *The Cultures of Globalization.* Durham: Duke University Press, 1998.

Jarraud, François. *Les Américains à Chateauroux, 1951-1967.* Arthon: Privately published, 1981.

Jarvie, Ian. *Hollywood's Overseas Campaign: The North Atlantic Movie Trade, 1920-1950.* New York: Cambridge University Press, 1992.

Kindleberger, Charles. *Marshall Plan Days.* Boston: Allen and Unwin, 1987.

Kipping, Matthias and Ore Bjarner, eds. *The Americanization of European Business: the Marshall Plan and the Transfer of U.S. Management Models.* London: Routeledge, 1998.

Kroes, Rob. *If You've Seen One You've Seen the Mall: Europeans and American Mass Culture.* Urbana-Champaign: University of Illinois Press, 1996.

Kroes, Rob, Robert W. Rydell, and Doeko F.J. Bosscher, eds., *Cultural Transmissions and Receptions: American Mass Culture in Europe.* Amsterdam: VU University Press, 1993.

Kuisel, Richard F. *Seducing the French: the Dilemma of Americanization.* Berkeley: University of California Press, 1993.

Lacroix-Riz, Annie. *La choix de Marianne: Les relations franco-américaines.* Paris: Messidor, 1986.

———. *La CGT de la liberation à la scission de 1944-47.* Paris: Editions Sociales, 1983.

LaFeber, Walter. *Michael Jordan and the New Global Capitalism.* New York: W.W. Norton and Company, 1999.

Lebovics, Herman. *Mona Lisa's Escort: André Malraux and the Reinvention of French Culture.* Ithaca: Cornell University Press, 1999.

———. *True France: the Wars Over Cultural Identity, 1900-1945.* Ithaca: Cornell University Press, 1992.

Leffler, Melvyn P. *A Preponderance of Power: National Security, the Truman Administration, and the Cold War.* Stanford: Stanford University Press, 1992.

Leonard, Mark, et al. *Public Diplomacy.* London: Foreign Policy Centre, 2002.

MacCanell, Dean. *The Tourist: a New Theory of the Leisure Class.* New York: Schocken, 1989.

MacShane, Denis. *International Labour and the Origins of the Cold War.* Oxford: Clarendon Press, 1992.

Maier, Charles S., ed. *The Cold War in Europe.* New York: Markus Wiener, 1991.

Mathy, Jean-Philippe. *French Resistance: the French-American Culture Wars.* St. Paul: University of Minnesota Press, 2000.

———. *Extrême Occident: French Intellectuals and America.* Chicago: University of Chicago Press, 1993.

Miller, Ronald and David Sawers. *The Technical Development of Modern Aviation.* New York: Praeger, 1970.

Milward, Alan. *The Reconstruction of Western Europe, 1945-51.* London: Methuen & Co., 1984.

Ninkovich, Frank A. *The Diplomacy of Ideas: U.S. Foreign Policy and Cultural Relations, 1938-1950.* New York: Cambridge University Press, 1981.

Nye, Joseph S. *The Paradox of American Power: Why the World's Only Super Power Can't Afford to go it Alone.* New York: Oxford University Press, 2002.

Peer, Shanny. *France on Display: Peasants, Provincials, and Folklore in the 1937 Paris World's Fair.* Albany: S.U.N.Y. Press, 1998.

Pells, Richard. *Not Like Us: How Europeans Have Loved, Hated, and Transformed American Culture Since World War II.* New York: Basic Books, 1997.

Piniau, Bernard. *L'action artistique de la France dans le monde: histoire de l'Association française d'action artistique (AFAA) de 1922 à nos jours.* Paris: L'Harmattan, 1998.

Pisani, Sallie. *The CIA and the Marshall Plan.* Lawrence: University Press of Kansas, 1991.

Pommerin, Reiner, ed. *The American Impact on Postwar Germany.* Providence: Berghahn Books, 1995.

Prevots, Naima. *Dance for Export: Cultural Diplomacy and the Cold War.* Hanover: Wesleyan University Press, 1998.

Rawnsley, Gary D., ed. *Cold-War Propaganda in the 1950s.* New York: St. Martins, 1999.

Rioux, Jean-Pierre. *The Fourth Republic, 1944-1958.* Translated by Godfrey Rogers. Cambridge: Cambridge University Press, 1987.

Roger, Philippe. *L'Ennemi américain: Généalogie de l'antiaméricanisme français.* Paris: Seuil, 2002.

———. *Rêves et cauchemars américans: Les Etats Unis au miroir de l'opinion public française (1945-1953).* Paris: Presses Universitaires du Septentrion, 1996.

Romero, Federico. *The United States and the European Trade Union Movement, 1944-1951.* Trans. Harvey Fergusson. Chapel Hill: University of North Carolina Press, 1992.

Rosenberg, Emily S. *Spreading the American Dream: American Economic and Cultural Expansion, 1890-1945.* New York: Hill and Wang, 1982.

Russell, Bertrand, John Lehmann, Sean O'Falain, et al. *The Impact of America on European Culture.* Boston: Beacon Press, 1951.

Saunders, Frances Stoner. *The Cultural Cold War.* New York: the Free Press, 1999.

Schain, Martin, ed. *The Marshall Plan Fifty Years After.* New York: Palgrave Macmillan, 2000.

Schlosser, Eric. *Fast Food Nation.* New York: Harper Collins, 2002.

Schopenhauer, Arthur. *The World as Will and Representation.* Trans. E.F.J. Payne. New York: Dover, 1958.

Sharp, Joanne P. *Condensing the Cold War: Readers Digest and American Identity.* Minneapolis: Minnesota University Press, 2000.

Shulman, Holly. *The Voice of America: Propaganda and Democracy, 1941-45.* Madison: University of Wisconsin Press, 1990.

Slater, D. and P.J. Taylor, eds. *The American Century.* London: Blackwell, 1999.

Soria, Georges. *La France deviendra-t-elle une colonie américaine?* Preface by Frédéric Joliot-Curie. Paris: Éditions du Pavillon, 1948.

Starr, Amory. *Naming the Enemy: Anti-Corporate Movements Confront Globalization.* New York: Zed Books, 2000.

Tomlinson, John. *Globalization and Culture.* Chicago: University of Chicago Press, 1999.

———. *Cultural Imperialism: A Critical Introduction.* Baltimore: Johns Hopkins University Press, 1991.

Trumpbour, John. *Selling Hollywood to the World: U.S. and European Struggles for Mastery of the Global Film Industry, 1920-1950.* Cambridge: Cambridge UP, 2002.

Urry, John. *The Tourist's Gaze.* London: Sage, 1990.

Urry, John and Scott Lasch. *Economies of Sign and Space.* London: Sage, 1994.

Vickers, Rhiannon. *Manipulating Hegemony: State Power, Labour and the Marshall Plan in Britain.* New York: St. Martin's, 2000.

Wagnleitner, Reinhold. *Coca-Colonization and the Cold War: The Cultural Mission of the United States in Austria after the Second World War.* Trans. Diana M. Wolf. Chapel Hill: University of North Carolina Press, 1994.

Wakeman, Rosemary. *Modernizing the Provincial City: Toulouse, 1945-1975.* Cambridge: Harvard University Press, 1997.

Wall, Irwin M. *The United States and the Making of Postwar France, 1945-1954.* Cambridge: Cambridge University Press, 1991.

Weber, Eugen. *Peasants into Frenchmen: the Modernization of Rural France, 1870-1914.* Stanford: Stanford University Press, 1976.

Wexler, Imanuel. *The Marshall Plan Revisited: the European Recovery Program in Economic Perspective.* Westport: Greenwood Press, 1983.

Wheatcroft, Stephen. *The Economics of European Air Transport.* Manchester: Manchester University Press, 1956.

Wylie, Laurence. *Village in the Vaucluse.* Cambridge: Harvard University Press, 1964.

Zieger, Robert H. *The CIO, 1933-55.* Chapel Hill: University of North Carolina Press, 1995.

INDEX